# Shadows in the Sun

## HEALING FROM DEPRESSION AND FINDING THE LIGHT WITHIN

GAYATHRI RAMPRASAD

PENGUIN BOOKS
An imprint of Penguin Random House

PENGUIN BOOKS

USA | Canada | UK | Ireland | Australia
New Zealand | India | South Africa | China | Singapore

Penguin Books is part of the Penguin Random House group of companies whose addresses can be found at global.penguinrandomhouse.com

Published by Penguin Random House India Pvt. Ltd
4th Floor, Capital Tower 1, MG Road,
Gurugram 122 002, Haryana, India

Penguin Random House India

First published in the United States of America by Hazelden 2014
This edition published by Random House India 2014



10 9 8 7 6 5 4 3 2

This publication is not intended as a substitute for the advice of health care professionals.
Some names, details, and circumstances have been changed to protect the privacy of those mentioned in this publication.

ISBN 9788184005196

Interior design: Kinne Design
Typesetting: BookMobile Design & Digital Publisher Services
Developmental editor: Sid Farrar
Production editor: Mindy Keskinen

For sale in the Indian Subcontinent only

Printed at Repro India Limited



www.penguin.co.in

FSC www.fsc.org MIX Paper from responsible sources FSC® C047271

This is a legitimate digitally printed version of the book and therefore might not have certain extra finishing on the cover.

THIS IS A WORK of creative non-fiction. The events are portrayed to the best of the author's memory. While all the stories in this book are true, some names and identifying details have been changed to protect the privacy of the people involved.

The conversations in the book all come from the author's recollections, though they are not written to represent word-for-word transcripts. Rather, the author has retold them in a way that evokes the feeling and meaning of what was said, and in all instances, the essence of the dialogue is accurate.

Depression and the medications and electroconvulsive therapy used to treat it can seriously damage recollection. Where the author's memory has failed her, she has interviewed family members to fill in the gaps.

Advance Praise for *Shadows in the Sun*

"Gayathri's colorful, harrowing, and ultimately uplifting life story transcends memoir and becomes history"

—Julie A. Fast, author, columnist, and winner of a Mental Health America media award

"Superb"

—James Boehnlein, MD, professor of psychiatry, Intercultural Psychiatry Program, Oregon Health and Science University School of Medicine

"Anyone reading [*Shadows in the Sun*] will gain valuable insight into what it is like to struggle with serious emotional and mental disorders, as well as receiving a most precious gift—reason to believe that such a harrowing journey can lead to hope and healing"

—John Head, author of *Standing in the Shadows: Understanding and Overcoming Depression in Black Men*

"By her courageous willingness to share her most private horrors, Gayathri Ramprasad will touch many hearts"

—Patricia B. Nemec, PsyD, CRC, CPRP

"A deeply moving travelogue of two remarkable journeys: from India to America, and from the depths of mental illness to the forefront of wellness advocacy"

—Jeff Bell, author of *Rewind, Replay, Repeat: A Memoir of OCD* and founder of the Adversity 2 Advocacy Alliance

"A must read, even if mental illness has not touched your family"

—Jessie Close, BringChange2Mind.org

"*Shadows in the Sun* reminds us how closely we are interconnected and how we all have a stake in the mental wellness of everyone on our planet"

—Cinda Johnson, Ed.D., coauthor of *Perfect Chaos: A Daughter's Journey to Survive Bipolar, A Mother's Struggle to Save Her*

"*Shadows in the Sun* illuminates us all with fierce truth and beauty, and inspires us to our core"

—Janine Francolini, founder of the Flawless Foundation

"For us, and for anyone, Ms. Ramprasad's efforts offer hope"

—Brandon Staglin, schizophrenia survivor and communications director of the International Mental Health Research Organization

"A truly masterful piece of work!"

—Delaney Ruston, MD, Fulbright Scholar, Filmmaker, and Mental Health Advocate

"This book is a true gift to all those struggling with a mental disorder and those of us who love them. In writing it, Gayathri Ramprasad establishes herself as an international voice of hope"

—Pete Earley, author of *Crazy: A Father's Search through America's Mental Health Madness*

"Shadows in the Sun is a courageous journey from adversity, apathy and depression toward action and advocacy. Gayathri's memoir, written in beautiful prose, is a must-read for anyone who has suffered from, cares for or wants to learn about severe mental illness"

—Matcheri S. Keshavan MD, Stanley Cobb Professor and Vice-Chair for Public Psychiatry, Department of Psychiatry, Beth Israel Deaconess Medical Center and Massachusetts Mental Health Center, Harvard Medical School

"A true and moving story of healing from depression. Her book can help all of us to find our own effective, integrative, and life-transforming path. She is an inspiration."

—James S. Gordon, MD, Author of Unstuck: Your Guide to the Seven-Stage Journey Out of Depression, and founder and director of The Center for Mind-Body Medicine.

*To my parents, for giving me the gift of life;*
*To my husband, for his undying love and support;*
*To my daughters, who are my reason and reward for living.*

*And, to you, my dear readers, let us come together to create a world of understanding, compassion, and inclusion, where every man, woman, and child suffering from mental illness is provided the love and support they need to thrive in life.*

Into my heart's night
Along a narrow way
I groped; and lo! The light,
An infinite land of day.

— *Rubaiyat of Rumi*

# CONTENTS

# ACKNOWLEDGMENTS

Birthing this book has been like birthing a baby. It is the culmination of a long-cherished dream—a dream that has been nurtured by a community of collaborators, friends, and family.

Thanks to my wonderful agent, Susan Lee Cohen at Riverside Literary Agency, for her love and steadfast faith in me and my story. Thanks to my editor, Sid Farrar at Hazelden Publishing, for his dedication and support in helping me share my story with the world. Thanks to production editor Mindy Keskinen and to Betty Christiansen for copyediting the manuscript to enhance its narrative flow. Thanks to Alison Vandenberg, Jill Grindahl, Wes Thomsen, and the marketing team at Hazelden for overseeing the launch of the book, from the beautiful cover design to the promotional materials.

Thanks to my dear friends Barbara Maloney, PhD; Julie Fast; Patricia Nemec, PsyD, CRC, CPRP; Gina Nikkel, PhD; and James Boehnlein, MD for nurturing my story from its conception to its delivery. I am grateful to each and every one of them for taking time in their busy lives to read early drafts of my manuscript and helping me sculpt it into the book I dreamed of.

Thanks to Jennifer Thompson and Quinn Fariel at Perseus Books Group for facilitating the partnership with Random House India.

Thanks to Archana Shankar, Caroline Newbury and their dedicated team at Random House India for making it possible for me to share my story with my brethren, the *beautiful minds* of India, and fellow countrymen. As the daughter of India and a mental health advocate, I sincerely pray that my story will inspire us to end the silence about mental illness and start the conversation about mental health. If not for us, we have to do it for our children's sake.

Thanks to Dr. Vikram Patel for his valiant efforts to ensure *mental health for all*, and for his insightful preface.

Thanks to my family for their eternal love and support. I am forever indebted to their courage and compassion in sharing our story with the world.

Thanks to the many friends, healers, and health care professionals who have helped me recover and thrive in life.

To every person around the world who is struggling to recover from a mental illness, you give me hope and inspiration. I wish you a life of wellness.

Namaste!

# PREFACE

I cannot recollect precisely when I first communicated with Gayathri Ramprasad but I will never forget when we first met at an international congress on mental health in Bengaluru. I knew that she was a passionate advocate for bringing mental health out of the closet, not least in countries like India where it has often remained hidden or shrouded in mystery and fear for centuries. I knew that she had launched an organization, ASHA International, devoted to this cause and joined the Movement for Global Mental Health, a network of organizations and individuals committed to a better life for people affected by mental illness around the world. What I did not know was the power of her ability to communicate, which I only discovered when I had a face-to-face conversation with her and realized that I was in the company of an extraordinary woman. A woman who was not only passionate but also fearless and determined to walk the extra mile to achieve her goal. I knew instantly that I wanted to walk with her.

It was only a matter of course, then, for Gayathri to write this moving account of her life, moored around her struggle with mental illness from an early age. She was fortunate in many ways: she was surrounded by a sympathetic and loving family; had access to quality mental health care; and perhaps, most importantly, had innate capabilities and resources to cope with the torment of her illness and emerge whole and fulfilled. Still, she acknowledges that "recovery is a journey, not a destination."

Mental illness is, unlike other health conditions, more than just an impairment on one's health. It is, at its core, an impairment of one's being. There is no correlation between feeling that life is not worth living anymore and a boil on one's back, no equivalence between hearing voices tell you that your neighbour is spying on you and being told by a doctor that you have high blood pressure. Mental illness profoundly influences one's own identity, one's mooring in the world we live in. Not surprisingly, then, recovery is not just about getting past the tormenting symptoms of illness, but attaining the same desires and dreams as any other person, whether it is to be fulfilled at work or in one's intimate relationships. As Gayathri shows so vividly through her beautiful prose, this is truly a journey, an epic one for many, and one she has navigated through storms and calm to emerge with remarkable humility and poise.

Mental illness is not just a statistic. It is a reality that millions, hundreds of millions, of people around the world live with every day. It is equally a reality that a majority of these people do not receive the care, including medical treatment, that we know can help transform their lives. This is especially true of countries like India, the country of Gayathri's birth. Worse, people with mental illness suffer some of the worst abuses and indignities witnessed in modern times and die much earlier than their compatriots, not just through suicide but also due to the poorer quality of care they receive when they suffer physical health problems. Most governments spend less than one percent of their health budgets on mental-health care. In many countries, prisons, colonial-era mental institutions and the streets have become the dumping grounds for people with mental illness. Despite this, there is barely any attention to this global health-crisis. Quite simply, mental illness is not a sexy topic for politicians, foundations, celebrities or the media. Though the tide is turning, we have a very long way to go, not least in the poorest countries of the world.

I am convinced that there is one key ingredient needed to turn this tide into an unstoppable wave. It was an ingredient which transformed the global response to HIV/AIDS. And it is the voices of those who are directly affected. It is in this way that I see *Shadows in the Sun* becoming a beacon of, and the author a champion for, the empowerment of people who have lived with mental illness. It shows the power of and reason for them to speak out about their experiences, both of suffering and recovery, and forces those who should act to do so by moving their hearts and minds. But this is not just a book for advocates of global mental health; it is a book for anyone who cares about human suffering and justice, and should serve as a call to arms for them to join the movement to achieve a better life for those living with mental illness today.

Vikram Patel
London School of Hygiene & Tropical Medicine; the Public Health Foundation of India; and Sangath
New Delhi
August 2014

# PROLOGUE

I grew up in a world anointed by the sweet, scintillating fragrance of jasmine and sanctified by the Hindu gods and goddesses who graced and guarded our family. Ganesh, the elephant-faced god, removed all obstacles and impediments. Saraswathi, the goddess of learning, blessed my efforts in school. Lakshmi, the goddess of wealth, was generous to us; Krishna, the god of love, watched over us; and always we revered among others the righteous Lord Rama and his devout consort Sita, the epitome of womanhood. Mine was a world of otherworldly tales, castles, flickering oil lamps, and fragrant sandalwood dreams.

At some point in a fairy-tale life, I suppose, it should come as no surprise to discover dragons, demons, and dungeons in the dark corners of the kingdom. What was surprising was to discover that all the scariest creatures were *within me,* and that the castle of my dreams could become a prison from which the only escape was death. Later, I would discover that these demons had names: *anxiety disorder, suicidal depression, postpartum depression, mental illness.* But for nearly a decade of my life, I had no words for it. "It" was me. In that fairy-tale life, I turned out to be both dragon and dragon slayer, but it did not start out that way. In the beginning, I was a princess.

# PART 1

# Bright Beginnings

CHAPTER 1

# Diwali at Rama Iyengar Road

"HAPPY *DIWALI,* PRINCESS," Appa says, peeking out of the bathroom, drying himself off briskly with a white-and-blue-checked cotton towel. "It is time to rise and shine." He pecks me on my head and tousles my hair lovingly. It is a rare treat to be awakened by my father. He is usually off to work at Binny's, the local textile mill, by 5 a.m. It is Diwali—the festival of lights, and all of us have holidays.

"Happy Diwali, Appa," I reply through my yawns, snuggling back under my sheets. I glance at my older brother, Ravi, and little sister, Chitra, curled up in their beds on the floor next to mine. I wonder why Appa and Amma always wake me up first. *Why not Ravi? After all, he is older than I.*

The scent of jasmine and sandalwood incense swirls through the house. I hear the tinkling of bells and my mother chanting *mantras* invoking the gods to awaken. Just as I try to close my eyes and sink back into slumberland, I catch a glimpse of my mother lighting the *nandadeepa.* Her hair, still wet from her bath, lies coiled at her fair nape, drawing designs on the back of her blouse.

One of my fondest memories of Amma, ever since I can remember, is of her lighting the nandadeepa, a brass lamp ornamented with a beautifully carved peacock. It is an ancestral lamp passed down through many generations on my father's side of the family. Suspended from the ceiling by a thick brass chain, the lamp hangs solemnly by the family altar, paying homage to the many gods and goddesses holding court in a *mantapa,* a miniature rosewood temple tucked in the right-hand corner of our kitchen.

Each day at the crack of dawn and at dusk, as the light of day embraced the dark of night, Amma religiously filled the belly of the lamp with sesame oil and adjusted the cotton wick to ensure that it stayed aglow all day and night. Today, the light from the nandadeepa casts a luminous glow on my mother, and I marvel at her serene grace. She looks radiant in her new *sari.* It is the most beautiful sari I have ever seen. I remember how excited Chitra was when Appa came home two days ago with a package wrapped in brown paper.

"What is it, Appa?" she had asked, as soon as our father had parked his Java motorbike in the front yard and turned off the ignition. "Is it for me? Are they my new dresses?"

"I am sorry to disappoint you, darling. It is just my work clothes," he had insisted, scooping her up with his right hand, the package clutched in his left hand. Later that evening, after dinner, Amma had asked Appa if he would like her to unwrap the package, iron his new work clothes, and set them out for him to wear the next morning.

"Thanks, Popsi," Appa had replied casually.

"Popsi" was my parents' nickname for each other. As Amma carefully opened the brown package, Appa had shouted, "Surprise!" From Amma's trembling hands cascaded the gorgeous sari. It was six yards of silk dyed in the most regal of purples, with stars of gold sprinkled throughout. The sari looked as though all the stars in the constellation were sewn into the rich colors of a glorious sunset. There were parading peacocks woven into the gold borders on either side of the sari that spilled into a breathtaking *pallu.* This was by far not only the prettiest sari in Amma's meager collection; it was also the most expensive. Appa had been awarded a handsome Diwali bonus at work, and he had splurged on an extravagant sari for Amma this year. As tears of joy trickled down Amma's flushed cheeks, Appa had drawn her into his arms and said, "Happy Diwali, Popsi."

Each year, my cousins and I wait with great anticipation for Diwali to arrive. Unlike all the other Hindu festivals, Diwali holds the promise of a great party without the prolonged prayers. And it almost always brings with it the gift of two or more new outfits, instead of just one as we got for other festivals or our birthdays. Over the four-day celebration, our family of twenty-three—grandparents, uncles, aunts, and cousins—gathers with friends and neighbors to frolic with firecrackers and feast on mounds of mouthwatering *mithai,* sweets. Each night, we deck our homes with hundreds of clay lamps called *diyas* to celebrate the triumph of good over evil, light over darkness.

"Happy Diwali, Gayu," Amma says to me. "Wake up, it is time to get showered and wear your new clothes. Your cousins are already in the courtyard bursting their firecrackers."

I rub my sleepy eyes and jump out of my bed at the thought of my cousins in their new clothes.

"Happy Diwali, Amma," I say, running to the bathroom to brush my teeth.

I hear Amma and Appa waking Ravi and Chitra. We roll our mattresses carefully and pile them up neatly in the far right corner of our bedroom, which morphs into a living room by day. Amma hands us steel tumblers filled with warm milk with a touch of saffron and sugar.

"Drink up, my darlings. It is time for your oil bath now," Amma says, deftly applying a dot of vermillion between our eyebrows. Appa hands her a little bowl filled with warm sesame oil. She gently rubs the soothing oil into our scalps and proceeds to massage us from head to toe, following the ancient ritual of *abhyanga.* By the time she is done, we are almost lulled back into sleep again.

"The water is ready, Popsi." Appa gathers fresh towels and heads back into the bathroom. He props a little ornate teakwood plank on the bathroom floor for us to sit on.

"I want to go first, me first!" Ravi, Chitra, and I squabble, each of us wanting to be the first to get bathed. Finally, we settle that I should go first since I was the first to get up.

Before I head to the bathroom, I go into the kitchen and stand in front of the God's altar where Amma had carefully placed all our new clothes on a silver tray. Amma had anointed them with a dot of vermillion the night before, seeking God's blessings before we wore them.

For months, we had shopped for fabrics and finally settled on a pretty multicolored silk brocade that looked like dainty plumes of peacock feathers. Chitra and I always got matching outfits. Amma thought we looked cute in them. Besides, it made life easier, she said, since Chitra and I always fought about having the same dress as the other had.

"Sew as many gathers as you can into the dress," Amma had told the tailor. "Add a net of tulle underneath, and line it with the softest muslin so it won't scratch their skin. I want the girls to look like Cinderella." After countless trips to the tailor, we had finally gasped in joy as he handed us our gorgeous new frocks, and another pair of red-and-white polka-dotted chiffon dresses Amma hadn't told us about.

For Ravi, Amma had chosen a pair of navy blue shorts with a red, white, and blue plaid shirt, and another pair of khaki shorts with a brick-red shirt. She was thrilled to find a pair of suspenders that coordinated with both of his outfits. And for Appa, she had bought a soft, cream-colored silk pajama and *kurta*. There they were, all our new clothes piled high, in front of the God's altar, blessed and ready for us to wear after our oil baths. I carefully pull my "Cinderella frock" from the pile and place it gently on the stool by the bathroom, along with my petticoat and panties.

"Come on, Gayu, we need to get going now," Appa calls out from the bathroom. I squat on the teak plank, ready for my bath. Amma wraps an old sari around her to keep her new sari from getting wet. She settles down beside me with a bowl of *shikakai* paste made with soap nut powder and water. I hate the shikakai paste. It always gets into my eyes, stinging them and making them red for hours.

"Why can't we have shampoo, Amma?" I pout, enticed by all the glamorous advertisements for Sunsilk shampoo I had seen in the newspaper Appa used to read.

"Shikakai powder is good for you, *bangara*," Amma insists. "It's much better than any shampoo. It will make your hair soft and bouncy." There is no arguing with Amma and her steely velvet way of cajoling us into her way of life.

Appa pours warm water over my head, making sure he soaks my thick mane and body. Amma scoops a handful of the shikakai paste and scrubs my hair. Appa rinses it with water, making sure all the oil is washed out. Amma lathers her hands with a bar of Mysore sandalwood soap and hands the sweet-smelling oval bar to me. She scrubs my back, as I scrub the rest of my body.

"All done." Amma tucks my wet hair into a sheer cotton towel and coils it into a turban on top of my head. Appa wraps me in a thicker terry towel. "Send your sister in for her shower," he says, patting me on my derriere.

I slip into my petticoat and panties and pull my dress over my head, careful not to topple the turban. I run back to Amma and ask her to help me with the buttons on the back.

"You look gorgeous, Gayu," she says, twirling me around.

"You look like a princess," Appa chimes in.

I feel beautiful, just like a princess.

When Chitra is done with her bath, I help her into her matching new dress. Together, we sing *Ring around the rosie, A pocket full of posies, Ashes! Ashes! We all fall down!* We twirl in circles and collapse into giggles, over and over again, our dresses cascading around us as we plop on the smooth, cool, red-oxide floor. Soon, Ravi is done with his bath and looks dashing in his new khaki shorts, brick red shirt, and Amma's favorite suspenders. Amma slicks Ravi's hair back with a touch of coconut oil and brushes my hair and Chitra's into a bouncy bob. She gently dusts Pond's talcum powder on our temples, cheeks, and nose with a fluffy powder puff, and applies a tiny black dot on our right cheeks.

"To keep the evil spirits from casting a spell on my angels," she proclaims, encircling our faces with her hands and cracking her knuckles by our ears.

Amma dries herself, removes the old sari that she had draped on top of her beautiful new one, and proceeds to the kitchen to help us with our prayers.

Every day, Amma insists that we shower and say our prayers before we eat our breakfast. Today is no exception. Appa changes into his new silk kurta—tunic and pajama—and squats on the kitchen floor beside us. Together, we devour the delicious mango *kesaribhat*—a delectable concoction of Cream of Wheat, diced mangoes, milk, and sugar, seasoned with crushed cardamom and saffron—that Amma has prepared for us this morning. As soon as we have eaten, Chitra and I nudge Ravi. Together, we dart out of the kitchen and into the courtyard before our mother can ask us to put our dishes away.

Tatayi, our paternal grandfather, has just completed his morning prayers and is settling into the wicker chaise in the courtyard. He is wearing a crisp white *dhoti* and undershirt. A red-and-white-checked cotton towel is tossed over his right shoulder. Round brass-rimmed glasses perch on his nose. Atta, our grandmother, is sitting next to him, doling out instructions to our maid, Akkamma.

"Happy Diwali, Tatayi. Happy Diwali, Atta." Ravi, Chitra, and I are prostrate at our grandparents' feet, seeking their blessing. "God bless you," they say, caressing our heads.

My three aunts, two uncles, Amma, Appa, and all fourteen of my cousins, ranging in ages from eight to twenty-eight, soon gather around to wish each other a happy Diwali.

"New pinch, new pinch!" We cousins chase one another, pinching each other for the new clothes we are all wearing. The commotion rattles Tatayi's calm.

"Ummmm . . ." he clears his throat, motioning us to be quiet. At eighty-four, Tatayi looks frail, almost skeletal. Yet he has a commanding presence, compelling adults and children alike to stand up straight and remain silent. Tatayi reminds me of a coconut—hard on the outside, sweet and tender on the inside. At four feet tall, Atta is short compared to Tatayi. She is as dark as he is fair. Tatayi is the master of our clan. And Atta is undoubtedly the matriarch of the family.

We often heard the happy clatter of keys Atta wore knotted into the ends of her pallu, the tip of her sari, before we saw her. There were keys for attics, keys for the many doors in our home, keys for the collection of Godrej cupboards where she stored the family silverware and jewelry, and keys for the small, handcrafted cedar pantry where she stored cloves, cinnamon, cardamom, cashews, almonds, raisins, saffron, and other spices. Atta usually sat on the divan in the main dining room, doling out instructions to Amma and my aunts about the myriad chores that needed attention. The sunlight streaming through the windows danced off her dazzling diamond earrings and nose ring, bathing the walls around her in a rainbow of colors.

"Go on out to the front yard and be careful playing with your firecrackers," Atta advises us. "Your grandfather needs to rest now."

We run into our rooms, gather our stash of firecrackers concealed in secret places, and join our cousins and neighborhood friends. We play for hours with pop-its, snakes, rockets, and trains, then Amma and our aunts ask us to help set up for the festive lunch.

Ordinarily, Amma and my three aunts cook in independent kitchens. But during festivals, they become a chef brigade operating seamlessly under Atta's supervision. Together, they cook for hours, chatting and laughing, creating elaborate meals that make our mouths drool. The aroma of their culinary delights wafts through the house and escapes into the street, suffusing it with the scent of exotic spices.

Today, as on all other festival days, we will eat in the grand hall, which also serves as the main dining room. This is where the Shastry family of twenty-three gathers to celebrate festivals and ceremonies. It is a huge room with high ceilings. The walls are lined with ornate frames housing temple art etched in vivid colors and filigreed in gold leaf depicting elaborate scenes from the *Ramayana* and *Mahabharata*—the ancient epics of India. A regal rosewood swing hangs from one of the thick teak beams. My cousins and I love to compete to see who can swing the highest and touch the ceiling with our toes. Our pursuits are often foiled by Tatayi's walking stick tapping on the walls, warning us to slow down or risk losing our turn on the swing. The grand room has been witness to many a homecoming, wedding proposal, bridal shower, baby shower, and cradling ceremony.

Six of us girls, the granddaughters of the family, gather the freshly cut plantain leaves stacked on the floor and lay them in two tidy rows facing each other. We spread finely woven wicker mats behind each plantain leaf, set out shiny steel tumblers at the far left-hand corner of the leaf, and carefully pour water into them from stainless steel jugs. Once everything is set, the men of the household and the grandchildren, eighteen of us in all, settle into our designated spots on the floor, as the chef brigade of 400 Rama Iyengar Road begins its choreographed parade.

Our plantain leaves are soon covered with a traditional South Indian feast. Tatayi offers a prayer and blesses our food. A brief hush descends upon the room as we dig into our Diwali meal. Amma serves us fresh, tangy salads made of lentils, carrots, and cucumbers, kissed with lemon juice, garnished with chopped cilantro, and seasoned with black mustard, red chilies, and *asafetida.* Little mounds of pearly white rice are served in the middle of the plantain leaf ladled with *sambar*—a savory lentil stew cooked with eggplant. Aunt Shubha serves a dollop of *ghee* on top of the sambar, along with delicious lemon rice sprinkled with golden roasted cashews, luscious homemade yogurt, spicy lemon pickle, and a variety of fried *papads*—deep-fried lentil wafers. But the highlight of the Diwali meal is undoubtedly the dessert. Our mouths water as we catch a whiff of the *payasam,* a rich milk pudding made of roasted poppy seeds ground up with a dash of soaked rice and fresh grated coconut, simmered to perfection with brown sugar and a touch of finely crushed cardamom.

"How about just one more ladle of payasam?" Aunt Lakshmi asks at the end of the meal.

"No, thanks," we answer, crossing our hands over our nearly empty plantain leaves, motioning that we are full. She serves us an extra ladle anyway. My cousins and I clutch our stomachs, wishing they were larger to contain my aunt's extra serving of love. One by one, we excuse ourselves and wobble to the tap in the central courtyard to wash our hands and rinse our mouths.

A short while later, the men retreat back to the veranda, where a silver tray is set with lush green baby betel leaves; an ornate bowl filled with *supari,* a special blend of candied sugar, spices, and betel nuts; a handful of cloves; and a little box of fine lime paste. Appa and his older brothers, Ramesh and Suresh, recline on the *charpoy* in the courtyard and ask me to make *paans* for them.

While my siblings and the rest of my cousins help with the cleanup, I kneel beside Appa, cleaning the betel leaves gently on a napkin placed over my right knee. I spread a small dab of the lime paste in the center, heap a teaspoon of supari on top, and wrap the leaf into a tight little package. I place it into the second betel leaf, fold it into a triangle, and secure it with a single clove to make a paan. I proudly hand it over to my uncle.

"You are the best *paanwali* I have ever met," Uncle Suresh says, smiling, tossing the paan into his mouth. Puffed up with pride, I make more paans for Appa and my uncles who are waiting for theirs with outstretched hands.

"One more, one more," they encourage each other. "It will help you digest your food better." When Chaitra, my cousin, wants a paan, however, our uncles chide her. Amid peals of laughter, they wink at one another and say, "You can't have one. Not yet. You will need to wait until your wedding night to savor your first paan." Confused by their adult humor and disappointed, Chaitra settles for the candied sugar instead.

Meanwhile, Amma and my aunts huddle in the kitchen, serving each other and eating their lunch. When done, they put away the leftovers and slowly trek back into their bedrooms for a well-deserved nap. Appa and my uncles join their wives. Atta and Tatayi retreat to their bedroom off the courtyard, as we children sprawl around in the veranda arguing about who has the cutest clothes and the most firecrackers this year. In minutes, we drift into sweet slumber, dreaming of sparklers and flowerpots that will festoon the dark sky tonight.

Hours later, the aroma of coffee swirls through the veranda, tickling our nostrils awake. Amma and my aunts are back in the kitchen again, passing around trays of piping hot coffee to arouse the rest of their sleepy kin. One by one, we make a beeline to the bathroom to wash the sleep out of our eyes and freshen up for the festivities of the evening.

As I meander into the bathroom in the backyard, I notice hundreds of diyas—clay lamps—arranged carefully in rows.

Each year before the holiday, Atta unlocked the doors to the attic and had my uncles help her retrieve wooden chests filled with diyas, carefully nestled amid shredded paper and straw. For weeks preceding Diwali, I joined my cousins in dusting the diyas and placing them in rows by the giant curry leaf tree in the central courtyard of our home. For days, Amma and my aunts twirled cotton between their thumb and forefinger, making hundreds of wicks to light the diyas with, while Atta made sure there was enough oil to fill them on Diwali day. Each year, I look forward to helping my cousins and aunts with the task of adorning our home with the magical glow of countless lamps.

I wash my face, careful not to wet my pretty new dress, brush my hair, powder my nose, and make it back in time to join the annual lighting of the Diwali diyas. It had taken us hours to line the entire length of the compound encircling our home. With the last of the diyas in place, and our evening prayers said, our clan of twenty-three assembles by the front gate to admire our little kingdom awash in light. My eight-year-old eyes dance with joy at the grandeur of the sight I behold. This is the palace of my dreams!

The wrought-iron gates stretch their arms open, inviting us to enter through the front door. The threshold is adorned with colorful *rangoli*—intricate geometric designs drawn with milled stone to welcome the good spirits to our home. Garlands of marigolds bedecked with sprigs of tender mango leaves drape the top of the door frame. The sweet smell of jasmine climbing the trellises surrounding the front yard fills the night air, while the melodious sounds of Bismillah Khan's *shehnai* emanating from the Phillips radio across the hallway triumphantly heralds the arrival of Diwali.

My reverie is broken with the sounds of rockets exploding into sprays of magical colors. The night sky is soon awash with brilliant gold, red, blue, green, purple, yellow, pink, and silver. The noise of fireworks bursting nearly deafens us, and the smell of gunpowder fills the air, cloaking us in a dreamy haze.

For hours on end, we dwell in the delights of Diwali, until it is time for our parents to herd us back into the house. Reluctantly, we bid goodnight to our friends and family with promises of resuming the fun at the crack of dawn for the next three days. That night, tucked safely within the womb of my ancestral home, my family and I are completely oblivious to the dark winds of depression that will one day threaten to destroy our lives.

By the fourth and last day of Diwali, the streets are carpeted with confetti—remnants of aeroplanes, rockets, sprinklers, flowerpots, and snakes. Together, we children survey the neighborhood to proclaim the winner of this year's Diwali, for the street with the most trash claims the coveted honor. We scream in delight when we learn that the children of Rama Iyengar Road are the winners this year!

The next morning, we resume our daily routines. My cousins and I go back to school, our fathers go back to work, and our mothers busy themselves with their labors of love.

The magic of Diwali continued for a few more years, until the day my grandfather, Tatayi, died.

For the first time in my life, Amma didn't light the nandadeepa that night. When I asked her why, she explained amid tears that it was to honor Tatayi's dearly departed spirit, and to mourn the loss of his life. For thirteen days, the house fell silent, weighed down by the grief of my grandfather's demise. No longer did Tatayi's *Vedic* chants resonate through the house. My cousins and I missed wishing him adieu each morning before we left for school, and we longed for the lemon drops he doled out to us each day.

Appa and my uncles shear their hair, cremate their father, and visit the crematorium each day. Atta, now a widow, is stripped of her *mangalsutra* (the wedding necklace), the *bindi* (the traditional red dot on her forehead), her toe rings, and the cluster of colorful bangles that had long adorned her hands—all sacred symbols of her married life. On the thirteenth day from Tatayi's passing, priests arrive at the crack of dawn, and amid chanting, the nandadeepa is lit once more. A host of relatives and neighbors gather to pay their last respects to my grandfather. Each of us grandchildren is carefully instructed to seek his blessings and pray for his departed soul. A team of cooks scurries around the house cooking a traditional meal for the hundreds of guests who have arrived. As I help my cousins lay the plantain leaves in neat rows in the grand hall again, I feel the overwhelming absence of our beloved grandfather. I am filled with sorrow knowing that he will never again be in our midst, sanctifying our meals with his prayers and blessings.

With Tatayi's passing, the talisman that had held our family together comes undone. A veil of sadness descends on 400 Rama Iyengar Road and remains stubbornly in place for months to come. One day, I inadvertently overhear Appa and my uncles consulting with Atta about selling our house.

Within months, we prepare to move into rental homes spread across Bangalore. We pack our belongings into boxes and bid farewell to our family and friends. As I hop onto the back of Appa's motorbike and turn around to catch one last glimpse of our beloved home, the palace of my dreams, I realize that Diwali will never be the same again.

CHAPTER 2

# Mantras and Miniskirts

MY FAMILY AND I change homes and schools twice within two years. In the spring of 1974, we finally settle into a two-bedroom rental home, part of an apartment complex in Jayanagar 1st Block, a few miles away from our ancestral home. Nestled beside a commercial nursery, the apartment named *Shanti* embodies its name—peace. The front gates welcome us into a lush garden. Banana, guava, and papaya trees line the compound surrounding the four apartments, two on the ground floor and two more on the second floor. Sweet-smelling flower bushes of *parijatas* and *spatikas* skirt the apartments, leaving plenty of room for us to play hopscotch and hide-and-go-seek. A prickly cotton tree is tucked into a far corner of the front yard, and two garages with tin roofs and metal doors stand watch opposite. Over the years, they morph into the neighborhood playhouse and dance studio.

At first, I miss my cousins, uncles, aunts, Atta, and our friends. But in time, the three other families, tenants at Shanti, become an extended family. The Nair family of four lives right across from us on the ground floor. Their daughters, Puja and Anuradha—Anu for short—are just a couple of years younger than Chitra and me. Mr. and Mrs. Nair both work full time and, therefore, have a couple of live-in maids, Jaya and Meena, who are from their hometown in Kerala, to help raise the girls. The Nairs also have a couple of cute white Pomeranian dogs, Raja and Rani. The Rao family of fourteen lives in one of the apartments on the second floor. And Mr. Menon, a confirmed bachelor, lives in the other.

We hardly see him, except on holidays, especially Diwali, when all twenty-four residents of Shanti gather to celebrate the festival of lights.

Although my uncles, aunts, and their families live in rental homes within five miles from ours, we don't celebrate festivals with them anymore, not even Diwali. We do, however, visit each other once a month and gather as a clan every year to celebrate my grandfather Tatayi's *tithi*—death anniversary. Atta takes turns living with each of her three sons. Gradually, we settle into our new homes and a new life.

Amma seems happier ever since the move to Shanti. There is a spring in her step and a lilt in her voice as she goes about her day. Perhaps it is a celebration of her newfound freedom. For the first time in her life, she is the mistress of our humble mansion. No longer under the vigilance of her mother or mother-in-law, she asserts her independence and sets out to chart our lives and create a cozy home for us. Amma had been barely eighteen when she met and married my father in June 1959. Appa was twenty-four. My parents were a study in contrasts. My mother was fair like the full moon and my father was dark as the night sky; she was steady like the earth and he was restless like the wind. She was deeply religious and he was almost an atheist. She was traditional and he was modern. She was pragmatic and he, a wild dreamer. Their differences complemented and completed each other; their love was real and long lasting.

"Marriages are made in heaven, Gayu," Amma always said. "God knows who to pair." Although she wasn't born rich, Amma exudes an innate regality that transcends all worldly wealth. She is a woman of virtue and unflinching faith. A strong and resilient woman, she had grown up determined to right the wrongs of her childhood. Even as a young girl, she had resolved to live a life of righteousness and raise morally upright children. Her determined love and steely strength arose from the broken shards of her childhood. Raised by a mother whose river of love had long dried by the overwhelming demands of raising four young children singlehandedly on a shoestring budget, and a father who was away at work as an accountant in the Forestry Department, Amma had sworn that her children would never be left wanting for love.

My grandmother had been an emotionally distant woman; my mother loved us with intensity. My grandmother had been reserved and critical of her husband; my mother doted on hers, treating him like a prince. My mother worked tirelessly and prayed incessantly. Her faith became the impenetrable fortress that protected our family.

As an eight-year-old, my mother had chosen Rama as her beloved deity among many other Indian gods, for he was the only monogamous god of them all, she often explained. Each Saturday evening, it became a tradition for our family to visit the local Rama temple to seek his divine blessings. Appa often called Amma "Sita," likening her to the beloved bride of God Rama, a compliment Amma cherished. It was her fond hope that her daughters would grow up to be like Sita, the revered epitome of Indian womanhood. She prayed that Chitra and I would evolve into pious, self-sacrificing, ever-loving women of grace.

Within five years of marrying, Amma had been blessed with motherhood three times over. She had nearly died giving birth to my older brother, Ravi. "A monkey without a tail," she used to tease him. A five-pound, three-ounce baby born prematurely in the seventh month of pregnancy, he could barely breathe, and she had nearly bled to death. A year and eight months later, I had arrived, a full-term, seven-pound, seven-ounce baby, calm and content, except for the occasional flaring temper and inconsolable crying spells. Apparently, even as a toddler, I would crawl behind the sofa and whine for hours until I fell asleep sucking on the middle and index fingers on my left hand to seek solace. Two years later, my sister, Chitra, had come kicking and screaming, eager to claim her spot as the comic of our family.

Like Chitra, my father was the baby of his family. Ambitious and hardworking, he had grown up with four siblings in a highly orthodox Hindu family. Early on, he had rebelled against the ancient traditions of India and worshipped all things American, emulating his favorite American hero, Gregory Peck. My grandmother used to tell us that his slicked-back hair, crisply ironed shirts, gabardine pants, polished patent leather shoes, and perfect English had earned him the nickname "Englishman." But his great love was not England, but America, an intimacy borne of books and celluloid. His greatest disappointment had been to be kept at home, and his greatest hope, therefore, was for his children to one day migrate to the land of his dreams. Appa's hope became Amma's mission, and our lives a dress rehearsal for the grand finale—life in America!

Ravi, Chitra, and I were sent to a private school—Sri Saraswathi Vidya Mandira. As an "English medium" school, SSVM used English as the language of instruction. The cost of tuition, school uniforms, and supplies took a large chunk of Appa's salary. There were times when Amma was left scrounging for grocery money by month's end, but she always managed to provide us with three wholesome meals a day, even if it meant that she ate leftovers or went hungry sometimes. My parents made sure we had new clothes for our birthdays and festivals, even though they had to forgo buying themselves anything new for years. Amma mended her blouses until they were tattered, and Appa had his shirt collars reversed to extend their wear. Sometimes, when hard pressed for fabric, Amma let Chitra and me tear up her saris to bring our dream fashions to life. Appa worked ten- to eleven-hour days at Binny's, and Amma worked even longer at home. But neither of them ever complained. Their sacrifices, they believed, were the stepping-stones to our success. My parents were convinced that investing in a private, English-medium education for their children was the first step in realizing their dream for them to one day live in America, the land of opportunities.

All our cousins and most of our neighbors attended Kannada medium public schools where the regional language was used, and they often badgered us for being prissy snobs. Attending a private English medium school, however, had its advantages. For starters, a huge city like Bangalore attracts residents from all over India. Many of our neighbors couldn't speak Kannada, so English became our shared language. Speaking English was also considered highly fashionable and instantly elevated our social status. My siblings and I, however, realized the most important advantage of our English-based education in the years to come. Our Americanization, of course, did not stop with us attending English medium schools. It was a total transformation, from head to toe. Although it was against cultural norms for girls to cut their hair short, Appa now drove Chitra and me to the neighborhood barber to have our hair cut in bouncy bobs, just like Julie Andrews's in our favorite movie, *The Sound of Music.* And once a month on Sundays, there were makeup sessions and etiquette lessons at our favorite restaurant—Mavalli Tiffin Rooms (MTR).

After Chitra and I were showered and dressed in our Sunday best, Appa would sharpen a black Lakme eyebrow pencil and fill in our eyebrows and line our eyes. "Gorgeous!" he would exclaim, admiring his artistry. "You girls look just like Elizabeth Taylor in the movie *Cleopatra.*" Dressed in our bright floral miniskirts and strappy white sandals, Chitra and I felt extra chic. Amma was also included in Appa's makeover. Once he was done dolling up Chitra and me, my father would sculpt my mother's hair into a beehive and give her the *Cleopatra* eye treatment. Amma would slip into her sleeveless blouse, chiffon sari, and high heels while Chitra and I watched her every move admiringly. Ravi and Appa would dress in their weekend best, and off we went to our Sunday brunch at MTR.

MTR was no ordinary restaurant, and everyone in and around Bangalore knew that. To get a table at the famed restaurant, we often had to wait up to an hour or more. The owners of MTR did not believe in taking reservations. But their customers rarely complained, since the food at MTR was always worth the wait. Their legendary *masala dosas*—delicious, crisp crepes of rice and lentils served with savory potato and onion curry and spicy coconut chutney—made our mouths water.

"Five masala dosas, please," Appa would request of the waiter in starched whites. And when they finally arrived, he would ask for a volunteer to demonstrate the proper use of the silverware. Always eager to please my father, I would volunteer. Appa would unfold and spread the napkin on my lap, and place the fork in my left hand and the knife in my right hand.

"Watch and learn," he would say, guiding my right hand to cut a piece of masala dosa with the knife, and with the fork in my left hand, he would help me dip it gently into the chutney and place it in my mouth. "Now, all of you eat with your cutlery and chew with your mouths closed," he would instruct before helping himself to his lunch.

Amma would glance at us and nod her head silently, prodding us with her eyes to follow Appa's lead. My mother's eyes always spoke volumes without words.

"Like this, Appa?" I would ask, showing off my newly acquired skills, hoping to make my father proud.

"Good job, Princess!" he would exclaim, patting my head and ordering Mysore coffee for himself and *masala chai* for Amma. Ravi, Chitra, and I always ordered pistachio ice cream for dessert. Our tummies full, we would arrive home looking forward to our afternoon naps. Later in the evening, as my siblings and I played with our neighborhood friends, our parents often went to visit friends and family or see a film. A movie buff, Appa made sure that he and Amma never missed an American film playing in town.

Amma told us that as a young bride, Appa had insisted that she learn to read, write, and speak in English. Although Amma had been a bright student and completed high school, she had attended a Kannada medium school and was very rusty with her English. Before leaving for work, my father often assigned her a story to read in the latest edition of *Reader's Digest.* And when he came home, Amma had to recount the essence of the story to Appa—in English. Amazingly, Amma had learned enough English to converse comfortably and understand most of the dialogues in the movies. But when it came to spelling, she made us laugh. For instance, *bulbs*—lightbulbs on the grocery list—was always spelled *blubs.* No matter how often we corrected her, she believed she was right.

It wasn't merely the school we attended, or how we dressed or ate, that showed our embrace of the American way. Appa truly believed in Thomas Jefferson's philosophy that all men are created equal, and Amma shared his belief. Regardless of whether a person was Hindu, Muslim, Sikh, or Christian; priest, beggar, housekeeper, or milkmaid, our parents insisted that we treated one and all with love and respect.

Born and raised in a country infested by the caste system, we found that the ability to love and respect all people as equal was one of the many precious gifts our parents gave us. "You are no different from any man," Appa often reminded Chitra, Amma, and me. "You are just as capable."

While my aunts were relegated to domestic duties at home, Appa encouraged Amma to step beyond the threshold and go to the bank and then pay the bills at the electric and water bureaus. He took her to company parties and encouraged her to be independent, treating her as a partner in every way. Unlike his brothers and many Indian men of his generation, he also let her handle the family finances.

Appa's love for all things American extended to his taste in music as well. He took great pride in the Phillips stereo system in the living room and his extensive LP collection—Frank Sinatra, Louis Armstrong, Elvis Presley, and Barbra Streisand. When Appa returned home from work and often on weekends, he often removed an LP from its cover, placed it on the turntable, and set the needle gently on the track. He serenaded along with Frank Sinatra singing "My Way" and swayed with the soulful trumpeting of Louis Armstrong's "What a Wonderful World." He often grabbed Amma in a bear hug and pestered her to dance with him. Amma always wiggled her way out of his arms. Sometimes, he scooped Chitra or me into his arms and slid us gracefully around the room. We clung to him like little chimps.

Appa was also an avid reader. He had read all the American classics. Ernest Hemingway was one of his favorite authors. Twice a week, Chitra and I walked to Ganesha Library with Appa's book list in hand. Mr. Joshi, the librarian, often joked that he couldn't keep up with Appa's appetite for American books. Appa also loved to read magazines—*National Geographic* was his favorite. Perched on my father's lap, gazing at the crystal blue waters of the Pacific Ocean, the expansive, palm-lined streets of Los Angeles, and the majestic cliffs of the Grand Canyon, I could almost picture myself in these far-off places. "Gayu, one day, you will send me pictures of you visiting these places," Appa would say, planting a kiss on my forehead. I believed my father's dream would come true.

While Appa encouraged us to wear miniskirts and makeup, Amma insisted on teaching us mantras. Although she supported our Americanization, she stood steadfast in inculcating all things Indian in us. By the time we could barely speak, she taught my siblings and me many mantras—prayers in praise of the Hindu gods and goddesses that presided in the altar in our home. "No prayers, no breakfast," was my mother's motto.

Over the years, Amma taught me how to sweep and wash the threshold at the entrance of our home first thing in the morning, and draw rangoli—intricate geometric designs made with finely milled stone—to welcome the gods and goddesses to sanctify our home.

Now, as a teenager, however, my most cherished chore is to wander into Ramayya's Tota, the commercial nursery across from our home, to gather flowers for Amma's morning prayers. Surrounded by birdsong and the sweet scent of flowers, I fall in love with the serenity of the garden, a love that would nurture my soul in the years to come.

During summer breaks, Amma instructs Chitra and me in the domestic arts. We make cotton wicks for diyas, and we learn the art of stringing flower garlands. While I sit transfixed, gently pinching the pale green stems of jasmines together in my left hand, struggling to weave a string of cotton yarn under and over with my right hand knotting the flowers together, Chitra is busy climbing the guava tree in our front yard and picking fights with the neighborhood boys.

Amma also teaches us how to cook a complete meal. "Gayu, the way to a man's heart is through his stomach," she insists. "It's not enough to know how to do calculus. It is also important to know how to cook." I recall being eight years old, barely tall enough to reach the granite countertop in our kitchen, when Amma first recruited me as her apprentice. At fifteen, I had now become her constant companion in the kitchen. I love everything about cooking—chopping vegetables, roasting spices, grating coconut, and making *chapattis.* I take great pride in rolling out the little disks of whole-wheat dough into perfect circles and watching their golden crusts puff up as Amma flips them on the hot *tava,* a heavy cast-iron griddle. Most of all, I love to work alongside Amma, while we sing in chorus with our favorite songs lilting through the Phillips radio in the living room.

*Mangalada e sudhina madhuravagali*
*Nimmoluve e maneya nandadeepavagali*
*Anuragadha raga male nimmadagali*
*Apaswaradha chaye yendu kaanadaagali*
*Shruthiyodane sahagana leenavagali*
*Shubha shanthi mereyali*
*Tande tayi daari toro kannugaleredu*
*Avara prema dooravage makkalu kurudu*
*Mamate eruva maneyu sadha jenina goodu*
*Ade shantiya beedu*

*May this auspicious day become a day of fond remembrance*
*Let your love be the everlasting guiding light of this house*
*May the garland of love be forever yours*
*Let there never ever be the shadow of discord in your life*
*Let the melodious hum of life enrapture you in its folds*
*Let goodness and peace prosper*
*Father and mother are the two eyes that guide us through the path of life*
*Bereft of their love, children become blind*
*A home filled with affection is forever cozy like a beehive*
*It is an abode of peace.*

Amma has a way of teaching me life lessons through lyrics.

Ravi, Chitra, and I eventually make our way through high school and enter pre-university. And Appa climbs the corporate ladder of success. Amma is blissfully happy. Life hums along in harmony, at least until my siblings and I enter the choppy waters of adolescence. Chitra begins to flounder in math. Our parents chalk it up to her failing interest. Ravi starts smoking clandestinely, cutting classes, and getting mixed up with local gangs. Amma becomes his corrections officer counselor. She keeps a close vigil on his every move and stages an intervention at school with his teachers and the principal. Determined to make a decent student out of him, she arranges for each of his teachers to attest to his attendance in class, and starts tutoring him at home. When Ravi fails to show up at home for dinner, she sends Chitra and me to patrol the neighborhood and his friends' homes until we find him. Appa threatens to throw him out of the house or send him to an army boot camp if he doesn't mend his ways. But Amma, insisting that it will boost Ravi's self-esteem, convinces Appa to buy him a motorbike and offer him an allowance as incentives for staying out of trouble and earning good grades. While Ravi is given free rein to explore the city and enjoy his perks, Chitra and I are granted none of these privileges. Instead, Amma keeps us contained within a five-mile radius, expecting us to be home before dark. "I trust you, my darlings. It is the world I don't trust," she insists when we argue to stay out late.

As I emerge into adolescence, the disparate ideals my parents have for me become clear. While my mother's goal is to groom me into a god-fearing domestic diva, my father's vision is for me to become a modern, ambitious woman who is unafraid to follow her dreams. My life therefore, becomes a mixture of mantras and miniskirts—a dizzying blend of two cultures, two continents, worlds apart: the ancient East, India, and the modern West, America. A born pleaser, I strive to please both my parents and succeed, at least until I am around eighteen, when my budding sense of style and independence coupled with my growing irritability and dark moods meet with the disapproval of both my parents.

Amma abhors my fascination with fashion, and I rebel against her archaic views—an act that she perceives to be extremely disrespectful. She wants me to grow my hair long and braid it, cover my arms and legs, and be cautious of the attention I elicit from boys. We argue incessantly about the flare of my bell-bottom pants and the style of my tops. She prefers they have sleeves and cover my arms and crotch line, and I insist that they are sleeveless and sit at my hip. Much to my mother's fury, I start experimenting with makeup and cut my hair in a boy cut. In Amma's world, a woman can either have style or substance, never both. And, more than anything, she wants me to be a woman of substance. Appa and I, on the other hand, believe a woman can have both.

I still remember the day my father took me to Collette's, the brand-new beauty parlor in the shopping complex in Jayanagar 4th Block. "Can you please cut my hair in layers like hers?" I had asked the Chinese hairdresser, showing her a picture of Bollywood's sizzling-hot heroine Zeenat Aman, on the cover of the latest *Stardust*—a popular fashion magazine. An hour later, I had emerged from the store ecstatic, loving my new hairdo.

"You look gorgeous, Gayu, just like Princess Diana," Appa had said, making my heart sing. But when we got home, Amma shrieked. "Look at your hair shorn shorter than your brother's! You look like a mad dog! No decent Indian boy will ever marry you!"

"What's wrong with you?" she had scolded my father. "I expected you to have more sense than to let your stupid daughter do as she pleases."

"I think she looks beautiful," Appa had chuckled. "If no Indian boy wants to marry my princess, we'll just have to find her an American boy."

Weeks later, I watch my cousin Chaitra tweeze her eyebrows into an arch. I sneak into her room after she leaves and pluck my eyebrows hiding behind her bed. I tiptoe back home later that evening and try to conceal my handiwork. But it doesn't work. Nothing escapes my mother's eyes.

"What did you do to your eyebrows, you stupid child?" she explodes. "You look like a prostitute. Don't you dare do it again!" She raises her hands, ready to slap me.

I duck and run out of the house, careful not to come back until Appa returns home from work. I squeeze between the washing stone and the trash can in the backyard, bury my head between my knees, and sob my heart out. I press my palms to my ears and try desperately to drown the world out. But I can't.

*Prostitute, prostitute, prostitute* . . . the word splinters me into smithereens. It rings in my ears, ricochets in my head, and rips through my heart. *Perhaps my mother is right. Perhaps I am a whore.* I feel filthy, like the trash in the red plastic pail sitting next to me. I can't believe my own mother has called me a prostitute. The very thought unleashes a fresh torrent of tears. Crying, I am learning, is my only way to cope with my mother's rage.

"Have you two been fighting again?" Appa asks when he gets home, sensing the tension in the air.

"Look what she has done to her face!" Amma glares, pointing toward my eyebrows.

"They look beautiful," says Appa, coming to my rescue again. "Perhaps you and Chitra should get your eyebrows shaped as well."

A week later, Amma and Chitra go to Collette's and get their eyebrows professionally tweezed. I am absolutely enraged. "Prostitute!" I want to scream at my mother, but the word stays stuck like hot coals charring my throat. I know better than to evoke her anger. When the endless arguments and screaming fits fail to sway me into her way of life, Amma unleashes the ultimate weapon in her arsenal of child rearing: the silent treatment. She stops talking to me for days, sometimes a week or more. I had grown up hearing the adage "Sticks and stones can break my bones, but words can never hurt me." Now, at nineteen, I have learned otherwise.

Lately, the catcalls of strangers on the streets and the taunts of my classmates make me feel like a freak. Ever since I had emerged into puberty, I had become prey to boys and men alike. It didn't matter if they were as old as me or old enough to be my father, I was fair game to their sexual fantasies. I wonder if they, like my mother, measure my merit and morals by the length of my miniskirts and short hair. While their words hurt me, Amma's silent treatment digs daggers into my heart. I cry for days on end, begging my mother to forgive me, until my eyes shrivel into mere slits in a swollen face.

"Is everything okay with you and your mother?" our neighbor Mrs. Rao asks when I go to throw out the garbage. "We haven't heard you sing lately."

"Everything is fine," I nod my head, avoiding to meet her inquiring eyes. Saving face and safeguarding my family's honor, I know, is my sacred duty. I do not want my neighbors to know about my altercations with my mother. And, even if they did, they would judge me to be a disrespectful daughter—the immeasurable shame of which had begun to suffocate me slowly.

At first Amma and Appa rationalize the changes in my behavior as nothing more than adolescent angst. But when the constant arguments and crying spells spill into days and weeks, their disapproval turns into disgust. In a household where strength is measured by how well one can suppress emotions, not express them, my weakness is seen as a personal misgiving and a sign of disgrace. Even my father, who had long supported my independent spirit and sense of fashion, begins to detest my melancholy.

"Stop it!" he yells. "Get a grip over yourself."

Unfortunately, the more I try to control my errant moods, the less in control I feel. I slowly submerge in a sea of conflicting emotions. Unable to think clearly or cope, I withdraw into a shell of sullen defiance. Not knowing what to do, my parents ignore me. With each passing day, the stone wall of alienation grows thicker, taller, and more impenetrable between us, until I feel completely abandoned. I need their approval as much as a sunflower needs the sun. Devoid of it, I begin to wilt—physically and emotionally. Blinded without their love and acceptance, I stumble through the first two years of my undergraduate studies, barely able to function. Unbeknownst, depression seeps into my life and tangles my relationships. Day by day, the sweet symphony of our family's life becomes but a distant memory. Our home, once a cozy cocoon filled with love and affection, becomes a place of despair and discord.

Like millions of people across the world, neither my parents nor I realize that the changes in my behavior are not just a normal phase of growing pains, but also the symptoms of adolescent depression—a highly prevalent, debilitating disease that affects millions of children and adolescents around the world. Looking back, I see that our ignorance was perhaps both a blessing and a curse. Had I been diagnosed with depression as a teenager in India, it might have defined me and limited my life. But not knowing what ailed me would ultimately lead me and my family through a harrowing journey. Having no knowledge of the disease that holds me in its teeth, or even a word to describe it, my family and I fail to understand or address it.

PART 2

# Veil of Darkness

CHAPTER 3

# Tomb of Terror

IT'S APRIL 1981. A throng of students stands buzzing around the bulletin board in the hallway by the chemistry lab at Vijaya College, where I have just completed my second year of undergraduate studies. It is a beautiful summer day—a perfect beginning for our long-awaited summer break. The annual results were posted earlier today. I spot my friend Jaya in the crowd and wave to her. She and I have been best friends since kindergarten. For weeks, we have been making plans for our vacation—matinees at the neighborhood Nanda theater, trips to the new shopping mall in Jayanagar 4th Block, savoring scoops of our favorite pistachio ice cream, and most important of all, two whole months of lazing around without a single book to read or an assignment due. We fight our way through the crowd and stand on tiptoe trying to locate our roll number and name on the list.

FAILED, it says in red ink, next to my name, M. K. Gayathri.

My mind goes dark. Tears streaming down my face, I dart across the campus, my heart pounding like the hoofbeats of a pack of wild horses. The world speeds by. I feel dizzy, faint. Nothing makes sense. A good student since kindergarten, I have never failed in my life.

"Wait," Jaya calls out, trying to catch up with me.

I don't look back.

I don't stop.

I am so ashamed. I want to disappear. I want to die.

I leap across puddles of cow dung on the street and rush past Ganesha Bakery, panting for breath, a couple of stray dogs chasing after me.

"Are you trying to get yourself killed, lady?" an auto rickshaw driver screams, tooting his horn loudly. "Stupid kids these days, they don't stop to see where they are going," he curses. "And then they blame us for the accident."

I race home on wobbly legs. I shut the front door and collapse on the chair at the dining table, wailing.

"What's wrong, Gayu?" Amma asks, putting down the basket of green beans she was stringing.

"I *failed*!" I blurt out between sobs.

"What?" she asks, stunned.

"I failed," I repeat, burying my face between my knees.

FAILED—the six-letter word shatters my world.

"Work hard, Gayu," Appa had always preached. "It doesn't matter if you are a girl. You can be anything you want to be."

I had believed him. Of the three children, I was the strongest academically. While my brother and sister stumbled through school, I had continued to focus on my studies and garner good grades. And, ever since I had won first place at the science fair in sixth grade for my papier-mâché model of the human heart, demonstrating the workings of the circulatory system, I had secretly dreamed of going to medical school and realizing my father's dream of becoming a doctor. When my tenth-grade scores had earned me a seat in the selective pre-university science program at Vijaya College, I had kept my fingers crossed about becoming the first female physician in my entire extended family. Disappointed that I hadn't scored high enough in my second year of pre-university to qualify for direct admission into Bangalore Medical College, I had held on to the hope that I might apply to medical school after completing my undergraduate program.

But with this one failed grade, I know now that I have destroyed our dreams—Appa's and mine.

I feel sick to my stomach. I clasp my mouth and run to the bathroom, retching.

"It must be a mistake, Gayu," soothes Amma as she rushes behind me. "Perhaps you misread the results," she says, handing me a cup of cold water. "Calm down. Everything will be all right. I can have Ravi check your results again if you like. I am sure it is a mistake."

"I *failed,* Amma. I *failed!*" I scream, crawling into a corner of the bedroom between the stack of mattresses and the large mahogany armoire. Filled with shame, I just want to disappear.

Amma tries coaxing me out to join her for lunch. I don't budge.

"Come on, let's have lunch," Chitra says, crouching beside me. "It's no big deal. Remember, I failed my accounting class last year." She shrugs her shoulders dismissively. "It's not the end of the world. You can take the supplemental exam and pass it. Come on!" She tugs at my hands, trying to pry me off the floor.

I sit motionless, mute. Bored, she leaves.

Ravi comes home during his lunch break. Amma busies herself serving my siblings their lunch. Ravi is now a first-year student in the electrical engineering program at BMS College of Engineering, a miracle considering his near-failing grades in high school. Amma's vigilance and tutoring had paid off. After an entire year of pleading with the admissions department at BMS, Amma and Appa were hard-pressed to pay the donation the college demanded. In the end, they decided to sell a plot of land they had purchased with dreams of building their own home, to essentially buy my brother a place in the program—yet another sacrifice to ensure my brother's successful career and future in America.

"It's no big deal, Gayathri. Come and join us for lunch," Ravi insists. I don't respond.

"It's okay. Let's give her some time alone," Amma says. "She'll eat when she is hungry."

Hours go by. I don't feel hungry. The pit in my stomach grows deeper and darker, churning with grief as I sob for hours. Over the last couple of years, even as my errant moods tangled my relationship with my parents, my good grades were my only source of pride and solace. They were the only redeeming factor that continued to please my parents and make them proud of me. And, now, with the failing grade, I believe I have severed my chances of ever earning their love and respect. Having disgraced myself and my parents, I see no purpose to live.

*How could I possibly have failed?*

*What will Appa say when he finds out?*

*I bet all my classmates know.*

*How can I ever go back to college again?*

*Do our neighbors know?*

*Will Ravi and Chitra tell them?*

*Oh, my God! I can't ever go out of the house again. Never!*

The thoughts keep whirring in my brain, like an audiotape gone awry—rewind, replay, repeat; rewind, replay, repeat.

Ravi returns to college. Chitra runs out to play with her friends in the neighborhood. Amma lies down for a nap in her bedroom next door. I feel sorry for her. She is usually worn out by midafternoon. I sit still and muffle my sobs with my fist. I don't want to disturb her. She needs her sleep. Except for Sundays, Amma wakes up at four thirty, showers, and cooks a complete four- to five-course lunch in time for Appa to take it with him to work by six thirty. Ever since Appa had a mild heart attack when I was in seventh grade, Amma has taken extra measures to ensure he eats healthy meals every day. She makes three chapattis—whole-wheat flat bread—a vegetable curry, rice, and sambar—lentil stew. She packs it in a four-tiered, stainless steel Tiffin carrier along with a couple of scoops of cool, creamy homemade yogurt in a little glass jar, and packs a few pieces of Appa's favorite lemon pickle in a tiny little steel box. She places them along with a red-and-white-checked cotton hand towel in the dark khaki-colored canvas lunch bag she has sewn especially for Appa. By six, Amma sets Appa's lunch on the dining table beside his work clothes, which she pressed and hung on the chair the night before, and polished black shoes and a pair of clean socks.

Appa wakes up at five every day, even on Sundays. He is a restless sleeper, a habit from working graveyard shifts. He shaves, showers, dresses, and sips a piping hot cup of coffee that Amma hands him.

He browses hurriedly through *Indian Express,* the daily newspaper, before waving good-bye to Amma at six thirty, setting the lunch bag into the metal storage box on his motorbike, and zooming out to work at Binny's, the textile mill where he has worked for the last twenty-one years.

Once Appa is off to work, Amma wakes us up, offers her morning prayers, serves us breakfast, and toils through the household chores until we come home from our classes.

Engulfed in the quicksand of my mind, I don't hear Amma's footsteps when she comes to get me.

"Get up, Gayu. It will be dusk soon. It's a bad omen to sit in the dark and cry. Appa will be home any minute. Come, help me make chapattis," she says, turning on the radio and walking into the kitchen.

I scramble to my feet reluctantly and follow my mother.

"Wash your face and say your prayers," she says, adjusting the cotton wick in the nandadeepa and lighting it.

I step beside my mother, fold my hands by my heart, and chant the evening prayer that she taught my siblings and me when we were toddlers.

*Shubhambhavathu Kalyani*
*Arogyadhana sampadham*
*Mama shatru vinashaya*
*Sayamjyoti namostuthe*

*I offer obeisance to you, dear Goddess*
*May you bless us with health, wealth, and happiness.*
*I offer my respects to the light of knowledge,*
*And pray that it destroys the enemies within.*

As a curious five-year-old, I remember asking my mother who the enemies were.

"Fear, sorrow, despair, doubt, apathy, anger, hatred, jealousy—they are our most formidable enemies," she had replied, caressing my head.

Now I lay my head by the God's altar and shudder, knowing that the *enemies within* have laid siege on my soul.

"Don't worry, Gayu," Amma says, wiping the tears rolling down my cheeks with the tip of her sari and handing me the rolling pin. "Everything will be fine. Lord Rama will relieve you of your troubles."

Amma's faith in her beloved God Rama had always comforted me, rooted me. But today, my faith is shattered. I doubt if even God Rama will forgive me for destroying my parents' dreams.

Amma's dream of going to college was torn to shreds by her father, who had insisted that she adhere to tradition and marry right out of high school. A brilliant student, she often told me the story of how she had walked barefoot for five miles on the day of her high school graduation to bring home a college application.

"It will be impossible for me to find you a groom if you go to college. No man wants to marry a woman more educated than him," her father had argued, tearing the application form into bits.

It was 1959. In India, young women from ordinary middle-class families were forbidden to go to college. Once married, Amma had hoped that her modern husband would help her achieve her dream. But with each passing year and the birth of yet another child, she had reluctantly made peace with the strictly prescribed role of a dutiful daughter-in-law and devoted wife and mother. And when she was blessed with daughters of her own, she had promised they would go to college.

Appa's dream was to become a doctor. But his dreams were dashed by his own father, who had paid the tuition to the textile school, where admissions had been announced before the medical school admissions. Although Appa had secured admission to Bangalore Medical College, he was never allowed to attend it. And, so, when I showed promise in my science classes, Appa had hoped that I would bring his dream alive—a dream that I know now will never come true.

I pick up the rolling pin and start rolling out the dough like a robot. Amma sings along with the radio, nudging me to join in. I can't. The words are stuck in my throat. Tears sting my eyes. I feel woozy with the pain and guilt of letting Amma and Appa down.

I hear Appa's motorbike in the driveway. My heart pounds faster and faster until it feels like it will jump right out of my chest.

"Hello, Princess," Appa greets me, pecking me on my head from behind. "Did you get your results today?" he asks.

I bite my lip to keep from bawling. It doesn't work.

"She failed," Amma whispers. "She has been crying all day."

"It's not the end of the world, darling," Appa says, drawing me into his arms. I bury my face in the crook of my elbow, too ashamed to look at him.

"Don't worry, Gayu. Did you know I failed in college more than once?" he asks, recounting his troubles as a student. "Trust me, you will come out of this stronger," he says. "I know it doesn't feel like it to you now." He draws me onto his lap and wipes away my tears. Tucked in the warm safety of my father's arms, I desperately want to believe him. But I can't. A deep dread sweeps through my body.

"Let's eat. I am starved," my father says, heading to the bathroom to wash up before dinner. I force myself to my feet and start setting the table.

I recall the day Appa brought home the dining table. It was on a Sunday, soon after my seventeenth birthday. Our neighbors peeked out of their windows to see what all the excitement was about as Appa helped the truck driver unload the table and eight matching chairs. The table was big and beautiful. It had a Formica top that looked like fine marble and felt like silk to the touch. Appa had also bought a soft, fluffy, peanut-shaped cleaning sponge and drilled all of us with precise instructions on the proper care of our newfound marvel. I adored the table and was filled with a snobbish pride knowing that we were the only ones in our entire extended family and among the elite few in the neighborhood to eat at a dining table—just like Americans—while the rest of them ate squatting on the floor. Appa insisted Amma join us at the table, instead of serving us first and eating alone in the kitchen later, as most Indian mothers did. Amma sat at one end of the table, and Appa held court at the other. Chitra and I sat on one side of the table, and Ravi across from us. Eating at the table was yet another of Appa's tutorials to teach us Western etiquette.

Amma took great care in the meals she prepared, and Appa took pride in our growing appetites. He often rewarded the child who ate the most and challenged the other two to follow suit. Ravi held the coveted title of the "family hog" for a while, but by the time I was eighteen, I was giving him a fight for the crown. Mealtimes had become a cherished tradition, a time to catch up with our lives, while relishing Amma's divine cuisine.

"Wash your hands, say your prayers, and join us for dinner," Amma calls out to Ravi and Chitra, who are lingering with their friends in the front yard.

I pass the chapattis around. Amma serves a scoop of brinjal curry on each of our plates and settles into her chair.

"I got picked to play on the university basketball team," Ravi announces excitedly, listing all the sports gear he needs to buy within the next week before practice starts.

"Wow! Congratulations," Amma, Appa, and Chitra wish in chorus. I sit quietly, lost in oblivion.

"Congratulations," I finally mumble, forcing myself back to the table.

I spot a look of concern floating through my mother's eyes. I bet she is worrying how she will be able to afford all the sports paraphernalia Ravi needs. Money is tight. But, she is a magician at making ends meet.

"Can I go to the movies this weekend, Amma?" Chitra pleads.

"I'll think about it," my mother says. "Can I serve you another chapatti?" she asks Appa.

"Thanks, Popsi, the curry is delicious," Appa says, serving himself more.

I tear a piece of chapatti, scoop a little bit of curry, and place it in my mouth. I taste nothing, except a fear that churns my stomach and hammers my head with pain. The room, the table, the dishes, Amma, Appa, Chitra, Ravi . . . everything around me begins to spin. I feel nauseated. I can't breathe. I am afraid I am going to die.

"Are you okay?" Appa asks, sensing my discomfort.

"Yes," I nod my head, clutching the table, not wanting to cause a scene. I cup my mouth with my hands, squeeze my eyes tight, and pray I don't puke. My prayers aren't answered. I throw up all over my plate. It splatters onto Ravi and Chitra's plates as well. It smells awful, like stale fish and rotten eggs. Ravi and Chitra plug their noses and flee from the table. I begin shaking violently. The floodgates of tears break open again. I hate myself for ruining everyone's dinner. Amma had cooked for hours to prepare dinner, and Appa had worked hard all day and was enjoying his meal.

My parents stare at me in concern.

"I am sorry," I say, grab my plate, and stumble into the bathroom.

I wash my plate and splash cold water on my face, and rinse my mouth over and over, trying to get rid of the awful taste. Not wanting to stink up the special peanut-shaped sponge, I wet a rag and scramble back to the table to clean it up.

Amma and Appa have already cleared the dishes off the table. The sight and smell of my vomit on the tabletop makes me want to throw up again. I pinch my nose with my left hand and wipe the filth off with the rag in my right hand.

"Don't worry, Gayu. It must be the evil eye," my mother says to comfort me. "Wash up and come sit by the God's altar," she says. "I'll perform *dhrishti.*" She grabs a pinch of rock salt and a couple of dried red chili peppers in her left hand. Up and down, she waves her clenched hand encircling me three times from head to toe, muttering a spell to chastise the evil spirits away. She taps her fist on the ground by my feet and tosses the salt and chili peppers into a little bonfire made of broomsticks on the concrete bathroom floor.

"There, Gayu, you will be just fine by morning," she says as the chili peppers pop.

Chitra rolls out my mattress. I crawl into it.

"Good night, Princess." Appa kisses me on my feverish forehead.

"Good night, Appa," I mumble, pulling the sheets over my head. Ravi and Chitra chatter into the dark. I am convinced they are talking about me.

*Will our friends and neighbors find out?*

*Does everyone in college know?*

*What if I never pass the supplemental exams?*

*What if I don't graduate with my classmates?*

*I am such a loser. I will never amount to anything in life.*

*Will Amma and Appa ever forgive me?*

I cower behind my sheets and try to shut out the thoughts racing through my head. No matter how hard I try, I cannot silence them or fall asleep. I toss and turn in bed all night. It is the longest night of my life. Finally, by the time night breaks into day, I begin to drift into a fitful sleep.

"Good morning, Gayu. Time to rise and shine." Amma wakes me with her sing-song voice.

I don't want to get up. I have a splitting headache. My stomach is still sore from the night before. Chitra and Ravi are sprawled awkwardly on their mattresses next to mine, arms flailing, sheets crumbled.

"I have made *idlis* for breakfast," Amma says. "It will be good for your upset stomach."

I feel guilty for sleeping in and not helping Amma with breakfast. I reluctantly roll over to my right side and sit up in bed. I squint at the grandfather clock in the dining room. It is eight-thirty on Sunday morning—a day for cleaning and scrumptious meals. Appa has a chore for each of us. Ravi has to clean the fish tank, I have to help Amma with the meals, and Chitra has to dust the furniture. Appa is busy washing his motorbike, singing "Hello, Dolly" along with Louis Armstrong's LP, loud enough to entertain the entire neighborhood. They don't mind.

One by one, Ravi, Chitra, and I shower, dress, and say our morning prayers.

"Gayu, can you help grind the coconut chutney?" Amma calls out from the kitchen.

I have always loved grinding chutneys at the old grinding stone mounted on the granite counter in our kitchen. And coconut chutney is my favorite. But today, I find the very thought of food repugnant. Not wanting to disappoint Amma, however, I arrange the pieces of freshly grated coconut Amma has set aside along with a few springs of cilantro, a tiny sliver of ginger, a pinch of rock salt, and a grape-sized portion of tamarind around the grinding stone. I sprinkle some water and turn the grinding stone around and around, feeding the array of ingredients into the pit of the mortar. I grind the chutney into a smooth concoction and scoop it into a stainless steel bowl.

"Chitra, please set the table, bangara," Amma calls out, adding a sizzling seasoning to the chutney: black mustard, curry leaves, halved red chili peppers, and a dash of asafetida.

My stomach somersaults at the smell of spices. Soon, our family of five gathers around the table for breakfast. I pass the idlis and chutney around and serve myself last. I tear a little piece of idli and place it hesitantly in my mouth. Instead of the usual chatter at the table, I sense a silent unease. Even without lifting my head, I can feel everyone's eyes boring holes through me. I know that they are worried I will puke again. My stomach revolts with every bite. I am terrified my family's fears will come true.

*Take a bite, chew, and keep it down,* I chant silently. My heart quickens and my stomach tightens. I feel dizzy and begin to choke. The more I try to calm the mounting waves of nausea, the more violent they grow. Visions of the night before keep flashing through my tired mind.

"You are going to throw up again, aren't you?" Appa glares at me.

I don't want to throw up. I don't want to anger my father. I want to please him more than anything in the world. But I can't. In an instant, the queasiness that I had tried hard to quell becomes a clear and present danger. I clutch my spastic stomach and run to the bathroom just in time for my breakfast to meet the floor. My chest tightens. I gasp for breath. *Am I having a heart attack? Will I die?* I collapse on the wet concrete floor, crying uncontrollably. My body is on fire. I splash cold water on my face to help calm down. Spent, I sit in a pool of water and vomit, longing for my mother's hands to caress my aching body and splintered mind. I want my father to hold me in his arms, assure me that everything will be okay, and tell me that he loves me despite my dark moods and failing grade. Instead, I hear my parents arguing loudly at the table.

"What in the world is wrong with her?" Appa screams. "For God's sake, she is nineteen years old. One failed grade, and she is acting like her life is over."

"Calm down, Popsi," Amma tells Appa. "Perhaps she has an upset stomach. Give her a few days. She'll be fine."

A gnawing threat grips me throughout the weeks ahead; each day is a torturous repeat of the day before. I cannot keep any food down. Not even the bland buttermilk and rice that Amma mashes up for me to eat. I survive on tender coconut water and fresh watermelon juice. I grow weaker by the day, become withdrawn, and spend hours in bed. I become paranoid about leaving home, ashamed about my failing grade, afraid I might throw up or, worse yet, lose control in public. My best friend, Jaya, stops by to visit me a couple of times. I refuse to see her.

Concerned, Amma and Appa take me to Dr. Mahesh, our family physician.

"What brings you here this morning, Gayathri?" he asks, motioning me to lie down on the examination table, peering through the gold-framed glasses perched on the bridge of his nose. Amma and Appa recount the events of the past few weeks.

Dr. Mahesh palpates my stomach and asks my parents a battery of questions.

"Nothing to worry," he says, handing a piece of paper to Appa. "Here is a prescription for antinausea medication. Children these days lose hope at the smallest setbacks, don't they?" Dr. Mahesh says, shaking his head.

"Gayathri, you can't get so upset at a failed grade. Life is full of ups and downs. I am sure you will do well next time," he says, helping me off the table. "Follow the prescription. You will be absolutely fine in a couple of days."

But I don't get better. The pills Dr. Mahesh prescribed do nothing to suppress my nausea or slow my pounding heart and racing thoughts.

"Buck up and be strong, Gayu," Appa admonishes. "You can't be weak and hypersensitive. You can't give up on life just because you failed once. You have to force yourself to eat so you can get your strength back," he insists.

"I can't," I cry. If there is one thing my father can't stand, it is tears. To him, they are the ultimate sign of weakness. Unfortunately, for me, they are my only solace.

"At this rate, we will have to hook you up to an IV tube and force-feed you," he shouts, storming out of the room. Appa's temper tantrums are legendary in our family. So are his sullen retreats, but no one ever questions them. We just accept it as a man's prerogative.

Later that evening, my father brings home a box of Threptin biscuits—high-protein biscuits fortified with minerals and multivitamins. They taste like sawdust. I pretend to nibble at one when he is around and toss it in the trash once he leaves.

"You are stronger than you think you are," he argues day after day, extolling me with heroic tales of World War II veterans. "Gayu, you have to get a grip over your mind," he cautions, "or it will destroy you."

*I hate you. I don't care about your heroes!* I want to yell. I don't. Over the last couple of years, I have caused my parents enough grief. The least I can do to atone for my sins, I decide, is to remain quiet and respectful.

"Gayu, pray with a pure heart," my mother coaxes me. "Why don't you chant *Sri Rama* a hundred and one times each day? Perhaps you should also write *Sri Rama* a hundred and one times a day," she says, handing me a notebook.

Lately, I have lost faith in God. In fact, I have begun to wonder if there is a God. And even if there is, I cannot fathom how a kind and loving God can inflict such pain upon me. Yet in my hour of need, I instinctively turn to God as a newborn turns to her mother's bosom. I chant *Sri Rama* incessantly and beg for his mercy. But regardless of my prayers, fear remains a constant companion: fear of failing again, fear of being mocked at college, fear of losing control in public, fear of throwing up, fear of disappointing my parents, and fear of being ridiculed by my brother and sister, who think it is endearing to call me *Vaikal Rani*—

queen of vomit. I am afraid that I will have a heart attack and die. And most of all, I am terrified that I am losing my mind. I don't tell Amma and Appa about my fears, not even Ravi and Chitra. I am scared they will think I am crazy. Instead, I get into meaningless fights with my siblings, jealous that they continue to live their carefree lives while I lie confined in a body and brain gone awry. I spend my days buckled over in the bathroom, or curled up in bed while my siblings are out with friends at the movies or the mall, enjoying popcorn and ice cream cones, living the life of my dreams. I hate my life. I hate everyone in it. I cannot understand how everyone can go on living when my life is in shambles.

Summer creeps painfully along. Even as the sun bathes everything with its golden kiss, my days are filled with darkness. I grow skinny. My hip bones jut out, and I can count my ribs.

"I can fill a measure of rice in those cavities," my mother says, pointing to the sunken hollow behind my collarbones as she helps me shampoo my hair one day. My arms have grown too weak to wash my hair.

"What's wrong with Gayathri?" my aunts, uncles, and cousins ask. "She looks like she has lost a lot of weight." At 5 foot 4 inches, I weighed ninety pounds the last time Dr. Mahesh checked at his clinic.

"She has a stomach upset," Amma reassures them. "The doctor says there is nothing to worry about."

Something is wrong with me, I know. And it is certainly not my stomach that is sick; I suspect I am going mad. I am terrified I will end up like the short, bald man living up the street behind the barbed-wire fence, pacing up and down all day, mumbling to himself. I have seen the neighborhood boys pelt stones at him, call him *huccha*—madman. I have heard him scream, begging them to stop. But they don't.

Days roll by, and I remain sick. When the bland diet and antinausea medications fail to revive me, Amma and Appa are baffled. Amma asks the priests at the neighborhood temples to perform *abhishekas*—special prayers in my name—and anoints my forehead with the sacred vermillion. Appa insists on getting a second opinion and a third. After performing a series of blood tests, a barium-meal X-ray, and many other explorative procedures, the physicians all unite in their opinion that there is nothing wrong with me. Dr. Karanth, a reputed physician and senior colleague of Dr. Mahesh, concurs, summing it up as adolescent angst. He insists that I am being a typical teenager—a drama queen asking for undue attention instead of navigating the road bumps of life with maturity and grace.

"Children these days aren't resilient like we used to be, Mr. Kasinath. They are not built like their parents and grandparents," Dr. Karanth lectures. "They can't stomach failure." He prescribes "tough love" to strengthen me for life. Amma and Appa dole out a healthy dose of it each day. But I can't stomach it, much like the food and water that my body rejects. Deep inside, I know Dr. Karanth is wrong, just like Dr. Mahesh and all the others. But I say nothing. In a country where doctors are revered as gods, I don't dare contest his opinion. Neither do my parents.

*None of us realize that my symptoms are characteristic of highly treatable, commonly co-occurring mental illnesses—generalized anxiety disorder, panic disorder, and depression. We are also unaware that, left untreated, my symptoms could become chronic or recurrent, and could impair my ability to have a functional, meaningful life. It isn't that my parents and physicians don't care; they are utterly ignorant about mental health issues, just as many parents and physicians are, even today.*

Intellectually, I understand that the deep sense of disappointment and shame I feel at my failed grade is out of proportion, but I can't comprehend or control the emotional maelstrom it has unleashed. In a culture where the emotional aspects of a human being are rarely talked about or addressed, my family and physicians focus only on my physical symptoms, and completely ignore the very real psychic pain.

My parents force me to get a grip over my emotions and move on with life. My brother and sister go on with their daily drill, mere spectators in the saga of my life. Even the thought of getting out of bed and showering seems daunting to me. But I struggle to put on a façade of normalcy and brave through my days. Every day is a battle. I feel constantly judged, my every move analyzed. Regardless of how well-intentioned my parents are with their persistent concern and criticism, their actions exacerbate my symptoms instead of alleviating them.

Day after day, Appa sits at the table, lips pursed tight, teeth gritted. "You are going to do it again, aren't you?" He glares at me. And sure enough, I do. The vicious cycle repeats itself.

It takes my family and me nearly a decade to discover that my suffering is not just an extreme reaction to a failing grade, adolescent angst, or bad behavior. In time, we learn it is caused by the complex web of genetic, gender, psychosocial, hormonal, and neurobiological factors that define clinical depression and anxiety. But for now, ignorance imprisons us all in the blame game. My doctors and parents blame me for being a hypersensitive, weak, ungrateful, self-centered, immature teenager, and I blame them for their lack of understanding and compassion. I have no one to share my struggles with. As a child, I used to be my mother's little doll and my father's little princess. But now, I feel orphaned, like a pariah in my own home.

My parents, who had long appeared godlike in my childhood eyes, emerge into mere mortals, flawed and imperfect. Our home, which had been an abode of peace, becomes a place of peril, and my family becomes strangers I fear. No longer do mealtimes mean love and laughter. The table that had been a source of pride and a place of togetherness becomes a symbol of alienation.

When our summer vacation ends and classes resume in June, I dread going to college. The fifteen-minute walk to college exhausts me. I suspect all the students know about my failing grade. *Just look at her! There she goes*—stylewali—*all style and no substance*, I imagine them mocking me.

*I bet they think I am stupid.*

*What if I fail again this year?*

*What if I don't graduate with my class?*

*What if I throw up in class?*

*What if? What if? What if?* I can't shut off my anxious thoughts.

I take a deep breath, hold my head high, and march past the students lounging in the hallway, careful to avoid any eye contact. Despite the terror that rises in my chest, I struggle to project a picture of calm confidence. I walk into my physics class, the first class of the day, and carefully pick an aisle seat right next to the door, just in case I need to make a quick exit to the bathroom. I open my textbook and pretend to be engrossed.

"Why wouldn't you let me visit you over the summer?" Jaya punches my back gently and slides into the seat beside me. "What's wrong with you? You used to be a chatterbox. But now, you hardly ever speak to me anymore. Why are you so quiet?"

"I am fine," I say, peering through the textbook. "Do you have the syllabus for this course?" I ask, trying to divert Jaya's attention.

"Have you heard the rumors?" Jaya whispers scooting closer, cupping my ears with her hands. "Apparently Gopal has been gloating about making you fail in math."

"What?" I cry in disbelief.

"Shhhh . . ." she motions me to be quiet and asks, "You know why he did it—don't you?"

In a flash, it comes back to me. For much of the past school year, Gopal, my classmate and the student body president, had pestered me to be his girlfriend. Having absolutely no interest in him, I had thwarted his romantic pursuits. Scorned and enraged, he had exploded.

"You think you are too good for me, don't you? I know exactly how to bring you to your knees. Believe me, you will soon be falling at my feet, begging for mercy," he had hissed, cornering me just outside the college gates, a couple of weeks before finals. His friends had stood around jeering, hands folded by their chests.

I was alone. Jaya had left for home earlier that day. Determined not to cry or give in to his threats, I had walked straight through the band of bullies, hoping that Gopal wouldn't hurt me. Other than a couple of classes that he and I shared, I hardly knew him, except that most students feared him and his ability to buy his way into anything he wished for, including admission to our college, the student body elections, and good grades.

"Apparently, Gopal bribed the registrar's office to make you fail," Jaya explains.

Anger surges through my chest. I want to drag Gopal into the quadrangle and slap him in front of all the students. I want to make him confess his wrongdoings publicly and apologize to me. I want him to restore my math score to the one I had earned, not the one he had concocted. But, as a young woman born and raised in India, where men reign supreme, I realize I am helpless. I know any reaction from me, other than total submission, will only incite Gopal's rage further. I am fully aware that as a young man in India, with the means to bribe his way into anything he desires, Gopal has the power to not only deter me from graduating, but also to destroy my life.

"There is also gossip that Gopal is planning to rape you during the final-year field trip," Jaya adds, her face ashen. "I think it is best you stay out of his way and don't go to the field trip."

"Messing around with boys is like dancing with fire, Gayu," my mother had warned me ever since I had blossomed into a teenager. "In the end, girls, like fireflies, will surely get burned." I had internalized my mother's warnings and accepted my powerlessness in a society where girls and women were sexual objects routinely victimized by men who got away with their crimes.

I make Jaya promise not to tell anyone about Gopal and his threats. I don't tell anyone, either, not even my mother. Afraid that she would fault me for provoking Gopal's wrath by the way I dressed and behaved, I bury my fears deep within the troubled waters of my mind, and reluctantly make peace with my only option: to avoid contact with Gopal at all costs and immerse myself in my studies. My only redemption, I believe, is to pass the supplemental math exam and earn a First Class in my final year as an undergraduate. But my goal is easier set than achieved.

Every day is a test of endurance. By day I dwell in a restless frenzy, and at night I lie awake in a tired stupor. I find it harder and harder to concentrate on my studies. Simple things like showering and dressing deplete me of my energies. I have no will to live, nothing to look forward to. Some days, I can stomach a meal or two, and on others, I can't keep anything down. Yet I persist, behind my mask, eventually growing adept at ignoring my inner world, just so I can function in the world outside.

Triumphant that he has broken my spirit, Gopal ignores me and turns his attention on pursuing other girls.

September crawls by. It is time for the supplemental exams. Stricken with fear that Gopal might make me fail again, I barely make it to the exam room. *Sri Rama, Sri Rama,* I chant, trying to rid my mind of the intrusive thought. *Calm down, Gayu. Calm down. Just focus on the problems. You will be fine,* I silently repeat to myself. Hands shaking, mind blanking, I somehow manage to finish the exam and make it back home. Miraculously, I succeed in getting a passing grade. Encouraged, I throw myself into my studies with a newfound confidence, determined to realize my goal to pass with a First Class in my final year at college. I read and reread my textbooks and toil harder on my projects than ever before. Homework that used to take hours to complete in years past now takes days or even a week to finish. Months blur by. Amma insists I enroll in typewriting and shorthand courses to enhance my value in the job market.

"My dream is to find you a good husband who can provide for you like a queen, Gayu," my mother says. "But you never know what life has in store sometimes. It is always good to have some skills to fall back on to sustain yourself."

"Appa, will you please take me to check my results?" I ask.

It is Saturday morning, April 1982. Appa has taken the day off. He is relaxing in his favorite wicker chair beneath the coconut tree in the front yard, a glass of frosty lemonade in one hand and a *National Geographic* magazine in the other.

"Sure, Princess," he says. "Give me a couple of minutes to change."

I hop onto the back of Appa's motorbike and tighten my grip on his shoulders as he snakes through the morning traffic.

"Are you all right, Gayu?" Appa asks, sensing my mounting tension.

I nod my head and stammer, "Uh-huh."

"Don't worry, darling. I bet you have passed with flying colors. I know my girl," my father says, patting my hands. I cling to him tighter. I want Appa to be right. I desperately want to make him proud. Minutes later, Appa and I fight through the crowds of students to get closer to the bulletin board. My legs grow wobbly, my vision foggy.

"Can you please check my results, Appa?" I plead. "I don't want to look."

"Sure, Princess," he says, peering over the students. At 5 foot 11 inches, Appa towers over most of the students. Seconds tick by. I hold my breath and look away.

*Dear Lord Rama, please let me pass with a First Class. Please . . . please . . . please . . .* I press my palms to my heart, lower my head, and pray quietly.

"Congratulations, Gayu! You did it!" Appa scoops me in his arms and tosses me in the air. The students stop, whisper, and stare.

"Are you sure, Appa?" I ask, giddy with relief.

"Yes! See for yourself," he walks me closer to the bulletin board.

PASS, FIRST CLASS, it says in black next to my name.

I stare at it for minutes, blinking back tears.

"I did it!" I whisper to myself. "I did it despite you, Gopal."

Later, I run into the house, screaming. "I passed! I passed! I passed with a First Class, Amma!"

"Didn't I tell you that Lord Rama will answer your prayers?" Amma says, smiling.

"Let's celebrate!" Appa says, "Let's go to dinner at MTR tonight."

While my family relishes our favorite masala dosas and *jamoons* at MTR, I pick at my food praying not to puke. Ever since my failed grade the year before and the nightmarish ordeal it had unleashed, I have grown fearful of life at large, and feel like I can't trust anyone anymore. I am, however, most afraid of being out in public, and around food and my family. The mere presence of either triggers terrifying flashbacks of the days I have since endured. I push my plate aside and say I am not hungry. No one asks me why. The last few years have taken their toll on me and my family. At twenty-one, I stand five feet four inches tall and weigh a mere ninety-three pounds. But my family and I no longer discuss my gaunt body or my errant emotions.

Over the past year, my family and I have become experts at the *dance of denial*, pretending I am fine when I can barely function. And I have perfected the art of concealing my fears and tears behind a mask of makeup and smiles. Before stepping out of the house, I spend hours fussing with my hair and makeup. I dab on a thick layer of Lakme foundation to freshen up my pale face, dust it with Pond's talcum powder, line my eyes with kohl, and smear Vaseline on my lips. I push my shoulders back, stand as tall as I can, hold my head high, and practice fake smiles in front of the mirror. The mask complete, I promise myself never to let my guard down. It works most of the time, especially when I am on my own, far away from the prying eyes of my family. No one knows of my mysterious malady or my family's misery—it is a secret tucked safely within the folds of my family.

Although my mask protects me and lets me function in the world, it sickens me to the very core of my mind, body, and soul. Yet I live behind the veil in constant fear that it might fall to reveal the crazy woman that I have become. And then, I am certain, I will be shunned by my own family and ostracized by my community.

Ravi and Chitra return to college in June. A few of my classmates continue on to graduate school. Jaya secures admission into a master's program in physics.

"I pray I can get you married this year, Gayu," Amma says. "But I want you to keep your options open. You never know if you will need a job to support yourself."

Like many of my classmates, I take the entrance exam for employment in a bank. I also enroll at the Davar's College of Commerce to earn a Personal Assistant's diploma. In December, I graduate from the program and start applying for jobs.

Over the next several months, Amma and I slip into a new routine. We start our day with an hour-long walk through Lalbagh, the famous botanical gardens of Bangalore, which is a mere ten minutes from our home. Despite the turmoil that has tested our relationship in the last few years, Amma and I find peace strolling through the tranquil landscapes. Amma usually returns home after the walk, and I head to the local market to pick up vegetables and fruits for the day. I help her cook the day's meals and leaf through the newspaper for job leads. After lunch, when Amma naps, I go to the post office to mail my applications, or I lose myself in a romance novel. Week after week, I await the mailman, praying to receive a job interview. Nothing arrives. I feel dejected at life and its irony. Having once nurtured dreams of becoming a physician, I am now struggling to find a job as a personal assistant.

"Would you like to become a model or a stewardess?" Appa tries to cheer me. "You can live a glamorous life filled with travel and adventure."

"Stop messing her mind with stupid ideas," Amma admonishes. "With Lord Rama's blessings, she will be married within the year."

Weeks later, I receive a letter inviting me for a job interview at Motilal and Sons, a stationery company. The general manager, Mr. Rao, is in need of a personal assistant.

I arrive at the interview a nervous wreck. Mr. Rao, a plump man in his fifties, sits in a high-back chair upholstered in red velvet behind an imposing mahogany desk. A large sunburst pendant dangles on a thick gold chain resting on his protruding belly.

"Good morning, Ms. Gayathri. Have a seat," he says, smiling, exposing a couple of gold-capped teeth. "Are you proficient in shorthand and typewriting?" he asks, tipping his face down, peering through my application.

"Hundred words per minute in English shorthand and forty-five words per minute in English typewriting, sir," I manage to mumble.

"Did you bring the three recommendations we asked for?" he asks. I hand him the letters. "When can you start?" he asks, browsing through them.

"As soon as you please, sir," I answer, startled.

*I can't believe I got the job!*

"I knew you could do it!" Appa hugs me when I get home. Amma is relieved I have found a job. She insists I dress in saris now that I am a working woman. Regardless of how uncomfortable I feel in them, I comply, knowing that it is also the dress code required at work. Soon, I find all the filing and phone calls boring. But I am most bothered by the way my boss undresses me with his eyes each time he calls me into his office to dictate the mundane letters that make hardly any sense—he pays more attention to the design of my sari blouses than my secretarial skills. Having no other job offer on hand, I decide to put up with the nuisance.

CHAPTER 4

# American Knight

MY FATHER ARRIVES HOME from work one evening in March 1983, excited about an opportunity to become the general manger at a new textile mill in Tanzania, Africa. After weeks of serious discussion, Amma decides to accompany him, but only after getting me married, she insists. Barely twenty-one, I am considered to be at my prime in the marriage market. I wonder, however, if my mother has gone mad. I cannot believe she thinks she can find me a groom and get us married in less than three months. Within weeks, however, her prayers and persistence pay off.

"Wait until you see the picture of the handsome prince who will marry you, Gayathri," Amma's coconspirator, my aunt Shubha, teases, waving a picture at my face.

My sister, Chitra, leaps at my aunt and grabs the picture from her hands, almost knocking her down. She studies the photo, grins, and runs. I chase her, begging to see it.

"After all, he is supposed to be *my* husband," I say, tackling her to the ground.

"What is all the commotion about, girls?" asks Appa, coming home from work.

"You will never believe our luck!" Amma grins, clapping her hands together. I went to propose Gayu to Shekar, a scientist working in Mumbai. But his grandmother took one look at Gayu's picture and insisted that she would be perfect for her *other* grandson, an engineer living in America! Can you believe it? America!" she gushes.

Apparently, the young man was returning home to Bangalore shortly to attend his younger sister's wedding and his family decided this would be an opportune time for him to marry as well. "His name is Ramprasad," Amma continues. "They call him Ram at home."

I marvel at both my mother's efficiency and her luck. Ramprasad literally means "the gift of Rama."

"Well done!" Appa notes. "He is named after your favorite god."

Amma's grin widens. "And he was a gold medalist in the engineering program at the Indian Institute of Technology"—India's Caltech and MIT. "He has not one, but two master's degrees in computer science. And he is working at Intel in Portland, Oregon. He also comes from a prominent family," Amma adds, and she sighs, deeply content.

I stare at the picture in my hand, unsure if the man staring back will be my future husband. His curly hair is parted on the side and combed neatly. His wide forehead—a sign of intelligence and nobility, I am told—sharp nose, and pronounced chin, make him look studious, even a bit too serious. But his smile exudes a boyish charm.

*I wonder if he will like me. I wonder if we will fall in love.*

My mind spins into a world of its own. I had always known that my parents would arrange my marriage as my mother's had been, and her mother's before her. But, carried away by romantic classics and Bollywood movies, I had secretly dreamed of one day being swept off my feet by a tall, dark knight, a handsome hero, all on my own. Today, very slowly, young Indian girls and boys are falling in love and choosing their own partners, but not when it was my time to marry. Now my mother pulls me briskly out of my reverie, like a magician pulling a cloth from a beautifully laid table.

"I left a picture of Gayu and her horoscope with Ram's parents," she tells my father as though I were not in the room. "They have promised to consult their priest and call us back in a few days. I have given them Mrs. Nair's phone number." Mrs. Nair, our next-door neighbor, will be the intermediary for this piece of business.

"The boy's grandmother loved Gayu's picture. She thinks she is perfect for her grandson and life in America," she adds, beaming.

Over the next couple of days, my mother prays often. Finally, on the third day, just as she finishes her morning prayers, the much-anticipated call arrives. Ram's mother informs Mrs. Nair that their family priest has found our horoscopes, Ram's and mine, highly compatible, and that she and her family would like to visit us the following Sunday.

Ecstatic, my mother plunges herself into sprucing up our house and preparing what amounts to a small feast for our honored guests. "Taste it and tell me if it is good," she pesters my sister and me every few hours, sweating over the stove.

Sunday morning, I cover the table with a white lace cloth and set a brass vase filled with colorful croton leaves and calla lilies in the center. Chitra helps me arrange the brand-new set of stainless steel Tiffin plates and cups, tall steel tumblers for water and little steel tumblers for coffee. I fan the spoons around the plates, and Amma sets out the kesaribhat and *uppama,* along with a Thermos filled with hot coffee.

"How many times have I asked you to grow out your hair, Gayu?" My mother studies me for a moment, one critical eye arched as she slowly waves a wooden spoon at me. My short, bobbed hair, trimmed with my America-loving father's blessing, makes me look more striking and contemporary, but is now a deficit to this master plan. Sweeping it into a bun on top of my head, Amma encircles it with a strand of sweet-smelling jasmine blooms and secures it with scores of bobby pins. "I hope it will not fall apart before they come," she frets.

"My head hurts, Amma," I say, "I feel queasy."

"Silly girl, you are just nervous. It's perfectly normal. Don't worry. You will be fine," she dismisses me as she consults her watch. "I remember when your father and his family came to see me for the first time. I was so shy and scared that I sat with my eyes glued to the ground the entire time. It wasn't until our wedding night that I even got a good glimpse of your father. Imagine that! Just be your normal self," she advises. "I am sure they will love you."

But by now, I am sure that there is nothing "normal" about me. There hasn't been for years now, and all this planning and wishful thinking manages to completely cloud the real issues that the prospect of marriage presents. The constant paranoia that I am going mad, the feeling of ants burrowing under my skin, my racing thoughts, my pounding heart, the nausea, the vomiting, the endless tears . . . we are all pretending it has never happened, or that it has somehow stopped.

But I know better, and I wonder if my mother and father have similar concerns. Am I really ready for marriage? Worse, I wonder if there is deception and deceit at work here. The young man and his family have no idea what they may be taking on with me. I think about honesty and fairness and our family's good name, a name that has always stood for decency. And then I wonder, *Can Ram's family return me if I turn out to be a damaged bride?*

My head begins to pound.

I don't want to burden Amma now with my worries.

"How old is Ram?" I ask my mother, diverting my attention.

"Almost twenty-nine," she replies, helping me drape my cotton sari. It is hot pink with a gold border, youthful and eye-catching.

"He is nearly nine years older than me, Amma. Doesn't that bother you?" I ask.

"It doesn't matter, Gayu," she answers, her fingers moving swiftly as she adjusts the sari. "Men stay younger longer. Besides, you should be thanking your lucky stars if he chooses to marry you," she replies and continues to instruct me. "When I ask you to serve our guests, remember to walk gracefully. Don't look the elders in their eyes. It is not respectful."

Soon, Ram's family arrives. One by one, parents, sisters, uncles, and aunts troop into our home ceremoniously. Ram's mother walks in first. She is holding a silver tray filled with coconut, fruits, and flowers. She places it in my mother's outstretched hands and rests her smiling eyes on me for a moment. She motions for me to sit beside her and settles into the rattan sofa in the living room. Ram's sisters, Mala and Gauri, settle on either side of me, examining me from head to toe. A quiet hush descends on the room. I feel suffocated. I turn around and see Ram's father and uncle sitting across from us. They seem very kind and friendly.

"I hope you did not have any problems finding our house," Appa inquires, breaking the silence.

"There was no problem, except we did not remember the house number," Ram's uncle answers. "We asked a young boy up the street if he knew where Mr. Kasinath and his family live. He said he did not know. But the minute we mentioned Gayathri's name he asked if we were looking for the *bob cut lady,* and walked us right to your house," the uncle chuckles.

Everyone shares in the laughter. I blush. In a neighborhood where most girls smooth their long hair with jasmine oil and wear it in plaits, everybody knows me.

"Would you like to serve our guests some snacks and coffee, Gayu?" Amma summons me with a smile. I pass around the tray of snacks and coffee, a smile plastered on my sweaty face, praying that I don't spill the hot coffee all over their laps. We nibble on homemade delicacies, which, Amma is sure to share with everyone, I have prepared—from scratch! For good measure, she tells the family how much I love children and how good I am with them. She is positively cooing. I sit back on the sofa next to my mother, palms crossed on my knees, and answer the slew of questions from my prospective in-laws: When did I graduate? What were my electives? Where do I work? What are my hobbies? Do I like to cook? Would I like to go to America? And, after what feels like an eternity, amid approving glances and satisfied smiles, Ram's uncle announces that they would like to return with Ram when he arrives home from America in a couple of weeks. I have passed the first hurdle.

Two weeks later, on *Ugadi,* the Hindu New Year's day, Ram and I set eyes on each other for the first time. At five feet six, he is just a couple of inches taller than I am. I am surprised at his simplicity. He is dressed just the way the magazines and television shows I consult tell me any young American male might dress on an ordinary day (which this is not!)—in a pair of blue jeans and a red-and-white-striped T-shirt. His curly hair is ruffled from the auto rickshaw ride, making him look a lot younger than he did in the picture, and a whole lot less serious. This is good, I think, peeking at him as he removes his flip-flops before entering our house. I like that there is something distinctly American about him, even down to the fresh scent of his cologne.

As Ram and his family make their way into our house, our neighbors gather at their windows trying to get a glimpse of the prospective groom. The men sit on one side of the living room, and the women settle into the other. Familiar with the drill, I ask our guests if I can serve them coffee and snacks before Amma bids me to do so.

"Hello!" I say, staring into Ram's eyes, serving him after his dad and uncle. I am dressed again in the pink sari that apparently worked so effectively before.

"Hello!" he responds, a little surprised by my boldness.

I bite my lip and avoid Amma's stare from across the room.

"Great coffee! Did you make it?" he asks.

"Yes," I answer, smiling.

"Our Gayu doesn't drink coffee. But she certainly makes a good cup of coffee. Doesn't she?" Amma calls out quickly. Ram and his family nod their heads in consent.

"Gayu actually cooked the jamoons as well," Amma boasts, trying again to impress my prospective groom and his family with my culinary skills. "I've never tasted better," she adds to fill the silence in the room as everyone enthusiastically chews.

"Could we please take Gayathri to my parents' house in Gandhi Bazaar?" Ram's mother asks hesitantly. "They live close by and would love to meet her."

"Sure," Amma agrees, and joins Ram, his family, and me as we ride in a couple of auto rickshaws to his grandmother's house. It is a beautiful ancestral villa. Ram's grandparents are old and frail. They welcome us warmly, and his maternal uncle and aunts gather around us as well.

"Come sit by me, child," his grandmother smiles sweetly, waving her arthritic hands. "Won't you sing a song for us?" she asks, stroking my head lovingly. I am worried that she might topple my bun. My heart skips a beat and my throat goes dry. I look at Amma pleadingly, begging her not to make me sing.

"Gayu, why don't you sing your favorite song for Grandma?" Amma insists instead. All eyes in the room close in upon me. I gather my courage, clear my throat, and sing a song in praise of my mother's favorite god, Rama, just as we had rehearsed. It is not uncommon for young ladies to be asked to sing for their future in-laws as, according to tradition, a beautiful voice is an expression of a virtuous soul.

"Beautiful, my child, you sing like a nightingale," compliments Ram's grandfather. "My dear child, Ramu, now that Gayathri has stolen your heart with her sweet voice, I suspect you shall be chanting the *Gayathri mantra* for the rest of your life," he quips. Everyone bursts out laughing at his poignant joke. The Gayathri mantra, after which I am named, is the most revered of all mantras in India, and is believed to have life-affirming powers. All Hindus, and especially young men inducted into Brahmanhood, are required to recite it three times a day—in the morning at sunrise, at noon, and at dusk.

"We will let you know of our decision soon," Ram's mother tells Amma discreetly as we rise to leave and she bids us good-bye.

The next few days drag as we wait anxiously to hear from Ram's family. I am intrigued by the idea of marrying Ram. He seems nice enough, and the possibility of being his chosen bride and living in America fills me with snobbish pride, especially when a distant relative, whose son is a good friend of Ram's, informs us of my competition. Evidently, the Ramprasads are reenacting this same coffee and song ceremony in a few more Bangalore living rooms.

"Don't have high hopes," I overhear her telling Amma, huddled in the kitchen one day. "Apparently, the boy's family has received a lot of proposals from girls who are much more accomplished than Gayathri—engineers, doctors, and postgraduates. Besides, a boy as accomplished as Ram can demand any bride he wants."

"I am sure he can. But, I know he will choose Gayu," Amma persists. "I know Lord Rama will answer my prayers."

Mr. Mohan, a mutual friend of our family and Ram's, arrives the next day. He is smiling. "The boy's family wonders if we could celebrate the wedding on the fourth of May," he asks. "I know it is just a week away.

But the boy has only ten days left of his vacation. He needs to return to America soon after the wedding."

"Thank you, God; thank you, Mohan!" Amma runs to the kitchen and returns with a pinch of sugar to offer Mr. Mohan to celebrate the good news. "Gayu, you are the luckiest girl in the world!" she exults, hugging me.

"Congratulations, Princess!" my father shouts, scooping me into his arms.

"Wow!" Chitra screams, squeezing me tight.

"Congratulations!" Ravi joins in.

But, as I lie in bed that night, I am hesitant. My sister had chattered away all night about America, with its malls, designer jeans, and washing machines. I know, however, there is more to marriage than small luxuries.

I am not sure if Ram is "the one" or if I am ready to marry at all. Yet I dare not voice my doubts. Soon after I'd graduated from college, Rakesh, a freshly minted doctor and a neighbor that I had grown up with, had proposed his eternal love and asked my hand in marriage.

"You think you are too good for him, don't you? You stupid child, don't kick God's gift in his face. At this rate you will never be married," Amma had fumed when I declined Rakesh's offer. She had stopped speaking with me for a week. And a week before Amma discovered Ram's family, Giri, another neighbor and a marine engineer, had sent his mother over to share his desire to marry me. In my imagination, I saw him as the tall, dark, handsome knight I had long dreamed of. But Amma had promptly dispelled that as infatuation. In the end, Appa helped me make my choice.

"Gayu, both Giri and Ram are wonderful young men. Knowing you, however, my darling, I think you will be happiest with Ram. Giri's job will keep him at sea nearly eight to ten months a year. I don't think you will be able to handle the loneliness."

In the days to come, Amma jumps into action. She transforms into a commander in chief and summons my father and uncles to secure a hall for the two-day wedding ceremony while she enlists a troupe of chefs to prepare the meals and hires the musicians. My aunts are handed extensive shopping lists filled with wedding essentials—flowers, fruits, vegetables, and gifts for the extended family. Amma also confirms with the family priest that he will be able to perform the ceremonies.

Ram joins our family for an afternoon of shopping. Within a couple of hours, he picks out his wedding suit, shoes, and a simple gold wedding band with GR engraved on it—the first letter of each of our names. We stop by Lakeview, my favorite ice cream parlor, to enjoy sundaes. As we finish our ice cream, I am relieved that I keep it down.

Over the next few days Amma, Chitra, and I trek through a shopping marathon. We go to Suvarna's, our favorite sari shop. For hours, we sit entranced as the salesperson shows us sari after beautiful sari. Amma sets aside a traditional white sari with red border for me to wear for the *dhare,* the main wedding ceremony, and lets my sister and me select our favorites for the rest of the wedding events. Chitra chooses a red sari with a navy blue border and a royal purple sari with a fuchsia pink border for herself. Of the five saris I will require, my favorite is a sky-blue ensemble strewn with stars of gold and with a navy blue border and pallu encased in a brocade of gold. I drape the sari around my shoulder and glance at the reflection in the full-length mirror.

"You will look gorgeous in it at the wedding reception, Gayu," Amma exclaims, clutching her heart, tears misting her eyes.

Amma purchases a sari for each of my aunts, my grandmothers, and Ram's mother and sisters as well. She buys Ravi and Appa matching pants and shirts for the wedding, and safari suits for the reception. The midafternoon sun blazes outside as we pay for our purchases and head toward the door, our hands overflowing with shopping bags.

"Would you all care for some cool drinks, madam?" asks the shop owner as everything is being wrapped. He is grateful for how we have filled his cash registers today.

Chitra and I slurp at our drinks greedily. All at once, my stomach churns into a sea of bile. The shop door has barely closed behind us before I buckle over in time for the soda to meet the scorching sidewalk. My sister looks mortified.

"Gayu, please get a grip over yourself," Amma sighs. "You'll be getting married in a few days. We have so much to do before then. Please, please be strong now and don't go back to your old ways," she says stroking my back.

Disgusted with myself, I wipe my face with the back of my hand and wobble back upright slowly. Over the next week, hundreds of invitations are printed and hand-delivered to scores of friends and family members. The entire neighborhood is abuzz with excitement; everyone pitches in as we prepare for my wedding. Amma and Appa go to bed bone tired but blissfully happy. The sweet solace of sleep, however, escapes me. I become increasingly jittery. I fear for myself, my secret, and the public humiliation my family will endure if I can't bring this off. I fear for Ram, who seems to be a good man, so sweet and unsuspecting. I limp through the next days, but my family is too busy to notice my suffering.

As the time for the wedding approaches, new items join the colorful stacks of saris and bangles displayed in front of the God's altar in the kitchen: a pair of glistening silver diyas, traditional Indian lamps; a large silver plate with five little silver bowls filled with turmeric, vermillion, *akshate* or rice confetti, camphor, and candied sugar; an intricate silver incense holder; and sparkling stainless steel dishes. For years, I had watched my mother skillfully trade in stacks of old newspapers and her tattered old silk saris for a collection of shiny stainless steel dishes. And, now, they are part of my wedding trousseau. Nestled in a beautiful jewelry box lined with red velvet are a pair of gold bangles, ruby and pearl earrings, silver toe rings, and the most sacred symbol of a Hindu marriage, the mangalsutra, my wedding necklace. Since the day I was born, Amma had stashed away Appa's bonuses and saved every rupee she could in anticipation of my wedding day and Chitra's.

I stand in the kitchen, surrounded by the gifts, embraced by the tokens of my parents' sacrifice and everlasting love. I am overcome with gratitude, yet filled with guilt at my inability to grant them their one wish—for me to stop being sick and to be a blushing bride.

A ceremonial tent adorns our front door. Tender coconut palms and stately banana leaves are tethered to four wooden poles draped in red and white streamers of cloth. Sprays of mango leaves and garlands of fragrant jasmine and marigolds festoon the festive entryway.

The prewedding ceremonies begin with gusto on May 2 and last through much of the next day. I stumble through them hiding beneath a joyous mask, praying to God that I don't let my family down.

The next evening, a caravan of cars makes its way to the wedding hall, which is actually Amma's former grade school. Unable to secure anything else during the busy wedding season, Amma's father, my grandfather, had begged the school's principal to allow us to use the space. The school's auditorium has been transformed into the wedding hall, and the classrooms into wedding suites. We settle in and begin to freshen up. Amma and my aunts ready themselves to welcome the groom's family. Ram and his entourage arrive at five to a rousing welcome. The next thirty-six hours blurs into an unending tableau of chants and rituals.

On May 4, the day of the ceremony that will join us, Ram and his parents sit on decorative wooden planks on one side of the canopied wedding platform. Amma, Appa, and I sit on the other side. The potbellied priests sit cross-legged across from us, orchestrating our every move. They chant Sanskrit mantras in unison and summon *Agni Deva,* the Fire God, to sanctify our holy union. At the conclusion of each mantra, they offer a ladle full of ghee, purified butter, into the fire, which rages resplendently. The billowing smoke stings our eyes.

More than three hundred guests dressed in their finest silks and gold jewelry gather to witness our wedding. The men and elders sit in collapsible chairs arranged neatly in rows. The women and children arrange themselves on the red, white, and green-striped thick canvas blankets spread on the floor. A few of the children chase each other around the hall. The cries of babies startled awake by all the noise and commotion compete with the *nagaswaram*—traditional wedding music accompanied by a live ensemble.

At ten-thirty, the *lagna,* the anointed time for our holy union, arrives. Ram and I stand facing each other, holding garlands of jasmine, separated by an *antarpata,* a curtain of fine muslin held aloft by a couple of my cousins. As the cheers of family and friends crescendo with the chanting of the *mangalashtaka,* the antarpata drops, and so does my heart. I am terrified that, like the antarpata, my façade of normalcy will drop to unveil the crazy woman that I truly am. I think again, as I have all week, of the dishonor my family and my husband's family will endure. I feel a desperate urge to duck and run. Seeing no escape through the assembled crowd, I take a deep breath and garland Ram.

"I suppose your bride will be the master of this marriage," Ram's older sister, Mala, teases him. It is believed that whoever garlands the other first will hold the upper hand in the marriage.

The priests instruct my father to place my hands in Ram's, transferring his responsibility for me to Ram. And Ram, in turn, promises Appa that he will protect me and love me for life.

"*Kanyadaan,* this act of giving one's daughter in marriage, is considered the noblest of gifts in Hindu mythology," the priest explains.

"God bless you, Princess," Appa says as he clasps my hands, tears rolling from his proud eyes. The musicians erupt in a jubilant song, and everyone showers us with akshate as Ram ties the mangalsutra around my neck.

The ends of my sari pallu are joined with the ends of Ram's dhoti, symbolizing our eternal union. Hand in hand, we circumambulate around the holy fire seven times, partaking in the ancient tradition of *saptapadi.* Each time we circle the nuptial fire, we beseech the gods for a specific blessing. With the first, we pray for the plentitude of pure and nourishing food and for a life that is noble and respectful. With the second, we pray for physical and mental strength, and fortitude to lead a healthy and peaceful life. With the third, we promise to fulfill our spiritual obligations, and invoke the gods to grant us spiritual strength. With the fourth, we appeal for the attainment of happiness and harmony through mutual love and trust, and a long joyous life together. With the fifth, we pray for the welfare of all living entities in the entire universe, and for begetting noble children. With the sixth, we pray for bountiful seasons all around the world, and seek that we may go through these seasons together, just as we would share our joys and sorrows. With the seventh and last, we pray for a life of understanding, loyalty, unity, and companionship not only for ourselves, but also for the peace of the universe. And then the saptapadi ceremony concludes with a prayer sanctifying our union as indissoluble.

Ten days from the day we meet, Ram and I become husband and wife. The guests are ushered to the lunch hall. It becomes crowded with hundreds of hungry people seated in rows. A platoon of cooks scurries around serving the traditional twelve-course wedding meal on lush green plantain leaves. Ram and I make our way to our designated spot where we sit side by side, cross-legged on the floor. Two large plantain leaves overlapping one another are served with an incredible array of delicacies. The leaves are surrounded by exquisite rangoli designs. Two tall shimmering silver diyas stand aglow on either end of the leaves. Their dancing flames beckon Ram and me to partake in our first meal together.

I feel famished. I haven't had a bite to eat since morning.

"It is auspicious for the bride to fast through the wedding rituals," Amma had explained. This is surely an interesting turn. My mother is actually discouraging me from eating. I certainly didn't want to upset her or displease the gods.

Many of our friends and family gather around Ram and me as we sit down to savor our meal.

"Feed her! Feed your bride!" they chant in merriment.

With a smile, Ram takes a *laddu* and feeds me.

"It's your turn now, Gayathri. Let's see if you will be more generous than your husband!" they tease. I break apart a piece of *peni,* and place it in Ram's mouth.

"Can you please do it one more time?" the photographer requests, wanting to make sure he captures the moment. Ram and I comply. Appeased, our friends and family leave us to finish the rest of our meal in peace.

"You have fifteen minutes before the afternoon rituals begin, Gayu," my mother rustles over and whispers in my ear.

"Okay, Amma," I answer, forcing a smile, wishing I could curl up and take a nap. I excuse myself from Ram and make my way to the bathroom to wash my hands. All at once, blood rushes to my head and my stomach does somersaults. Scared I will pass out, I hang onto the tap and plead for my meal to stay put. But it doesn't. I quickly close the bathroom door behind me and pray that no one has seen me. I rinse the bathroom floor with a bucketful of water. I splash my face with cold water and dab it with the end of my sari, careful not to rub away my bridal makeup. Minutes later I hear my mother tapping at the door.

"Are you okay, Gayu?" she asks.

"Yes, Amma," I reply immediately, careful not to rouse any suspicion. "May I please have a couple more minutes to freshen up?" I beg softly.

"Just five minutes," Amma relents. "The priests and your husband are waiting for you."

I pry open the door and peek out to make sure no one is around. I powder my nose, reapply the kohl in my eyes, and touch up my lipstick. I adjust my sari and stumble back to the wedding platform.

The priests engage Ram and me in a multitude of small games to help us get better acquainted. We fish for our wedding bands in a silver bowl and compete to be the first to win the bounty as our guests joke and cheer. We are given wooden dolls dressed up in wedding finery and are asked to play house and negotiate our parental chores.

Soon it is time for another ritual. My parents will relinquish custody of me as their daughter and invite Ram's parents to instate me as their daughter-in-law. Amma and my aunts sing tearfully in celebration as I sit awkwardly on my father-in-law's lap.

*Emmamaneyangaladi beledonda hoovannu*
*Nimma Madilolagidalu thandiruvevu*
*Kolliree Maguvannu emma mane belagannu*
*Nimma mane belagalu oppisuvevu*

*We have come today to bequeath in your lap,*
*A flower that blossomed in our courtyard*
*Please accept this beloved child of ours,*
*the light that had kindled our home*
*And, may she brighten your home forever more.*

I had grown up listening to my mother and aunts sing this song at every one of my cousin's weddings. Then, it had always moved me to tears. Today, even Appa is sobbing. Amma dabs my tears away gently with a handkerchief and suggests that Ram and I relax a bit before we get ready for the reception.

Ram looks truly handsome in his gray pinstriped three-piece suit. Two chairs upholstered with red velvet and trimmed in gold await us at the far end of the wedding hall. Deep burgundy satin drapes camouflage the school wall behind. Hundreds of collapsible chairs are arranged in neat rows for our guests.

"Princess!" Appa exclaims as I walk in, fussing with my upswept hair. "You look beautiful."

"What a striking couple you make," Amma gushes in pride.

Soon Chitra and my cousins, themselves beautifully attired for tonight's celebration, assume their positions at the entrance to the reception hall, each set out to provide our guests with a traditional welcome offering.

"Let us take the family portraits before the guests arrive," Appa says. The next hour is a blur of flashbulbs and smiles.

The guests start pouring in around seven o'clock. They greet Ram and me, hand us a colorful package, and pose to have their picture taken with us. But for a few close family members and friends, or colleagues from college and work, Ram and I hardly recognize most of our guests. Nonetheless, we graciously accept their blessings and generous gifts and smile effervescently as the evening wears on. My cousin Shanti's seven-year-old daughter starts piling up the gifts into a mountainous stack behind the reception podium. My uncles and aunts usher our guests inside to join the reception buffet.

By ten-thirty Ram and I smile wearily at one another, trying to rescue our aching lips from their frozen smiles. We sink into the chairs, toss our shoes aside and wiggle our sleepy toes awake. Having waved the last of our guests goodbye, we join our families for dinner. I stare in disbelief at the elaborate spread. My stomach recoils at the sight.

"Why aren't you eating?" Ram asks, as I sit beside him, picking at my dinner. "I am not hungry," I lie.

"The poor girl, she must be exhausted," Ram's aunt intervenes, much to my relief. "All she needs is a good night's rest."

Amma orders her troops to pack up and load the rental truck with all our belongings. The rental company dismantles the reception décor and leaves. A couple of taxis stand waiting to transport Ram's family and mine to his family home in Malleswaram.

"Good-bye, good-bye," everyone calls. "May God bless you both with a long and happy married life and a house full of children." Our relatives shower us with good wishes as we leave.

Ram's house is one of four structures circling a central courtyard, nestled within a spacious compound. His three uncles, a widowed aunt, and their families live in these homes. A couple of Ram's aunts greet us at the door and perform *aarti.* In their palms, they cradle a little silver tray with a pair of glowing, silver diyas set in a pool of water, reddened by a sprinkle of vermillion. Up and down they weave the lamps and sing a song to welcome me into my in-laws' home. A little tin pail filled with rice is placed at the right-hand corner of the threshold at the front door.

"Kick the pail of rice as hard as you can with your right foot, before entering the house," Amma instructs. I kick with all my might, and the pail flies to the far corner of the room, spilling the rice all around. This ritual, called the *grihapravesha,* marks my ceremonial entry into my wedded family. The scattered rice symbolizes the spread of wealth and prosperity that my good fortune will bring my new family.

"Step across the threshold with your right foot, Gayu," Amma reminds me again. Everyone cheers and welcomes me into my new home.

My mother and sister disappear to set up the bedroom upstairs for the wedding night. Ram's sisters serve tumblers filled with sweetened milk to everyone gathered. Their jobs complete, Amma and Chitra come down to join us. Soon the anguished moment of bidding farewell arrives. As tradition requires, Ram and I prostrate ourselves at my parents' feet.

"May you be blessed with a blissfully happy life filled with peace and prosperity," they recite. Appa helps raise me to my feet, then hugs me and kisses me on my forehead.

"Remember, Gayu, from now on, your husband is your god and your home is your temple. Be ever-loving and respectful to him and to your new family. Make us proud, bangara." Amma caresses my head as tears stream down her face.

"I promise I will make you proud, Amma," I say, hugging her tight.

Ravi gives me a quick hug and wishes Ram and me a wonderful life. Chitra cries uncontrollably, partly from exhaustion, partly from the emotion of departure. This is it. Our lives will never be the same. Her tears soak through my sari, mirroring the effusive dampness of my soul.

Suddenly I realize that I belong to a new family now. A family whose honor I am eternally pledged to strive to uphold. I am no longer a child, cradled amid the family of my birth. The thought frightens me, and tears that I have long withheld rush out in torrents. My mother-in-law and sisters-in-law brush away tears of their own with the tips of their saris, while the men of the household look into the distance with awkward silence.

"Send us off with a smile, Gayu," Amma pleads as she makes her way toward the waiting taxi. I muster a smile through my tears and wave good-bye. Although I stand surrounded by my new husband's family, I feel all alone. I stare into the darkness and wonder if I can keep the promise I made to my mother. Can I make her proud? Or will my secret leak out and spoil everything?

"We'd better get some sleep now," Ram suggests softly, climbing up the stairs. I wish my new family goodnight and follow him.

Our nuptial chamber is a romantic retreat. The room is suffused with the scent of burning incense. Sheets of soft satin are covered with rose petals and pillows covered in candy stripes invite us to sink into their comfort. Cozy, warm rose-and-navy-checked woolen blankets lie folded neatly at the foot of the bed. Amma had personally selected the bedding. Garlands of jasmine adorn the bed frame, and a silver tray laden with mangoes, bananas, pomegranates, and grapes sits glistening on the nightstand. A pitcher of warm milk stands beside another silver tray filled with lush green betel leaves and supari.

"Come, Gayu," Ram says gently, sitting on the bed and patting the spot beside him. His voice is low, like the moonlit tide. I sit beside him, my heart racing. He gently wraps his arms around me. I am startled by his warm embrace. I stay still. I can hear his heart beating next to mine. I can smell his cologne. Having never been intimate with a man before, I don't understand whether it is pleasure or panic that is coursing through my veins. Confused, I begin to cry.

Ram tips my face with his forefinger and kisses my eyes. "Don't cry, Gayu," he says. "Everything will be fine. I know you miss your family. You can visit them anytime you want," he whispers, kissing my tears away.

It is true I miss my family. But it isn't all that I am crying about. My family are the sole keepers of my secret. *What if Ram finds out about my secret illness? Will my marriage come crashing down? Will he forsake me? Or will he honor our wedding vows and stand by me in sickness and in health?*

My poor husband has no idea about my past, or of the fears hiding behind my veil of tears. And I don't have the courage to reveal it.

"Why don't you go to sleep now?" Ram says, pulling the blanket around me. "Everything will be better by morning."

As I lean to turn off the light switch by the nightstand, the betel leaves fanned out on the silver tray remind me of my wifely duties.

"Would you like me to make you a paan?" I ask, wanting desperately to be a good wife.

"I would love one, maybe more," Ram says, smiling sweetly.

He watches me as I deftly roll the supari into the betel leaves and secure it with a clove just as I had done making paans for my father and uncles ever since I was a child. Ram invites me to feed him, and then asks for more.

"Ah, Gayu, you can definitely make a great paan," he compliments me. "Are you not going to have any?"

"I love making paans," I say, returning his smile, "not eating them."

As I feed him the third paan, Ram holds my hand and draws me closer. I close my eyes. I imagine myself on the water, paddling up a narrow harbor. Ram holds my hand and draws me to him, kissing me tenderly on the lips—my first kiss. The harbor suddenly widens. I feel safe. I feel loved. I watch my secret sinking deep into the sea below me, slowly, slowly, soft bubbles rising to the surface until it is gone, and the water is calm again.

CHAPTER 5

# Passport to Paradise

TAP, TAP. TAP, TAP, TAP . . . I hear a faint tapping on the bedroom door. I jump up with a start, utterly embarrassed, realizing that I had overslept on my first day at my in-laws' house. Rajini, Ram's three-year-old niece, stands peeking through the bedroom door, smiling shyly.

I search for Ram under the crumpled sheets. He is gone. Amma had instructed me to rise before my husband and tend to his needs. Alas, I have already failed to meet my wifely duties.

"Thanks for waking me up, sweetie." I give Rajini a quick peck on the cheek and rush to the bathroom to shower. By the time I join my mother-in-law and sisters-in-law in the kitchen, they are already busy preparing breakfast.

"I remember you don't drink coffee. Why don't you have a cup of warm milk instead?" my mother-in-law says, offering me a cup of heated milk sweetened with sugar.

Ram, his brothers, and his father are sprawled on the floor in the living room, sipping coffee, reading different sections of *Deccan Herald*—the daily newspaper.

"Good morning," I greet them.

"Good morning," Ram replies, eyes glued to the newspaper. The rest of them simply nod and smile.

The smell of coffee makes my stomach sick. I feel weak. I haven't eaten a thing since my lunchtime disaster the day before. I am tired of pretending I am okay when I am not. I just want to crawl back into bed. But I can't.

Soon, the house echoes with the chants of priests and the air is thick with the scent of spices. A team of chefs is cooking up a feast. It is customary for the groom's side of the family to host the bride's family for lunch the day after the wedding. Amma, Appa, Chitra, Ravi, and a few of my aunts, uncles, and cousins join us for the celebration. Ram and I perform the *Satyanarayana puja,* our first together, to seek God's blessings for a happy married life. I push through the prayers with a smile, and join Chitra and my sisters-in-law in serving our guests. We roll up the plantain leaves after lunch and toss them in a dumpster behind the house where hungry cows stand waiting to graze upon them. Satiated, our guests relax on colorful charpoys to enjoy paan, and a few of them sprawl on the floor and take a nap.

"Why don't you girls eat?" Amma suggests, "Let me serve you. You have been working hard all morning."

Partway through my lunch, dread spreads through my body, and irrepressible talons of nausea tear through me. Terrified, I dash to the bathroom. I writhe in pain, praying not to puke. My prayers aren't answered.

"Gayu, open the door," Amma whispers, tapping on the bathroom door.

"Is she all right?" I hear my mother-in-law ask Amma.

"She must be worn out from the wedding," my mother reassures my mother-in-law. "I am sure she will be fine in a few hours."

"Perhaps someone has cast an evil eye at the wedding," my mother-in-law speculates. "Anyone would be jealous of her good fortune." She scurries to the kitchen to grab a fistful of rock salt and a few red chili peppers.

"Open the door, Gayu. Your mother-in-law is waiting to do dhrishti," Amma says, trying not to sound upset.

I wipe my face and open the door. I stand there, head hanging down, afraid to look into my mother-in-law's eyes.

"Lie down and rest for a few hours, Gayu. You will be fine," Amma says, escorting me to the bedroom upstairs. I hate her stoic calmness.

*How can she pretend I will be fine, when the past two years of my life have been a fiasco?*

Informed of the mishap, Ram rushes to my bedside. "What happened?" he asks, sitting beside me.

"I don't know." I shake my head, bursting into tears.

"You are shivering," he says, looking concerned, and covers me with the wool blanket by the foot of the bed. Not wanting to answer any more questions from Ram or my mother, I close my eyes and pretend to fall asleep. After a few minutes, Amma and Ram shut the bedroom door gently and leave.

Worries about Ram and his family finding out the truth and discarding me, and about my parents' disgrace, weave cobwebs in my head. The harder I try to claw through them, the more impenetrable they get. I feel scared and lonely. I had tried hard to keep my secret from ruining my marriage. But now, I know there is no escape from my past. Dejected, I cry myself to sleep.

Over the next two days, I withdraw into bed and stay there for much of the time. Concerned, Ram and my sister-in-law take me to their family physician, Dr. Veda.

Dr. Veda is a petite woman in her fifties. Her graying hair cascades in a silver halo around her weathered face. She measures my blood pressure, listens to my heart, and checks my pulse.

"Does it hurt here?" she asks palpating my stomach. "How long have you been sick?"

"Since the last couple of days," I lie. I hate myself for lying. But I don't have the courage to disclose the truth.

"There is nothing to worry about. She is just exhausted. Weddings can be stressful," Dr. Veda declares. "Let her rest and make sure she eats small meals frequently and drinks plenty of fluids."

"Will she be well enough to go on our honeymoon in a few days?" Ram asks.

"Absolutely!" Dr. Veda smiles, much to my relief and Ram's.

Once home, Ram makes sure I follow Dr. Veda's advice.

"It will heal your tummy," he says, forcing me to drink tender coconut water and fussing over my meals. Four days after our wedding, Ram and I leave to Kodaikanal for our honeymoon. We call Amma and Appa to say good-bye. They are busy packing for their trip to Africa.

"Have a great trip," they say, and ask us to visit them when we come back.

Tucked amid the folds of the verdant Pali hills in Tamil Nadu, India, Kodi—as Kodaikanal is lovingly called—was long heralded as a lovers' paradise. Our dreams for a romantic getaway, however, are dashed when we finally reach Kodi after a twelve-hour bus ride. A raging storm has knocked out power lines, blanketing the city with an eerie darkness. And the in-house restaurant in the hotel is closed. Starved, Ram and I satisfy our hunger with a couple of overripe bananas and a loaf of bread that he manages to scrounge from a bakery next door. All through the balmy night, we shift restlessly in bed swatting blindly at mosquitoes. The next morning, when the power does not get restored, Ram decides it is best for us to cut short our honeymoon and go to the American Embassy in Chennai earlier than planned, to turn in my application for the green card—my passport to paradise.

By noon, we join the serpentine line of hopeful applicants. It is the peak of summer in Chennai. Heat waves rising from the concrete sidewalks threaten to wilt even the sturdiest of sunflowers. After a nearly three-hour wait, Ram and I are finally summoned to file our papers. Ram flips open his wallet and offers a silent prayer to the picture of Lord Venkateshwara, his family deity.

"You should expect to hear from us in six months," the registrar says after examining our documents carefully. Then he waves for the next person in line to step up.

"Six months?" I sigh.

"Don't worry, the days will fly by," Ram says. "Make the most of your time in India. Take a few trips. Go visit my sisters. Spend time with your brother and sister. Have fun," he advises. "You never know how long it will be before you see your family once you leave India."

Later that afternoon, Ram and I return to Bangalore. The next evening, we join Ravi, Chitra, and a battalion of my uncles, aunts, and cousins at the Bangalore airport to bid bon voyage to my parents.

"Gayu, I have missed you so much," Amma says, hugging me tight. "I know we will miss each other terribly in the months to come. I will write to you often. And, your father and I will definitely be back to see you off to America."

"It'll be your turn next, Gayu," Appa says, kissing me on my forehead. "You'll soon be flying off to America."

"Happy journey, Appa," I hug him, fighting back tears.

Ravi and Chitra go home to start life on their own. And I return home with Ram to embrace my new role as a daughter-in-law. The following three days run by. Surprisingly, my symptoms had receded long enough that I can survive my honeymoon. Ram and his family are relieved to see me smiling, cooking, and mingling with the many friends and family who stop by to wish Ram a safe trip back to the United States. Ram's aunts, uncles, and cousins keep milling in and out of the house, bringing him treats, trying to spend as much time with him as they can before he returns to America. The two of us have hardly any time to ourselves.

Twenty days from the day we met, ten days from the day we wed, I stand next to Ram's distant cousin, Jai, at the Chennai airport and bid my husband good-bye. He waves back to me and disappears through the security gates without giving me a single hug. In the few days I had come to know him, I had learned that Ram was painfully uncomfortable with any public display of affection.

*Come back!* I want to scream. *Hold me in your arms one last time and tell me you love me before you go.* But it is too late. Adrift in an ocean of conflicting emotions, I try to make sense of the seismic changes in my life. Within the past three weeks, I have met and married a man I hardly know, my parents have moved to Africa, and my newlywed husband has returned to America. And I am now expected to change magically into a dutiful daughter-in-law and serve my in-laws while waiting for my green card. Much to my dismay, the symptoms of my secret past threaten to seep into my present. For years I have hidden behind a façade of normalcy, and now I fear that my mask is coming undone. I struggle desperately to continue to hide behind its safety.

"Call me when you reach Bangalore," Jai shouts, helping me board the Brindavan Express, the nonstop train to Bangalore.

I huddle by the window and sob silently.

"Why are you crying, my child?" asks an elderly woman sitting next to me.

"It's nothing." I shake my head and stare at the fleeting landscape.

"It's okay. You can talk to me. Perhaps I can help," she says stroking my back. Her gentle touch reminds me of Amma's caress, and I cry even harder, longing for my mother's embrace. I mumble about my wedding, my parents leaving for Africa, and Ram returning to America.

"It is hard to say good-bye, isn't it?" the lady says. "But time shall heal all wounds. I cried for days when my son Sham left for America for his graduate studies. I felt empty and lost without him. But it has been two years since he left, and my broken heart has begun to mend. Sham graduated recently and is working at a company called Intel in Portland, Oregon," she adds, pride dancing in her eyes.

"Did you say your son works at Intel?" I ask, utterly surprised.

"Yes. My husband and I are on our way to visit him for six months," she adds, pointing to the silver-haired gentleman sitting next to her with his face buried in a *Times of India* newspaper. "Do you know anyone in Portland?" she asks.

"Yes! My husband, Ram, has been working at Intel for the past couple of years," I answer, much to her amazement.

"It is a small world indeed," the lady's husband remarks, joining our conversation. "My name is Mr. Iyer."

"*Namaste,*" I say, folding my hands by my heart and bowing my head in respect.

"Mrs. Iyer and I would love to meet your husband when we are in Portland. Won't you kindly give us his complete name, address, and phone number?" he asks.

I search through my purse to find the piece of paper Ram had given me with his address and phone number, and hurriedly copy it on a slip of paper and hand it to Mr. Iyer.

"May I please have your name and your son's contact information in Portland? I would like to pass it to my husband," I request.

"Sure," Mr. Iyer says, and hands me the information scribed neatly in cursive.

The three of us are engrossed in conversation when the train pulls to a halt at the Bangalore railway station. Ram's brother Satish stands waiting on the platform to escort me home.

Upon my return, I immerse myself into my new responsibilities as the eldest daughter-in-law of the house. Having no knowledge of my prior troubles, my in-laws justify my lack of appetite, bouts of withdrawal, and crying spells as the lovelorn pining of a new bride; perhaps also, they say, I must be missing my parents. Fortunately, within weeks, my symptoms recede mysteriously amid the monotony of my daily routine. Each day, I rise at six-thirty and wash the entryway to our home with water and draw rangoli, just as Amma had taught me when I was a little girl. I help my mother-in-law with the day's cooking, wash dishes, sweep and mop the floors, and do laundry. Before I go to bed each night, I cut fresh fruits for my father-in-law and serve him a warm cup of milk sweetened with sugar. I sincerely do not mind the chores, except for the silence that surrounds me in my new home. No one sings or listens to music. I miss the way Amma and I used to sing while we worked in the kitchen before I became ill, and I long to listen to my father belting out his favorite tunes with Frank Sinatra and Louis Armstrong. Despite my struggles with my family in the years past, I miss the familiarity of my home and family. And, I especially miss the bedtime chats I shared with Ravi and Chitra. I hate sleeping all by myself. Having always shared a bedroom with my siblings, I feel very lonely and scared. Some nights, I bury my nose into my sheets, close my eyes, and try hard to recall the scent of Ram's cologne and his warm embrace.

My in-laws are loving and kind, but they are not demonstrative with their affections. Each lives in a separate world, distinct yet connected like islands in an archipelago. My brothers-in-law, Satish, four years older than me, Girish, two years my senior, and Ramesh, practically my twin—born on the exact same day—all work at local banks. They leave for work at eight and return home by five. My father-in-law works at a local Montessori school from nine to one o'clock. In the afternoons, quiet blankets the house. While my mother-in-law and father-in-law take a nap, I lose myself in a craft project. Many afternoons, I sit transfixed by the living room window, waiting for the postman to deliver a letter from my parents or Ram. I rejoice when the letters finally arrive, and read them over and over again. Finally, when satisfied, I number the letters and save them on the nightstand beside my bed. Soon after receiving the letters, I sit for hours responding to my parents and Ram, sharing every minuscule detail of my life.

Days turn into weeks, and weeks into months. Chitra's weekend visits are the only welcome distraction from my domestic chores. Together, we go to see our favorite Bollywood movies and browse through the aisles of Sapna Book House searching for the perfect romantic card for me to send Ram. Sometimes, we treat ourselves to one of our favorite meals—*chole-batura* at the Sri Rama Hotel in Majestic. Much to my relief, for the first time in years, I relish the taste of food instead of fearing it.

"I wish Amma and Appa were here to see you enjoy eating, *ma,*" Chitra says, using an affectionate term. "They would have been so happy."

"I wish they were here, too," I agree, hoping to make my parents proud.

Occasionally, I accompany my mother-in-law and father-in-law to a wedding or cradling ceremony.

"This is our eldest son Ram's wife, Gayathri," my mother-in-law introduces me to her friends and relatives everywhere we go.

"Is she the one going to America?" they ask, joyful and jealous at the same time. Marrying Ram had instantly elevated my status within our community, especially since he lives in America.

Soon, the festival season descends upon us. For the first time in my life, I celebrate Diwali without my parents or my brother and sister. I miss my family and Ram very much.

It's November 1983, six months since Ram and I had applied for my green card. When I don't hear from the American consulate, I write to Ram, concerned about the delay.

"The immigration policies have apparently changed recently," he replies two weeks later. "Unfortunately, I just learned that it will take another five months for you to get your green card. I am sure you are sad with the sudden change in plans. But please understand that there isn't anything I or anyone else can do to speed the process, Gayu. I suggest you keep yourself busy and occupied. Why don't you visit my sisters in Mangalore and Chandigarh? It will be a great distraction for you, and they will certainly appreciate seeing you again."

I am heartbroken with the delay. Lately, our neighbors and relatives have begun to inquire why I haven't joined my husband yet.

"My niece got her visa immediately after marrying," they tell me, not realizing the different types of visas. "Perhaps her husband had some influence," they suggest.

"Who knows? Maybe your husband already has a *white wife* in America," another neighbor teases. I don't find it funny.

Frustrated, I relent to Ram's wishes and visit his sisters. I spend a week in Mangalore with Ram's little sister Gowri and her husband. They have just learned that they are expecting their first child. I am glad to give Gowri a helping hand as she struggles through morning sickness. I cook and clean their home while Gowri and her husband go to work. On the lone weekend I spend with them, we all go to the beach and feast on spicy grilled corn on the cob as the cool sea breeze tousles our hair.

My brother-in-law Satish accompanies me to Chandigarh. We have a great time with Mala, Ram's older sister, and her family. It is delightful to be with Rajini, my little niece, again. Her childish banter and temper tantrums entertain us. The weather is beastly hot and we don't venture out during the day. Much to our surprise, we get accustomed to taking cold baths. Mala and her husband take a few days off from work and take us sightseeing to local museums and the famous Rock Gardens.

Ten days later, Satish and I are relieved to return to the relatively cool weather of Bangalore. Satish resumes his work at the bank, and

I return to my routine of cooking, cleaning, and anticipating the postman's visits.

In early March, the letter from the American consulate finally arrives, inviting me for the interview—one last formality before I am granted my green card. Ecstatic, I write to Ram and my parents immediately. They are thrilled.

Later that month, on March 23, my father-in-law is due to turn sixty—a significant milestone in a man's life in India, and a time to retake his wedding vows. My in-laws decide to celebrate the occasion at a neighborhood wedding hall before I leave for America. Over the next couple of weeks, hundreds of invitations are hand-delivered to friends and family, inviting them to partake in the momentous celebration.

"I am sure Ram will surprise us and come for his father's birthday," my mother-in-law prophesies day after day. "Besides, I am sure he will want to accompany you on your first trip to America."

I have my doubts. But I keep them to myself, not wanting to break my mother-in-law's heart.

Amma and Appa arrive in Bangalore on March 21, two days before my father-in-law's birthday bash. I meet them at the airport along with Ravi and Chitra. It feels wonderful to be reunited at last. I spend a few hours with them at home and return to help my in-laws with the preparations.

"It must be Ram," my mother-in-law announces each time there is a knock on the door. We hold our breath and wait to hear his voice, only to be disappointed. "He will probably come directly to the wedding hall," she says, remaining hopeful.

"I am sure he will," I say, trying to comfort her, although I suspect he might not come at all.

The next morning, amid chants and cheers, we celebrate my father-in-law's sixtieth birthday, and my in-laws retake their wedding vows. My mother-in-law's eyes continue to search, hoping to spot her son in the crowd.

"I suppose he won't be coming after all," she relents at last, tears brimming in her eyes.

That night, Amma helps me pack my bags and move back home to spend the last couple of weeks in India with my family. I prostrate myself at my mother-in-law's and father-in-law's feet and bid my brothers-in-law good-bye.

"We will miss her," my mother-in-law tells my mom. "The house will feel empty without her."

Ram's grandmother, uncles, aunts, and cousins gather at the compound gate to wish me bon voyage.

"Don't forget to write to us," they remind me.

"I promise I won't," I say, hopping into an auto rickshaw alongside Amma and waving good-bye.

That night, as I lay my head to rest, scenes from the years past race through my head. As I pull my sheets over my eyes, trying desperately to block out the traumatic memories, the old tentacles of fear and nausea rise to strangle me again. Although I long for my family and home to be a source of solace, they trigger the trauma that has entangled our lives. I toss and turn in bed all night, desperately wanting to prove to my parents that I had mastered my moods and grown into a mature woman. Yet with each ticking moment, the pit in my stomach grows larger and larger, until it threatens to swallow me whole.

The next morning, I reluctantly join my family for breakfast. Ravi, Chitra, and I sit transfixed as Appa recounts his adventures in Africa.

"One must experience the splendor of the Serengeti National Park," Appa proclaims, pounding his fists on the table describing the exquisite beauty of its exotic wildlife.

I try to lose myself in his vivid imagery. But, my brain begins to turn into fuzz. My heartbeat thunders louder than the drumbeats of Africa. I feel like a marked antelope soon to be the lion's prey. I know I need to fight or flee, but I remain frozen in fear. I feel sick to my stomach. I manage to make it to the bathroom before the mounting waves of nausea come crashing down. Even through the closed door, I can hear Appa screaming.

"There she goes again. What in the world is wrong with her? She was fine yesterday. What could have possibly gone wrong in one day?"

He is right. I cannot understand why I feel sick. All I know is that I am sick of feeling sick, tired of troubling my parents, and ashamed at my inability to please them. I had longed to see them for eleven months, and now, all I want to do is disappear. I reluctantly return to the table and sit with my head hanging low, tears streaming down my cheeks.

"Why can't you get your act together?" Appa shouts. "Do you want to spend the rest of your life tethered to an IV tube? At this rate, you will never be able to join your husband in America. What are we going to tell Ram and his parents?"

I feel frightened, worthless, and guilty for ruining our reunion, for "making" myself sick, for ruining my life, for disappointing my parents.

Amma, Chitra, and Ravi just sit and stare.

Later that afternoon, my parents and I leave to Chennai for my interview at the American consulate. On board the Brindavan Express, I lie crumpled on the seat while Amma tries to sustain me with watermelon juice and tender coconut water.

"Listen to me, Gayu, you and only you can help yourself," Appa says, shaking his fist in front of my face, "There is nothing wrong with you. Haven't all the doctors told you that?"

"The human mind is rather weak," he went on. "But you can *will* it to be strong. Look around you. You are surrounded by people who love you. Look ahead. You have a fabulous future ahead of you. Don't give in to your imaginary sickness. Amma and I have worked very hard to give you a life of dreams. I beg you, please don't ruin your life!" My father folds his palms and pleads with me, "Believe me, you are a strong girl. You can do it!"

Appa's words echo faintly in the sunken hollow of my mind. I glance at him and Amma, in part reverence and part repulsion. I love them for all that they have done for me, and yet I loathe them for failing to understand my misery. The conflicting emotions tear me apart.

"I can't do it!" I want to scream. But the words stay stuck in my parched throat. Growing up, screaming at one's parents or, for that matter, merely talking back to any one older than me was scorned upon as a sin. I could never bring myself to do it.

I wonder how and whenceforth my parents and I became strangers, unable to understand or inhabit each other's worlds. It is true they had given me life. Yet, over the last couple of years, they have had no clue about my inner life.

"Do you know how terrifying it is to be imprisoned in a body and mind paralyzed by fear?" I want to ask them. "Do you know how difficult it is to pretend you are normal when you know you are going crazy inside?" But I don't. I want to crawl into my mother's lap and let her hold me until I am well again. I want Appa to wrap me in the safety of his arms and chase away the demons within me. All I do instead is creep as far away from my parents as I can, and crouch by the window praying to die.

Hours later we arrive at the home of my father's older sister, my aunt Sarasa, in Chennai. I collapse into bed and don't say a word.

"What's wrong with Gayathri?" I hear my aunt ask Appa.

"Nothing, really; all the doctors say she is perfectly fine. But she certainly doesn't behave like she is normal," Appa says, his voice laced with anger. "It is best we don't fuss about her."

The next morning, I can barely stand up long enough to brush my teeth. I struggle to bathe and get dressed.

"Drink this lemon juice, at least," my aunt offers. I sip at it hesitantly.

"Make sure you have all the documents, Gayu," Appa reminds as we walk into the sweltering day. A few paces later, my eyes go dark and my legs buckle. I sink into the scorching sidewalk and pray it will swallow me whole. I don't have the strength to stand up and take a step. Forget about taking a trip to America!

"The bus stop is just a couple of yards away. Come on. You can do it. Get up now. Don't make a scene!" Appa shouts, lending me his hand.

"Please get up, Gayu," Amma says, trying to help me up.

I can't budge. A couple of women on the street gather close to us, watching the mounting drama.

"Is your daughter all right?" they ask in Tamil, the local dialect.

"Don't worry. She will be fine," Appa replies in Tamil.

"It must be the blistering heat. Poor child, would she like some water to drink?" one of them asks. I shake my head no, afraid I will puke again.

"Sit by the window, Gayu," Amma suggests when we finally make it onto the bus. "The breeze might revive you."

An hour later, Amma and Appa usher me through the long line of waiting interviewees.

"Your name, please," a spectacled man with a receding hairline asks, poring through the papers in front of him.

"May Sri Rama be with you," Amma whispers in my ear.

"Good luck, Princess," Appa says.

"Gayathri Ramprasad," I answer, my heartbeat quickening.

"Your date of birth?"

"Where are you traveling to?"

"The reason for your travel?"

"How long will you be staying?"

"Are you married?"

"What is your husband's name?" He runs through a list of questions in a mechanical drone. I answer him in a trance.

"Congratulations, Mrs. Ramprasad," he wishes, stamping my passport and handing me my green card.

"Congratulations, Gayu!" Amma and Appa applaud and offer a million prayers to God Rama.

I steady myself, green card in hand, thrilled I will join Ram at last, and terrified whether I can endure the trip. We return to Bangalore late that night. I call Ram and my in-laws from the home of our neighbor, Mrs. Nair.

"God bless you," my in-laws say.

"Congratulations, Gayu! I can't wait to see you!" Ram shouts through the static wires.

The next couple of days unravel in slow motion. Worry becomes a constant companion. My body is tied into knots, my muscles are sore, and my head hurts. I feel like a paper doll dragged through the shredder. The sight and smell of food and drink repulse me. I can barely sit through the abhisheka, the special puja Amma requested at the neighborhood Rama temple to ensure my safe journey. I concede to Appa's wishes and visit his mother, brothers, and their families to seek their blessings and bid them adieu. Every home I visit, they offer me food, a token of their love.

"Thank you so much. But I just had my breakfast before I left home," I lie, smile politely, and excuse myself.

I deteriorate rapidly over the next few days. I can't eat. I can't sleep. I am jittery and tearful. I retreat into bed.

It's April 8, 1984, three days before I leave for America.

"Take just one more sip, Gayu." Amma cradles me in her arms, forcing me to drink some glucose water. I can barely hold my head up. Concerned, Appa asks Dr. Mahesh to make a house call. Dr. Mahesh tugs at my eyes, pinches my skin, peers into my mouth, listens to my heart, checks my pulse, and squeezes my stomach.

"She is dehydrated," the doctor pronounces. "I can either administer IV at home, or you can admit her to Maya Nursing Home."

"She needs to leave for America in three days. Will she be well enough to travel?" asks Appa, anguished.

"Don't worry, Mr. Kasinath," Dr. Mahesh strokes Appa's back. "She will be fine."

Within hours, the bedroom is transformed into a makeshift hospital room. Dr. Mahesh deftly positions the IV needle in the crook of my left elbow, instructs Appa how to change the IV bags as needed, and leaves.

"Don't worry, Gayu, Sri Rama will heal you. You will join your husband soon." Amma strokes my forehead gently.

"Just get some rest, Princess," Appa pecks me on my head.

Amma leaves to pack my suitcases, and Appa leaves to confirm my airline tickets. As the roar of Appa's motorbike retreats into the distance, I lie in bed limp, neither awake nor asleep. Eventually, I slip into a restless stupor. It is dusk when I finally awake.

"How are you, ma?" Chitra asks, settling at the foot of my bed.

"I don't feel well," I sob.

"Don't cry," she says, wiping my tears. "You will be fine. How about I paint your nails?" she asks, whipping out a little bottle of burgundy Tips and Toes nail polish. "It matches your *churidar* perfectly," she says, referring to the outfit I had tailored for my trip to America. I bet *bhavaji* will fall in love with you all over again when he sees you at the airport," she says, imitating Ram swooning.

"I wish," I mutter, afraid I may never make it into his arms again.

She mimics the American accent of my future babies as she paints my fingernails. I chuckle, clutching my stomach, tears streaming down my cheeks. I have always marveled at my sister's comic streak and envied her carefree spirit. Although she is two years younger than me, she has always mothered me, comforted me, and made me smile, even through my tears. I wish I could be more like her.

"I will miss you, Chitra," I say, drawing her hand into mine.

"I doubt you will," she mocks. "I am sure you will forget all about me once you see your sweetheart and go gallivanting with your hero in Hollywood."

"I will write to you often and send you lots of pictures," I promise.

Chitra blows on my fingernails to help them dry faster.

"Why don't you rest for a while?" she says, pulling the blankets over my feet. She shuts the door softly behind her and leaves.

I sail into a fitful slumber, visions of a glorious life in America flitting through my tired eyes like golden rays of sunshine bursting through clouds of gray.

Dr. Mahesh stops by the next morning. He is a little concerned that I am not faring as well as he had hoped. "Just to be safe, let us admit her to Maya Nursing Home," he suggests. "Let us continue to keep her on the IV. I will order a few rudimentary blood tests to rule out any potential problems I might have missed."

Hours later, a young nurse dressed in a crisp white sari, her dark curls secured underneath a nurse's hat, stands beside me smiling, drawing a couple of vials of blood. "I hear you are leaving for America in two days," she says. "Lucky girl! I wish I could go with you."

"The blood tests are all negative, just as I had expected," Dr. Mahesh confirms later that evening. "Perhaps Gayathri is anxious about leaving all of you and starting a life with her husband in America," he adds. "Happy travels, young lady," Dr. Mahesh wishes me as he leaves.

I despise Dr. Mahesh, my parents, and my life. For almost three years now, anxiety and depression have plagued me, appearing and disappearing at their will. My heart pounds, thoughts race, and I feel eternally guilty, hopeless, and worthless. And no matter how hard I try, I cannot manage my moods. Yet nobody believes my pain, not my parents nor the doctors. They tell me it is all in my head and insist I can will myself to wellness.

"Are you all crazy?" I want to scream. I don't, afraid that I am the one who is going insane. Like the million other questions I had wanted to ask over the years, this one sinks into the dark hole in my heart filled with the stagnant waters of shame.

"Chin up, baby. What's the matter with you now?" Appa asks, peering into my fallen face.

"Nothing." I shake my head and climb into the waiting auto rickshaw.

I want to run away, far, far, far away. Far away from the penetrating gaze of my parents, far from the incompetent doctors, and even farther from the mysterious malady that holds me hostage.

"One last night," I tell myself in bed that night, knowing that in less than twenty-four hours I will be granted my wish. Thankfully, the IV has at least given me the strength to start my journey. I pray fervently that America will be my talisman to a life filled with love, health, and happiness.

The next morning, friends, neighbors, and relatives stop by to wish me bon voyage. Appa insists on having me pose for pictures with each and every one of them. I force fake smiles, concealing the cries inside.

Later that evening, my in-laws meet my family and me at the Bangalore airport. We stand around making small talk waiting for the boarding announcement.

"How are you doing?" my sister-in-law Mala asks. "All set for the big trip?"

"I am fine," I lie, relieved that my secret is locked safe in my heart.

My in-laws have no clue about how sick I have been, or the fact that I had spent the last couple of days tethered to an IV tube at home, and in the hospital.

The moment of parting finally arrives. Deeply relieved, I prostrate myself at my in-laws' feet, then hug my parents, Ravi, and Chitra good-bye.

"God bless you and happy journey," they wish me.

"Call us as soon as you reach Portland," Amma reminds me.

"Good luck, Princess," Appa says. "Remember! You are a strong girl. You can do it!"

"Leave us with a smile," my mother requests.

I brace myself, turn back, smile, and take one last look at my family.

"Namaste!" A couple of stewardesses stand smiling at the door of the airplane. "Welcome aboard Air India," they greet each passenger. Their batik silk saris are pleated perfectly and pinned in place. Their dark hair is coiffed in a bun atop their head, their eyes are lined with kohl, and lips are painted red.

"Namaste," I say, and make my way to my seat.

"Do you need any help?" asks one of the stewardesses, noticing me fumbling with the seat belt.

"Could you please show me how to buckle my seat belt?" I ask, embarrassed. I had turned twenty-two a couple of days ago, but I had never been on an airplane before. And, except for the train ride from Chennai to Bangalore, I had never traveled on my own.

"Thanks," I tell the stewardess, and check the back pocket of the seat in front of me for airsickness bags. Appa had told me where to find them, just in case I needed to use them. As the plane soars into the skies, I pray that I make it safely into Ram's arms.

PART 3

# Shadows in the Sun

CHAPTER 6

# A Welcome Respite

I ARRIVE IN AMERICA on April 12, 1984, with two green suitcases filled with silks and spices and a heart full of secrets. Ram, like his parents, has no clue about my mysterious malady or my recent hospitalization. And I am determined to keep it that way.

It is just before dusk when the United Airlines pilot announces our final descent into Portland, Oregon. *Breathe,* I remind myself as the plane breaches the clouds. *Pull yourself together.*

A blonde stewardess stops by my aisle seat one more time and asks if I need any help getting off the plane. I shake my head no. It is a miracle that I have survived the thirty-six-hour journey and maneuvered through two plane changes. During the flights, I cried so hard and vomited so frequently that my fellow passengers had begun to worry about me.

As the plane taxis, I try to steady my thoughts and my stomach. I check my wallet to make sure I have my passport and offer a silent prayer to the picture of God Rama and Goddess Sita Amma had tucked inside. I fish around my purse for my lipstick, paint on a thick coat of Plum Wine, and plaster a smile on my face.

"Mommy, look! She has an owie!" The little blue-eyed girl across the aisle tugs at her mother and points at my bindi. The mother shushes her child and smiles apologetically at me.

As people start to file off the plane, I stand and smooth the creases out of my *churidar* and *kameez*—custom-made silk trousers and tunic.

I reach into the overhead bin and pull down my carry-on bag. Jars of Amma's homemade lemon pickles and chutneys clank against each other as I swing the bag across my shoulder. I follow the other passengers down the exit ramp, heart pounding, feet wobbly from sitting for hours. Once in the terminal, I spot Ram instantly—the lone brown man in a sea of white.

"Hi, Gayu," he smiles nervously and stretches his arms, offering to carry my duffel bag. He hoists the bag onto his left shoulder and leans forward to give me a quick, awkward hug. Next to us, a young American couple kisses passionately. The young man's hand slides across the seat of his girlfriend's Lee jeans. I blush and look away.

Within minutes, Ram ferries me through the airport to the baggage claim area. He steps on the escalator and disappears. I stare at the contraption, not sure if I want to step on it. Although I have seen them in the movies, I have never been on an escalator before. Afraid I might lose my husband in the milling crowd, I edge forward reluctantly and hang on tightly to the black rubber rails, careful to jump off as it reaches the ground floor.

Relieved to see Ram standing by the carousel, I walk over and stand beside him. "What color is your luggage?" he asks. "Parrot green," I say, thinking about the afternoon a couple of days ago when Appa had surprised me with the set of two matching suitcases. Before long, Ram grabs my suitcases off the conveyor belt and walks toward the exit. I follow him closely through a turnstile and out into the cool night air. I take a deep breath and am surprised to smell . . . absolutely nothing. In India, the air was often thick with the competing aromas of cow dung, exhaust fumes, and curry.

We cross the street and enter a parking garage filled with hundreds of cars parked neatly in parallel rows. I have never seen so many cars in one place and can't believe it when Ram actually finds his car, a brown Honda Civic. He tosses my luggage into the trunk and opens the door for me. I slide into the passenger seat. As he leans across to fasten my seat belt, the scent of his Chaps cologne carries me back to our wedding night.

In minutes, we wind our way out of the parking garage. Once outside, I sit gaping at the sweeping expanses of velvet green lawns and pine trees lining the streets leading to the highway. Unlike in India, there are no cows wandering, no auto rickshaws honking and weaving through the bicycle traffic, no buses overflowing with people. There are no pedestrians darting across the streets or beggars hawking on the sidewalks, just hundreds and hundreds of cars sailing smoothly in a perfectly orchestrated parade. The headlights of the oncoming cars weave a magical necklace of diamonds, while the taillights of the cars in front of us create a beautiful strand of rubies.

Passing through downtown Portland, its multistoried buildings aglow with lights remind me of Diwali. As we continue south, the car approaches a bridge perched like a crown above the Willamette River. When we reach its center, Ram grabs my hand and squeezes it tightly.

"Welcome to America," he says.

"Thanks," I reply, surprised by his sudden show of affection.

I feel like I am in a trance as we leave the bridge and drive through a well-lit tunnel and emerge into an enchanted forest.

"Oh, my God! It is so beautiful!" I say over and over again.

Ram smiles, his eyes glued to the road ahead.

I am overcome with awe at the beauty that surrounds me. *Appa was right. This is God's country. It is prettier than all the pictures he had shown me in the* National Geographic *magazines. Amma was right. I am the luckiest girl in the whole wide world.*

Soon, Ram steers off the highway and enters an apartment complex—Rock Creek 185, the large letters inscribed on a huge slab of wood at the entrance. Ram parks the car in his allotted slot, picks up my luggage, and leads me through a dimly lit corridor and up two flights of stairs.

"Welcome home, Gayu," he says, unlocking the door to apartment 286. He props the door open with the suitcases and flips on the light switch.

There is no family swarming around to welcome us home with an aarti.

I unbuckle my sandals and set them by the door, relieved to be barefoot at last.

"You don't take your slippers off at the door in America, Gayu," Ram explains. "Please bring them in and leave them here in the coat closet."

I pause at the apartment door, sandals dangling in my left hand, puzzled to see that there is no threshold—just a scuffed metal strip where the shaggy brown carpet in the corridor meets the vinyl flooring in the apartment entry. There is no place to draw rangolis to welcome the good spirits into my home and no threshold to worship. Not knowing what else to do, I lean down and touch the metal strip with my right palm and press it to both my eyes and pray, *Dear God, may the secrets of my past never taint the future in my new home. Please bless me and my husband with a life filled with health and happiness.*

*Remember to cross the threshold with your right foot first, Gayu.* I hear Amma's voice reminding me across the oceans. I take a deep breath and step into the apartment with my right foot first carrying with me the hopes, dreams, and blessings of our families and ancestors.

"Would you like to see the apartment, Gayu?" Ram asks, excited to show me around. I nod and follow. Expecting to see a bachelor pad with clothes strewn around and dirty dishes piled high in the sink, I am surprised to see how clean and orderly everything is. To my right is a small kitchenette lined with oak cabinets. A beige refrigerator nearly as tall as me, a matching electric range, and a porcelain sink whiter than my wedding sari are flanked by Formica countertops. The kitchen leads into a larger room that is partitioned into a nook and a living room. A round oak table and four matching chairs stand in the nook. A royal elephant painted on a wicker mat hangs behind the table. Two brown vinyl sofas face a small television set atop a stereo system encased in a glass showcase. I am delighted to spot boxes of neatly labeled and numbered audiocassettes. I walk through a couple of sliding glass doors and onto a deck overlooking a picturesque courtyard. To my surprise, I see ducks paddling in a man-made pool surrounded by weeping willows and flowering shrubs. I close my eyes and soak in the ambience. It is so quiet, I can hear my heart beat in my chest and the crickets chirping in the distance.

Between the living room and nook is a short hallway leading to a pantry on the left and a bathroom followed by two bedrooms on the right. The pantry is stocked with brightly colored cereal boxes. A bag of Tilda basmati rice and Lakshmi whole-wheat flour lean on the floor.

"These are for you, Gayu," Ram says, pointing at several unopened boxes on the shelves containing a set of CorningWare dishes emblazoned in blue flowers, Farberware cookware, a set of stainless steel cutlery, and an Osterizer blender.

"Thanks," I smile. True, they weren't the dozen long-stemmed roses that I had hoped for. But I appreciate my husband's practical gifts nonetheless.

One of the bedrooms is empty. Ram's roommate, Das, had moved out a couple of days before I arrived. In the other bedroom, Ram had made the bed with brand-new sheets covered with ferns and butterflies.

"Would you like to wash up while I make you something to drink?" he asks.

"I'd love to take a bath," I say and dig through my suitcase for my clothes. The suitcase is jam-packed with plastic bags bursting with Amma's homemade curry powders, a stainless steel pressure cooker, a rolling pin, and ladles. I open the other suitcase and sort through the neatly folded saris, small silver idols of gods and goddesses, a couple of pairs of diyas, and boxes of *agarbhatti*—sandalwood incense sticks. Tucked underneath is the new silk pajama kurta Amma had sent Ram, along with the stack of Ram's letters to me secured with a pink ribbon. Underneath it all, I finally find my clothes.

"The soap and shampoo are here," Ram points to the shower and hands me a thick baby-blue towel. It is as big as a blanket and soft like a bushel of rose petals. Ram shows me how to turn on the shower. In an instant, hot water blasts from the spout, filling the room with steam.

"You get hot water 'round the clock here," Ram says. I can't believe it. Back home in Bangalore, we thought we were lucky to get running water throughout the day. More often than not, we were limited to a few hours of water supply each day. As for hot water, Amma woke up at five every morning to heat water for our baths in a copper boiler, and we were rationed two buckets of hot water per person at the most.

Ram pulls a knob on the faucet, and suddenly, water streams from a different nozzle at the top of the bathtub. I watch in amazement. I have never taken a shower like this in my life, and I long to let the warm water refresh my tired body. I wait for Ram to leave and close the door behind him. I strip bare, stare at myself in the misty wall-sized mirror, and cringe at the skeletal image I see. The last few weeks of hell have left their mark on my body. I run my fingertips over the purple bruise where the IV had been inserted, and pray that Ram won't notice it. I step into the shower, draw the vinyl curtain closed, and let the warm water wash away my worries. Minutes later, I reluctantly turn off the shower, get dressed, and step out of the bathroom.

"Hope you like strawberry milkshake," Ram says, handing me a tall frosty glass filled to the brim. Everything in America, I am learning, is super-sized, from the giant suitcases at the airport to the refrigerator in the kitchen to the towels and even the tumbler.

"Thanks," I say and sip tentatively, afraid I might not be able to keep it down. Besides, I hate milk. But I don't want to disappoint my husband.

"You'd better call your parents now," Ram says. "I am sure they are waiting to hear from you." He motions to his wristwatch and reminds me of the twelve-and-a-half-hour time difference between America and India. He dials my neighbor Mrs. Nair's phone number in Bangalore and hands me the phone. I settle next to Ram on the couch and listen to the ring tone.

"Hello, Auntie," I shout excitedly when Mrs. Nair answers the phone. I can barely hear her say, "It's Gayathri calling from the United States," over the crackling line. "Hello, Gayuma, your parents have been waiting for your phone call," she says, handing the phone to Amma. Mrs. Nair's Pomeranian dogs Raja and Rani yelp in the background.

"Hello, Gayu," Amma says, "how are you?"

"I am fine, Amma," I answer. "I reached Portland safely."

"Hello, Princess," I hear Appa's voice on the line.

"Appa, America is so beautiful. I hope you will get to see it for yourself soon," I say. I hear Chitra pleading to talk to me. Mindful that it costs about four dollars a minute to call India, I say a quick hello and promise to write soon. Placing the phone in its cradle, I realize the thousands of miles that stretch between my family and me, and I wonder when I will see them again.

"It's hard at first, Gayu," Ram says, as if reading my mind. "But you will get used to it. You must be tired," he says, caressing my hair. "Let's go to bed now." He turns off the lights and leads me to the bedroom. His hands brush against my hip bones as he covers me with a blanket. "Have you lost a lot of weight since I last saw you, Gayu?" he asks. My heart skips a beat. Fear rises into my throat. "Don't worry," he says before I can muster a response. "Everyone who comes to America gains weight." He chuckles. "It's all the fresh air and rich food." Safe in my husband's arms at last, I fall asleep, our bodies entwined like the ferns on our comforter.

"Good morning, Gayu," Ram kisses me on my forehead the next morning. "Look what my colleagues sent for you," he says, holding out a dozen long-stemmed red roses tied with a red satin bow. A little white envelope with a Hallmark gold seal peeks out from between the roses. I hug the roses and open the envelope: "Welcome to America! Hope your travels were safe. We look forward to seeing you soon. Best wishes, Julia Clemens."

"You can sleep in longer if you want to," Ram says, tucking the comforter around me. "This is not India. I don't expect you to get up before me and make me coffee and breakfast."

I smile and get up, shower, and unpack my suitcases. I set up a makeshift shrine in one of the kitchen cabinets with the silver idols of the gods and goddesses Amma had sent with me, along with a pair of silver diyas and incense sticks. I light the diyas and say my prayers. Ram joins me. I prostrate to God and then to Ram.

"You don't need to do that," Ram says, propping me up. "I am no God."

I am pleasantly surprised that, despite his traditional upbringing, my husband is a modern man who doesn't expect me to fall at his feet or cater to his every need.

It is Saturday. Ram has the weekend off. After breakfast, Ram's friends Das and Anil, who live in the same apartment complex, join us on a shopping spree at the Llyod Center. First stop, Nordstrom. Even before I can gather my wits about the sheer expanse of the store and its merchandise, Ram whips out his credit card and buys me Chanel No. 5 perfume and body lotion. I stare at the bill, converting it into rupees, and am shocked to realize that it is more than a month's rent my parents paid.

"Buy a couple of pairs of jeans and a few T-shirts, Gayu," Ram says, leading me to the women's section. "You should probably get a light spring jacket, too."

The salesgirl, a petite gal with flaming red curls, is all too happy to help.

"Will you need any help changing?" she asks, eyeing my sari.

"No thanks," I say, heading to the dressing room. I slip into a pair of Gloria Vanderbilt jeans and a red-and-white-striped polo T-shirt. I remove the bindi from my forehead and shake my hair loose. I like what I see in the mirror. It takes me a couple of hours to choose the rest of my wardrobe.

Anil, Das, and Ram help carry our shopping bags to the car. We stop at the pizza place across from our apartment complex for dinner. While the guys devour the pizza with extra jalapenos and red chili pepper flakes and wash it down with a jumbo serving of soda pop, I struggle to free my mouth from the stringy mozzarella cheese.

The next day, Ram takes me to Safeway, the neighborhood grocery store. The sterility and silence surprise me. I hear none of the shoppers bargaining. And there are no hawkers calling out to convince us that they have the freshest produce and the best prices. The variety of foods overwhelms me, and so I decide to follow Ram quietly.

"Can we buy a coconut and some cilantro?" I ask, hoping to surprise my husband with dosa and coconut chutney for lunch the next day.

"We have to go to India Bazaar in Beaverton for that," Ram says and takes me to a tiny little store off Highway 217. I am relieved to be surrounded by the familiar smell of *dhal* and spices. And a bit shocked to pay a dollar for a wimpy bunch of cilantro that would have been unacceptable to be sold in Bangalore, let alone fetch forty rupees.

Once home, I help Ram put away the groceries, and he gives me a quick run-down on how to use the stove and operate the stereo system, TV, and VCR. He teaches me how to use the vacuum cleaner and shows me how to work the washer and dryer in the Laundromat in the basement. He cooks rice, and we enjoy yogurt rice and lemon pickle, cuddled on the couch, and watch *Ek Dhuje Ke Liye,* our favorite Bollywood movie.

Dawn arrives the next day, heralding a new era in my life. Most days, Ram gets up at six thirty and leaves for work by seven forty-five. I sleep in until eight thirty or nine.

*It's a bad omen for a woman to wake up late,* I can hear my mother and mother-in-law chide from across the oceans. Both women had risen before their husbands and waited upon them devotedly. I was raised to do the same, but cut loose from my family and its cultural expectations, I loll in bed as long as I want and linger in the shower, singing to my heart's content. I light the diyas, say my prayers, and pour myself a bowl of corn flakes along with some milk and sink into the couch to visit with the guests on *Good Morning America.*

Some days, I clean the apartment, humming my favorite *ghazals* along with the audiotape of Chitra and Jagjit Singh playing on the stereo. I am amazed at the collection of cleaning products Ram has stowed in the cabinet underneath the bathroom sink. In America, I find even cleaning house is fun. I love the fresh scent of Pine-Sol, and the lemony burst of Pledge.

"Is it true that no one needs a maid in America?" Ram's cousin Sheela had asked me shortly before I left India, as we scrubbed dishes squatting on the stone floor in my in-laws' backyard. "I have heard that machines do all the work for you. You are a lucky girl, Gayathri," she had continued, her voice tinged with envy. "You will never have to work hard like the rest of us."

She had reason to be jealous. However, the "conveniences" of my new life in America sometimes threw me for a loop. A couple of weeks after I had arrived in America, I wanted to surprise Ram with *puris*—deep-fried whole-wheat bread and *sagu*—a mixed-vegetable curry. I remember rolling out the dough and sliding them into the simmering oil when all at once, I heard sirens going off. Terrified that the apartment complex might be on fire, I turned the stove off and ran out of the building as fast as I could, expecting to see my neighbors crowding in the parking lot and fire engines rushing to our rescue. To my shock, I found myself all alone. Minutes later, confused and still shaking, I returned cautiously to my shrieking apartment and called Ram. He came home within minutes and asked what I was doing when I heard the alarm go off.

"I was right here frying puris for your lunch," I explained, pointing to the stove, which sent him off into peals of laughter. "Don't worry, Gayu," he comforted me. "Just remember to turn the exhaust fan on when you cook from now on."

Another time Ram asked me to pick up a loaf of bread while he waited in the car. Fifteen minutes later, I had returned empty-handed, confused and unable to choose a loaf of bread among the fifty kinds lined up on the shelves. And I often struggled with using the key to our apartment, forgetting that I needed to insert the key the reverse of what I did in India.

Despite these little setbacks, I cherish the newfound solitude of my life. I thrive on the freedom America affords me in forging a new life. The very things that made me a misfit in India help me acculturate in America—my independent spirit; my untraditional looks; my love for jeans, short hair, and makeup; my need for personal space; and above all, my fluency in English and lack of shyness. I find my anonymity in America rather soothing. As the bruise from the IV needle on my arm disappears, so do my symptoms. Afraid that the mere mention of it would bring back my secret illness, I don't bring it up in my letters to my family. My parents don't inquire either. We are all happy to pretend it never happened. Instead, I write about my wonderful life with Ram, our weekend trips to the mall and excursions to the Rose Garden, Multnomah Falls, Mount Hood, Cannon Beach, and Seaside. I tell them about Das and Anil and a host of new friends—Kiran; Naveen; Bala and his wife, Neeru; Sham and his wife, Sunitha; Dinesh and his wife, Leela.

I tell them about my favorite chain restaurants—Hunan, Pizza Hut, and Taco Bell. I describe every nook and cranny in the apartment. Chitra is particularly impressed with my growing collection of perfumes, designer jeans, and Cover Girl cosmetics. With each letter, I tuck in a handful of pictures, which Ram loves to take.

Amma, Appa, and Chitra write back promptly, their handwriting tiny so as to ensure that all three of them can fit their messages in one aerogram. The letters are crammed with updates about our family and friends, reminders of upcoming festivals, and inquiries about Ram and our life together. Amma anoints each letter with *Sri Rama* inscribed on the very top. "I always knew Sri Rama would bless you with a wonderful life, ever since the day you were born," she writes.

Nestled in the cozy comfort of my apartment, I smile, recalling Amma's tale of the day I was born. Apparently my parents had gone for a walk that evening, and Amma was dressed in her finest silk sari. Midway through the walk, Amma had gone into labor and Appa rushed her to the hospital in an auto rickshaw just in time. I was born moments later, even before Amma could change out of her precious silk sari. From that moment on, Amma had predicted that I would live as I had arrived—in the lap of luxury.

"Gayu, your home is your temple; your husband, your God. Don't forget to greet Ram at the door when he returns from work," Amma reminds me in her letter. "There is nothing more soothing than your sweet smile and a warm meal to revive him after a hard day at work."

"Did you get your driver's license, Gayu?" Appa asks. "You're essentially crippled without it in America."

Ram doesn't necessarily agree with Appa's concerns. He insists on chauffeuring me everywhere I go.

"Have you met any Americans yet?" Chitra inquires. I write back and tell her about the beautiful red roses and the wonderful party Ram's colleagues at work had hosted upon my arrival. I describe their surprise at discovering I could speak English fluently, and the ardent wishes of a co-worker, Robert, to have Ram help him find an Indian bride.

"Americans are really friendly and open-minded, ma," I write, "but Ram and I hang out with other Indians most of the time."

Except for signing my birthday card, my brother Ravi never writes to me.

Even though I enjoy my life with Ram, there are times when the silence that surrounds me in my new home makes me long for the familiar chatter of my family, especially at mealtimes. Ram, like his family, is a man of few words. He prefers to eat dinner while watching the evening news. Soon enough, I discover my favorite TV shows: *Three's Company, I Love Lucy,* and *Family Ties.* As I let myself melt into the everyday drama of their scripted lives, the actors become my extended family. And I develop a secret crush on one of the stars of *Family Ties,* Michael J. Fox.

Some afternoons, Ram drops me off at a friend's apartment. We gals trade recipes and tips about where to find raw mangoes to pickle and fresh bunches of cilantro. Rarely, we venture into downtown Portland, daring ourselves to navigate TriMet—the local bus system—and spend hours window shopping. Our husbands usually join us for dinner, and together we relive our favorite memories in India through music and movies.

Eventually, we tire of our get-togethers and begin exploring educational and career opportunities. While a couple of my friends choose motherhood instead, I reluctantly enroll in a computer programming class at Portland Community College, not because I like the subject, but, like many other Indians, I believe computer science is the only path to success. Needless to say, 75 percent of the students in the class are Indians. While my fellow students revel in the beauty of binary numbers, I slouch in my seat, eyes glazed over, unable to comprehend the complex mathematical concepts. I bug Ram to help me with my homework and break into tears when he loses his temper.

"How many times do I need to tell you that you don't have to torture yourself through these courses, Gayu?" he screams. "For God's sake, I don't expect you to go out and earn a living. All I want is for you to be happy," he repeats over and over again, offering me a tissue. I don't know what it is about a woman's tears that rattle men. I fail to understand why they cannot accept tears as a form of self-expression and not a tidal wave of emotions to flee from.

The C grade in my C++ computer programming language class finally convinces me to quit computer science. Next term, I register for an accounting class and a course in watercolors. Just as expected, I spot a couple of Indian students in the accounting class, and none in my painting class. The pursuit of arts and humanities, most Indians believe, is a hobby, not a study.

Ram and I celebrate my first Diwali in America with more than a hundred other Indians at a party hosted by the India Cultural Association at a community center in Hillsboro. Dressed in our finest silks and jewelry, we gather in cliques across the party hall representative of the states that define and divide us. I find it rather ironic that even here in the United States of America, thousands of miles away from our homeland, we still struggle to overcome our differences and unite as a people.

Over winter break, Ram and I embark on a ten-day road trip across California. The Golden Gate Bridge takes my breath away—both by its magnificence and the winds blowing through it. We wander through Fisherman's Wharf and carefully navigate our brand-new Toyota Camry through the crooked contours of Lombard Street. Ram's childhood friend Satya takes us for a drive through the expensive neighborhoods of Palo Alto and to his alma mater, Stanford University, considered the academic holy land by many an Indian. In Disneyland, Ram and I romp alongside Minnie and Mickey Mouse and sing along while sailing through the wondrous waters of "It's a Small World" not once, but three times in a row. We feast on french fries, ice cream, and cotton candy as we huddle together to watch fireworks explode into magical starbursts illuminating the night sky. Driving down Sunset Boulevard, I sit wide-eyed, hoping to spot a star. No luck. At Universal Studios, however, I get the opportunity to pose as one. I insert my face in the life-size wooden cutout of the spirited Scarlet O'Hara embraced in the arms of Rhett Butler. Of course, I mail it to Amma.

"How did a daughter I raise turn out to be brazen enough to bare her bosom for the world to see?" Amma had lamented, looking at the picture. Chitra writes, "It took me hours to convince Amma that it wasn't a picture of you. And no matter how many times I explained to her that you had simply stuck your head in the plywood cutout of Ms. O'Hara, she just wouldn't believe me." I had a belly laugh when I learned of my mother's plight. Even Ram couldn't help smiling.

Everywhere I go, I wish Appa were standing beside me, basking in the beauty of his dreamland. I hope someday soon he will. But for now, I write to him about my travels and send him lots of pictures.

My parents are delighted by the pictures of my travels, but they are most happy to witness my blossoming body. Just as Ram had predicted, I have gained weight—almost twenty pounds in the eight months since my arrival in America. Ram, never knowing why I had been skinny in the first place, is pleased.

"Gayu, it doesn't hurt to hug you anymore," he teases.

On New Year's Eve, Ram and I join another friend of his, Varghese, in a midnight service at a Catholic church in San Diego. Raised by parents who believed in the unity of all people—Hindu, Muslim, Christian, or Jew—I revel in the beauty of our oneness.

Once home from our vacation, Ram and I settle back into our routines. But my life in America continues to feel like a vacation, a welcome respite. As the first anniversary of my life in America draws near, so does our second wedding anniversary.

"Is there any good news, Gayu?" Amma inquires in her letter, craving to cradle her first grandchild in her arms. Ram's mother has been praying for a grandson to carry on the family name since the day of our marriage.

"I want to have a baby," I say, cuddling Ram in bed one night.

"Are you sure you are ready to be a mother, Gayu?" he asks. "America is a lonely country. I don't want you to have a baby and feel overwhelmed in taking care of it all by yourself. This is not India, Gayu," he adds, his eyes filled with concern. "You can't go to your mother's house for months on end to get pampered while you learn how to be a mother.

Are you sure you want to be responsible for another life when you yourself are so young, and new to this country?"

"I'll be fine. I love babies," I say, "We can do it."

As winter turns into spring, daffodils and tulips poke their perky little faces from underneath the cold ground. The cherry blossom trees encircling our apartment complex burst into clouds of pink. Robins and blue jays chirp in the trees, and the evening breeze is kissed with the lemony scent of blooming magnolias. The world is bursting with life within me and all around me.

CHAPTER 7

# Blessed Motherhood

IT'S MAY 1985.

"Hello, Amma, you will be a grandmother!" I announce, calling my mother at our neighbor Mrs. Nair's house, a couple of weeks after my second wedding anniversary.

"Congratulations, Gayu!" Amma squeals in delight.

"Popsi, you will be a grandfather soon," I hear her tell my father.

"Congratulations, Princess!" he shouts from behind.

"How are you feeling, Gayu?" Amma asks. "Any morning sickness?"

"I am okay, Amma," I answer. "The baby is due on January 7 next year."

Ever conscious of the expense of international phone calls, Amma speaks quickly and breathlessly. She tells me to eat, pray, and rest for two. "Always think pure and loving thoughts, Gayu," she adds. "A mother's state of mind has a profound impact on the growing baby." Both of us know exactly what she means.

Within a week, Amma's letters filled with prenatal advice begin to flood my mailbox. "Gayu, soak a few sprigs of saffron in warm milk each night, add a pinch of sugar and crushed cardamom, and drink it first thing in the morning. It will clarify your blood and ensure that the baby will have a glowing complexion," she writes. "Chew on cloves if you get nauseous. Eat dates, prunes, figs, and almonds if you can't stomach a full meal. Drink plenty of milk and make sure you rest. Don't worry if the house isn't picked up or your chores aren't done. I am sure God Rama will bless you with a healthy pregnancy and safe delivery."

The thrill of being pregnant wears off when my morning sickness begins. For days on end, I lie in bed, retching and clutching my stomach. Ram feels completely helpless. He is saving his vacation for when the baby arrives and can't take time off from work. He sets up a makeshift nursing station beside our bed, complete with a stainless steel bowl, paper towels, a box of saltine crackers, and a bottle of chilled 7 Up.

"Call me any time," he says before leaving for work in the morning. Often, he returns home at noon to find me crumpled in bed, just the same as when he left me in the morning. The food and drink by my bedside remain untouched.

"You have to eat something, Gayu," he insists. "It's not good for you or the baby to starve."

The mere mention of food makes me want to puke, and the aroma of barbecued hot dogs and hamburgers wafting through the apartment complex assaults my senses. My appetite, however, isn't the only thing under attack. My thoughts are filled with fears.

*Is my secret illness seeping back into my life? What if I can't keep any food and water down like in the years past? Will I need to be put on IV again? Will I fail my baby? Will I suffer a miscarriage? What if Ram finds out about my past? Will he be angry? Will he ever forgive me for keeping secrets?*

Of course, I tell no one about my worries. Instead, I comfort myself that it is perfectly normal for a pregnant woman to be sick to her stomach during the first trimester. But my thoughts tilt back into paranoia. I recall my mother's experience when she was pregnant with her firstborn, my brother, Ravi. She couldn't keep any food or drink down well into her seventh month, when she gave birth to him prematurely. He had weighed four pounds, three ounces, and she had nearly hemorrhaged to death. *Would that happen to me, too?*

Fortunately, my nausea dissipates within weeks, and so do my fears. My appetite returns gradually. I crave cheese enchiladas, onion rings, and salads with pickled jalapenos and garbanzo beans. Ram finds it hilarious that although I am Indian, my cravings are not. With renewed energy, I promise myself to become the healthiest pregnant woman possible. I follow Amma's advice diligently, and study *What to Expect When You're Expecting* by Heidi Murkoff, Arlene Eisenberg, and Sandee Hathaway, and Dr. Benjamin Spock's *Baby and Child Care* devotedly. Despite my distaste for milk, I force myself to drink three glasses of milk a day, and eat plenty of yogurt, fruits, and vegetables. I religiously take the B12, folic acid, and other prenatal supplements my OB/GYN prescribes. While working around the house, I sing to my growing baby the lullabies that Amma used to sing to my siblings and me when we were kids. I nap each afternoon for an hour and take long walks after dinner with Ram.

"I wish every patient were as healthy and happy as you, Gayathri," Dr. Wess tells me during my twenty-week checkup as he scans my protruding belly with an ultrasound wand and listens to the fetal heartbeat.

"Can you see your baby?" he pauses and asks.

Ram and I stare at the pulsing mass on the monitor, mesmerized.

"Would you like to know the sex of your baby?" Dr. Wess asks.

"No!" Ram and I say in unison. We want it to be a surprise. I suspect strongly it will be a girl, which I know will please Ram greatly. I worry, however, that my in-laws will be disappointed not to have an heir to carry on their family name.

"Would it be all right with you if my parents came to help us with the baby instead of your mom?" Ram asks on one of our evening walks. "They have wanted to visit me ever since I moved to America."

His request unsettles me. But I nod and smile, trying not to show my disappointment. Had I been in India, I would have traditionally gone to my mother's house in the seventh month of pregnancy and returned when the baby was three months old. Although I live in America, far away from the dictates of my culture, I had hoped for Amma to come and help me welcome my baby into this world. I write Amma reluctantly about Ram's plan to invite his parents to come for the baby's birth.

"That's fine, Gayu," Amma replies. "As Ram pleases."

Still, her disappointment is clear. Ever since my wedding, she had dreamed of nurturing me through my pregnancy and childbirth. Despite her dreams and mine, the rules of patriarchy that bind us force my mother and me to honor the wishes of Ram and his parents.

In August, Ram's parents arrive. As I help them unpack, I am surprised to find that Amma has sent an entire suitcase filled with gifts for Ram, me, and our expectant baby: our favorite snacks, a year's supply of spices that I had difficulty finding in America, and Amma's homemade curry powders, chutneys, and pickles. Tucked within the crinkly folds of tissue paper enclosed in a plastic bag, I discover a stunning green Banares sari strewn with silver stars and an intricate floral border. Woven in India's holiest city, the sari is embroidered with threads of real silver. I recall Amma wanting a Banares sari all her life, but not being able to afford one. My eyes grow moist knowing that she had splurged a month's rent on this sari.

"Your mother sent it for your *seemantha,*" my mother-in-law explains.

My heart weeps thinking of my mother and how she had longed to perform my seemantha—the bangle ceremony performed in the seventh month of pregnancy to pray for the health and well-being of the mother and unborn child.

Amma had tucked in a four-page letter with careful instructions on how to perform the ceremony in America. Considering that there would be no priests to perform the prayers in America, she had sent audiotapes of them, and also included several sets of green bangles to give to my friends at the celebration—green to represent prosperity and new life. Had I been in India, Amma would have pampered me like a princess and invited our friends and family to celebrate the joyous occasion and hired cooks to prepare the festive meal. Here in America, I realize, however, I am both cook and queen.

Peeking from underneath the sari bag is a tiny snow-white sweater set. Even though I adore the sari, the dainty sweater, cap, and booties steal my breath away. Soon after learning I was pregnant, Amma had mentioned in her letter that she was learning how to knit so she could make a gift for her first grandchild to wear home from the hospital. Her description, however, had failed to capture its sweet essence. Holding the tiny garment to my chest, I am angry that I hadn't insisted that Ram invite my mother to come help us with the baby instead of his parents. To avenge my anger, I promise to name the baby Roshini, if it is a girl—a name that my mother had longed to give me and couldn't since she had to honor the dictates of the patriarchal culture of India, and allow her father-in-law, my grandfather, to name me.

Soon, Ram, his parents, and I develop a new rhythm to our lives.

"There is no need for Gayathri to get up and make coffee when she doesn't even drink coffee," Ram tells his mother. "I'll make coffee for us before going to work. Besides, she needs to rest as much as she can."

Although a bit perplexed about my lack of wifely responsibility, my mother-in-law insists on waking up before Ram and making the coffee herself. But I win her over with my dutiful diligence. I encourage her to rest, go for a walk, or watch TV while I cook, clean, and do the laundry. She is all too happy to relinquish her domestic duties. She'd been married shortly after her fourteenth birthday and had spent her entire lifetime caring for her husband's extended family of nineteen and her own brood of four boys and two girls, all born before she had turned thirty. At fifty, for the first time in her life, she has the opportunity to relax, and she is determined to savor every moment of it. After Ram leaves for work, she curls up on the couch with a shawl tucked around her and takes a nap while my father-in-law pores through our local newspaper, *The Oregonian,* for hours.

"I could have bought so many steel dishes trading these newspapers in Bangalore," my mother-in-law comments over and over again, amazed at the girth of the newspaper, especially the Sunday edition.

By midmorning, my in-laws shower, dress, say their prayers, eat breakfast, and take a stroll around the apartment complex. Of course, my father-in-law always stays several paces ahead of his wife. Initially, at lunch, my mother-in-law insists that we serve the men first. But eventually, at Ram's insistence, the four of us eat together at the oak table in the nook.

After lunch, when Ram returns to work, my father-in-law religiously watches *Perry Mason* followed by a movie on TV. He chides my mother-in-law for taking too many naps, but she plays deaf.

Soon after learning I was pregnant, Ram decided to build a home of our own. Now, after dinner each evening, he spreads the blueprints of our new home on the coffee table. For weeks, we had strolled through up-and-coming subdivisions in our neighborhood. After careful deliberation, we had chosen to build a house in Charlais, a housing development ten minutes from our apartment. Our friend Anil, who had been recently engaged, is also building a house a few homes away from ours. My in-laws and I gather around Ram as he walks us through the floor plan. It is a 1,840-square-foot Tudor with three bedrooms, two-and-a-half baths, a living room, a dining room, a nook, a kitchen, a family room, a walk-in pantry, a laundry room, and a two-car garage. Several times a week, we drive over to the construction site to check up on the progress. My father-in-law is filled with pride as he and Ram pace up and down the stairs, inspecting every detail. My mother-in-law beams with joy.

Some weekends, we spend our days choosing windows and doors, flooring, carpets, light fixtures, cabinetry, paint, trim colors, and appliances for our new home—tasks I love. On others, we take my in-laws sightseeing across the Pacific Northwest.

In late October, we move into our new home. I am delighted to have a threshold to decorate and worship at last. I draw elaborate rangolis in my entryway and hang garlands of roses on the front door. My mother-in-law, along with my friend Neeru, welcomes Ram and me into our new home with aarti. I remind Ram to step across the threshold with his right foot first. I set up the God's shrine in one of the kitchen cabinets, light the silver diyas, and boil over some milk in a saucepan, beseeching God to bless our home to overflow with abundance just like the boiled-over milk. We treat the construction crew to lunch and thank them for their graciousness in building our home. Ram rents a U-Haul, and our friends help us move and unpack.

The next weekend, we host our first party, my seemantha. I follow Amma's letter to a tee and organize the ceremony under my mother-in-law's watchful guidance. I make a makeshift shrine for God Ganesha in the family room and decorate it with bouquets of dahlias, roses, and chrysanthemums. I draw rangoli patterns with colored chalk on a two-foot-by-two-foot wooden board and prop it up at the base of the altar. I arrange five fruits: a banana, an orange, grapes, apples, and a coconut, along with a bunch of green bangles on silver trays to give as gifts to my girlfriends. I dress in the green Banares sari, follow the priest's chants and instructions on the audiotape Amma sent, and worship God with turmeric, vermillion, sandalwood paste, flowers, and akshate—vermillion-coated rice. I light the silver diyas and incense. Once the puja is complete, Ram and I prostrate to God and his parents to seek their blessing.

Having no furnishings to seat all our guests, Ram spreads blankets and bedsheets on the new beige carpet in the family room, dining room, and living room. More than fifty of our friends and their families squat on the floor and relish the traditional meal that my mother-in-law and I had taken days to prepare.

A couple of days after the party, I wear the green Banares sari again and join Ram and his parents for a portrait session at Olan Mills. As soon as we pick up the prints, I mail one to my parents.

Amma and Appa are ecstatic at my pregnant profile—my blooming body is tipping the scales at 157 pounds, my face is glowing, and my hair has grown long and lustrous, flowing to my knees.

"Gayu, you look resplendent like the full moon," Amma writes. "Please ask your mother-in-law to do dhrishti for you."

With the baby due in just a couple of months, I turn my efforts to transforming one of the bedrooms into a nursery. In India, it's considered a bad omen to buy anything for the child until he or she is born. But we live in America, I argue, and eventually convince Ram and his parents that I should keep up with American traditions and decorate the baby's room and purchase all the essentials. Each day after I finish cooking our meals, I hurry into the nursery to work. Ram helps me hang a wallpaper border with dancing teddy bears and clowns in vibrant costumes, cartwheeling with red, white, and blue balloons. After looking at scores of stores, I finally settle on a sturdy oak crib, matching dresser and changing table, and coordinating clown and teddy bear bedding, window treatments, and night-light at Toys "R" Us. Ram surprises me with a matching rocker. I stock the dresser with cuddly soft receiving blankets, sleepers, onesies, booties, and hooded towels and washcloths in pink, yellow, and blue. I place a framed picture of Rama and Sita on top of the dresser, right next to a big brown teddy bear, and I stack diapers, wipes, and baby lotion in the cabinet under the changing table. Ram takes pictures and videos of every detail, and we mail them to my parents. They are thrilled.

Soon, the garage fills up with the baby's car seat, infant carrier, stroller, and playpen, along with a beautiful white bassinet my friend Rani lends me. Ram and I attend Lamaze classes for eight weeks at the Kaiser Permanente offices in Beaverton. My mother-in-law is a bit shocked to hear that Ram will be joining me in the delivery room and helping me with the birthing process. Ram informs his boss that he will take a week off from the day I go into labor. I practice my breathing techniques, pack my suitcase according to the layette list given by our instructor, and include one of my wedding saris, a green silk sari with a red border, to wear when I bring the baby home from the hospital. And I make sure to pack the white sweater set that Amma had knit for the baby. I slip the picture of God Rama and Sita that I'd carried with me in my wallet twenty-one months earlier on my trip to America into the front pocket of the suitcase and place it in the coat closet.

We have Thanksgiving dinner with Ram's colleague Robert and his new bride, Katie, at their home in Hillsboro. Although it had taken Katie hours to prepare the traditional turkey dinner, she was sweet enough to have made sure we had enough vegetarian options. My in-laws, while very appreciative of her thoughtful cuisine, wonder if Katie had forgotten to add the spices and seasoning. I smile, knowing that for us South Indians, no meal is ever complete without a touch of turmeric, cumin, coriander, curry leaves, asafetida, and mustard seeds.

Ram takes an extra week off at Christmas break and takes his parents on an extended trip across California, Chicago, New York, and Washington, D.C. Not wanting to jeopardize my pregnancy with travel, I stay behind with our friends Neeru and Bala.

It's January 9, 1986, two days past my due date, and I still have no labor pains. I grow a little restless and irritable. The next morning, I wake up with an overpowering urge to clean. I start in the kitchen. I wipe down the counters, the cooking range, and the microwave. I sweep the floors and get on my hands and knees to mop them. I clean the bathrooms, change the sheets on our beds, and wash the laundry.

"Why don't you take a nap?" my mother-in-law suggests. "It's not good to exert yourself." I follow her advice and quickly fall into a deep sleep. I wake up around six o'clock, feeling queasy, a faint pain spreading across my back and abdomen.

"I think it is time," I tell Ram when he returns home from work.

"Really?" he says, jumping up and almost knocking himself off his feet.

"Yes," I nod calmly and smile.

"Let's time your contractions before I call the hospital," he says, shifting his eyes between his wristwatch and my crinkled forehead.

I retrieve the suitcase from the coat closet and set it by the door. My labor pains are fifteen minutes apart. Ram calls my parents in Bangalore to tell them that I am going into labor. They are busy preparing for Chitra's wedding on January 13, in three days. Much like my marriage, Chitra's was fixed in a hurry. Her fiancé, Shashank, lives in Dallas and was on a two-week vacation when he met and agreed to marry my sister. And so the wedding was arranged in haste, and there was no way I could attend it with a baby due any minute.

"God bless you, Gayu," Amma says. "May Sri Rama bless you with a safe and speedy delivery and a healthy baby." Although I can't see her, I can picture my mother standing in our neighbor's house, ears glued to the phone, eyes brimming with tears, right hand clutching her heart in prayer. I ache for her to hold me in her arms as I welcome my baby into mine.

"Good luck, Princess," Appa joins in. "We will miss you and Ravi at the wedding." My brother Ravi had recently arrived at Marquette University in Milwaukee, Wisconsin, to pursue his graduate studies in computer science.

"I will miss being at the wedding, too, Appa," I say, and hurriedly wish Chitra a wonderful wedding before it is time to hang up. Although

I am heartbroken not to be able to attend my sister's wedding, I am delighted to know that she will soon be moving to America.

"It is so much easier these days," my mother-in-law says as we eat dinner, and recounts the births of each of her six children.

Ram calls his friend Anil to ask if my in-laws can stay with them while he takes me to the hospital. My in-laws, a nervous couple in ordinary circumstances, are used to having the security of their extended family during times like this. Being alone in a house in America, while their son and daughter-in-law are at the hospital, is more than they can handle.

Anil's bride, Latha, who had arrived just a few days earlier from a visit to India, answers the phone and says they would be most happy to have my in-laws over. Ram drops his parents at their house at eight thirty and drives me to the hospital. By nine fifteen my contractions are less than five minutes apart. The nurse helps me settle into a raised hospital bed and connects my belly to a fetal heart rate monitor.

"Everything looks great," she announces, much to my relief and Ram's. "My name is Melinda," she says, "I will be your nurse tonight."

The thirteen hours that follow are a blur of intermittent pain mixed with fleeting moments of brief respite. I feel pressure, followed by a loud pop. My water breaks. The nurse changes my sheets. The pain intensifies. Ram and Melinda keep me focused on the breathing techniques I have learned in the Lamaze classes. My OB/GYN, Dr. Wess, is on vacation. The doctor on call, Dr. Scott, checks in on me. He suggests that I opt for an epidural to ease the pain. I look at Ram. He shrugs his shoulders and says, "Whatever helps, Gayu."

Within minutes of receiving the epidural, I grow numb from the waist down. My body relaxes and I quickly drift into an uneasy sleep. A little while later, I wake with a throbbing pressure in my pelvis and an urge to push. I frantically search for the buzzer underneath my blankets, press it, and wait for Melinda to come. I turn to wake Ram up. He is sprawling awkwardly on a chair beside my bed, deeply asleep. His eyeglasses are perched precariously on his knees.

The hospital is quiet except for the mechanical drone of medical equipment, the sound of footsteps receding in the distance, and a clock clicking on the wall across from my bed.

"Did you have a little nap?" Melinda asks, studying the fetal monitor.

"Yes," I say, "I feel like I need to push."

"Let's check and make sure you are ready before we page the doctor," she says, flicking on the lights. She pulls on a pair of latex gloves and checks to see how far I have dilated.

"Yep," she says, "you're ready. Time to wake up, Dad." She taps Ram on the shoulder. He wakes up with a start.

"What? Is the baby here?" he asks, confused, scrambling for his glasses.

"You'd better get scrubbed in fast or the baby will come before you are ready," Melinda teases, handing him a gown.

Ram flips his wallet, looks at the picture of God Venkateshwara, his family deity, says a silent prayer, and slips the gown on before he scrubs his hands.

"Just a couple of big pushes," Dr. Scott suggests.

Ram holds on to one of my knees and the nurse braces the other. I take a deep breath as they count. On the count of three, I purse my lips, exhale, and push with all my might. Then I do it again and again, a few more times.

Soon, I feel my baby slide into the world.

It is 10:18 a.m., January 11, 1986.

"She is gorgeous," the nurse says, swaddling our seven-pound, five-ounce baby girl and placing her in Ram's arms.

I look at Ram. His face breaks into the biggest smile I have ever seen, and tears roll down his cheeks as he peers into his daughter's eyes. I have never seen him happier.

"Congratulations, Gayu," he says and places the baby into my arms. I press her to my heart, lean down, and kiss her moist head. I stare at her perfect little fingers and toes, her button nose, and rosebud lips. I gently smooth back the wispy locks of black hair spotting her soft little head and kiss her over and over again. I wiggle my forefinger into her tiny fist, and am amazed at the power of her fingers as they grip mine. I look into her dark eyes and am drawn into a world of abiding love.

"Do you have a name for the baby?" Nurse Melinda inquires.

"Roshini," I answer.

"What does it mean?" she asks.

"A ray of light," I say, drawing my baby closer. "Roshini means a ray of light."

CHAPTER 8

# Postpartum Blues

"WOULD YOU LIKE TO EAT LUNCH while your baby is still asleep?" asks the nurse standing beside my bed. "My name is Susan," she says, wheeling the lunch tray to me.

I squint at the bright sunlight streaming through the partially opened vinyl blinds in the hospital room. Roshini is sleeping peacefully in the bassinet nestled by my bed. Ram has gone home to call my parents in India to inform them of Roshini's birth. Then he planned to shower, grab a quick lunch, and bring his parents to visit the baby and me.

"Yes," I say, nodding and propping myself up. I am starved. The vegetarian sandwich, potato salad, sliced apples, and strawberry Jell-O topped with whipped cream look appetizing.

"Be sure to drink plenty of fluids," Nurse Susan reminds me before leaving the room.

Soon another woman, thirtysomething with a quick smile, comes to the door. "Ready to nurse the baby, Mrs. Ramprasad? I am Grace, your lactation consultant. I will be happy to help you and your baby get started." She gently picks Roshini up from the bassinet and places her in my arms just as I finish my lunch.

"Sure," I say, wondering why on earth I need a lactation specialist to teach me how to nurse my baby. *Isn't it a God-given instinct that mothers and babies share?* Fortunately for me, Roshini seems to agree with my sentiments.

"Wow! You are a lucky mom. You and your baby are naturals at this,"

Grace says, looking pleased. "Please don't hesitate to call me if you have any questions," she says, leaving a brochure about breast-feeding on the nightstand.

I stare at Roshini cradled in my arms and know that I am the luckiest woman in the world.

The rest of the day is filled with visitors filing in and out of my hospital room. Ram returns with my in-laws and a bouquet of pink roses. Our friends arrive with pink balloons and teddy bears tucked with Hallmark cards that say, "It's a girl!" or "Congratulations on your new baby." Ram takes pictures of Roshini and me with each one of our visitors.

That night, I am up every few hours to nurse Roshini. I don't mind at all. Between feedings, I doze off, *happily tired*, as Amma used to say—bone tired, but blissfully happy.

"Good morning, Mom. May I please check your vitals?" A nurse's voice nudges me awake.

"Can I shower today?" I ask, propping myself up.

A sharp pain sears through the back of my neck and shoots through my head, jolting me back into bed. Even the pain of childbirth pales in comparison to the excruciating throbbing in my temples. Nausea splashes across my ribs. I shut my eyes tight and squeeze my head between my palms, hoping the pressure will relieve the pain. I clench my jaws so hard, I am afraid my teeth will fall out.

"Are you okay?" the nurse asks.

"My head hurts," I whisper hoarsely, gasping for air.

"You'd better lie down. I need to go find the doctor," she says, rushing out of the room. The sound of her receding footsteps thunders in my head.

Moments later, she returns with Dr. Thomas, an anesthesiologist. He asks me a few questions while shining a pencil-sized light into my eyes.

"I think you have a spinal headache, Mrs. Ramprasad. Your dura was accidentally punctured during the epidural, causing a leakage of your spinal fluid," he explains.

I can't see or hear him clearly, and I struggle to comprehend what he is trying to tell me, except that he can patch the leak with my own blood. A few hours later, I sit upright, braced by a couple of nurses holding me steady while the anesthesiologist creates the blood patch. I am advised strict bed rest and intravenous fluids for the next forty-eight hours.

"Avoid sitting up for the next couple of days, Mrs. Ramprasad," Dr. Thomas insists. "Your head won't hurt as much if you are lying down."

The doctor prescribes a narcotic to numb the pain. I refuse to take it, paranoid about the small chance that it could get into my breast milk and affect my baby. The nurse asks if she should move Roshini to the nursery so I can rest.

"She'll be fine with me," I insist, determined to care for my baby on my own. The initial euphoria after the birth begins to dissipate under a cloud of agonizing pain.

Two days later, with Ram's assistance, I wobble to my feet, shower, drape myself with the silk sari I had brought from home, and place a red bindi on my forehead. I dress Roshini in the snow-white sweater set Amma had knit and swaddle her in a lemon yellow waffle-knit blanket. I cradle her tightly in my left arm and clutch the teddy bears with my right hand as the nurse wheels us out to the car. Ram struts proudly beside us, suitcase in one hand, the bouquet of pink roses and balloons in the other. He straps Roshini into her car seat, and we pull out of the hospital parking lot and onto the freeway. My head hurts. I slump beside Roshini in the backseat, one arm across her car seat, wincing at every turn for fear it might jostle her.

"Are you both okay?" Ram asks, looking in the rearview mirror.

"We are fine." I muster a smile, and reach for his right hand and give it a gentle squeeze. "I love you," I say as we reach the belly of the Fremont Bridge.

"I love you, too, Gayu," he says, grabbing my hand tighter. Ever since the day that I had arrived in America, and the first time Ram had squeezed my hand and said "I love you" as we had crossed this bridge, it has become a ritual for us to lock our hands and pledge our love to each other every time we cross it. Despite the pain that envelops me today, I feel blanketed by the love that Roshini encircles us in.

Minutes later, we park the car in front of our house. Latha and my mother-in-law meet us at the door and perform aarti. They float a pair of silver lamps my mother had given me for my wedding in a small, round, silver plate filled with water reddened by vermillion powder. They circle the diyas up and down around Roshini and me, singing a devotional song and praying to God to bless us with health and happiness. With Roshini tucked tightly in my arms, I step across the threshold with my right foot first. I place Roshini gently on the countertop underneath the God's altar in the kitchen, and pray to God to bless her with health and happiness.

Soon, Ram helps Roshini and me settle into our bedroom upstairs. My mother-in-law takes charge of the kitchen. "You don't have to come down for your meals," she says. "It is not good for a new mom to run up and down the stairs. Ram will bring it to your bedroom."

Ram brings my meals on a TV tray and rocks Roshini in his arms while I eat. But I have no appetite. My in-laws peek into my bedroom to check on the baby and me a couple of times throughout the day. Each night before I go to bed, my father-in-law slices fresh fruits and serves me fruit salad in a fluted glass bowl. Yet amid all the love and attention, I feel lonely.

Days disappear into nights. Each time I sit up to nurse my baby or eat, my head explodes in pain. Between the spinal headaches, frequent nursing, changing diapers, and sleep deprivation, my moods begin to grow darker than the winter nights. I become increasingly restless and weepy, sometimes crying for hours on end. I feel exhausted, overwhelmed, and empty inside. Waves of worthlessness, hopelessness, guilt, and fear come crashing from the shadows of my secret past and choke me in their vicious grip. Having enjoyed a brief respite from these symptoms over the last couple of years, I feel deeply betrayed by my body and brain. I watch helplessly as the anticipated joys of motherhood turn into a painful, confusing reality, and the familiarity and safety of my family and home begin to fade into a strange and scary place.

*I am blessed with a beautiful baby and a loving family. Why can't I be happy? Is my old illness coming back? Will Ram and my in-laws find out about my secret past?* I feel the walls of my world closing in on me. But I have no one to turn to, nowhere to escape.

A week later, Ram returns to work and I go through the motions of motherhood like a robot. When friends stop by to visit Roshini, I pretend to enjoy their company, but all I want is to be left alone. And when I am alone, I am plagued with worries about unlikely worst-case scenarios.

*What if I drop Roshini on her head? Will she die from hemorrhaging? What if I fall asleep while nursing her at night, roll over her, and smother her to death? What if I don't hear her cry and let her choke herself to death?*

Incessant thoughts of inadvertently harming or killing my baby exacerbate the anxiety coursing through my ragged body and mind. Even as the gray skies of an Oregon winter give way to rays of spring sunshine, my moods continue to cast shadows in the sun.

I tell no one about my symptoms and scary thoughts. Not even Ram. And I definitely don't mention it in my letters to Amma and Appa. Even though a part of me knows it's irrational, I am afraid that if I do, they may deem me a danger to my baby and take her away from me. So I put on a façade of normalcy and send my parents envelopes filled with Roshini's pictures and tell them how blessed I am to be a mother.

"Dear Gayu," Amma writes, as if she senses my distress. "I understand how tiring it must be to be a new mom. I wish I were there to take care of you and Roshini Rani. Please remember, your love and patient nurturing are the most important vitamins for your growing baby. Although she may not be able to tell you, Roshini can pick up on your moods. If you are happy, she will be happy. If you are tired and irritable, it will make her cranky. Please don't exert yourself. Rest while the baby sleeps and let your husband and in-laws take care of the chores at home."

Instead of soothing me, Amma's words sting me. They make me feel guilty for being a bad mother.

It's March 1986, time for my in-laws to return to India. Ram and I decide to celebrate Roshini's cradling ceremony on March 15, before they leave.

Had I been in India, Amma and my aunts would have joined hands to celebrate the occasion on the eleventh day after the baby's birth. But, here in America, I have no such luxury. The task of planning the party and cooking for it overwhelms me. But I am determined to organize a cradling ceremony befitting my little princess. When she naps between feedings or after her bath, I make endless lists—guests, groceries, decorations, and paper supplies. It takes me a couple of days to make all the phone calls to invite our guests—twenty-one families in all. A week before the cradling ceremony, Ram and his dad shop for groceries, and I join Ram to pick up decorations at the neighborhood craft store.

Three days before the event, I start cooking the festive meal. My mother-in-law and my friends Neeru and Latha give me a helping hand. The refrigerator is soon overflowing with hundreds of *gulab jamoons,* eggplant curry, green bean curry, *bisibele bhat,* yogurt rice, tomato *rasam, vadais,* and homemade yogurt. The oven is stocked with a hundred deep-fried papads. Running out of space in my refrigerator, I ask Latha to store the fruit salad in her refrigerator.

The day before the cradling ceremony, I decorate our living room with red, white, and blue paper streamers and bouquets of pink balloons. I drape the white wicker bassinet with the sky-blue silk sari I had worn at my wedding reception. Worried that pushpins might scratch Roshini's tender skin, I string paper flowers around the bassinet and secure them with Scotch tape. Ram sets out the party supplies on the dining table and I arrange the puja ingredients by the God's altar—silver trays filled with fruits, flowers, and incense.

That night, I crawl into bed, exhausted. Just as I settle in, I hear Roshini crying. She is up for her bedtime feeding.

"Would you like me to get her?" Ram asks.

"Forget it. I'll do it myself," I snap at him, frustrated.

"What's wrong, Gayu?" he asks as I sit down to nurse Roshini. "Why are you so angry?"

"You want to know what's wrong?" I scream at him. "Let me tell you what's wrong! While you were at work resting your feet, I was standing on mine cooking all day. I am tired of this stupid country! I have to do everything myself—cook, clean, take care of the baby, and get ready for the party. I am tired of it all. I just can't do it anymore. I hate myself. I hate my life. I need a break!

"At least if my mother were here she would have helped me. But no, no, no—you had to go invite your parents to come visit us, didn't you? You don't care about me or what I want. All you care about is you and your family."

"Shhhh. Don't scream, Gayu." Ram frowns. "My parents might hear you."

"I don't care if they do!" I shout. Roshini starts to cry. She has been unusually fussy over the last couple of days. *Perhaps she senses my exhaustion. Perhaps Amma is right.*

"Is everything all right?" My mother-in-law knocks on the door.

"Everything is fine," Ram replies, glaring at me, motioning me to remain quiet. I burst into tears.

"Don't cry, Gayu," he says. "You are just tired. How many times have I told you not to stretch yourself so thin? Don't forget, you are in America, not India. You don't have ayahs, cooks, and maids here. You are it!" he exclaims. "I understand how excited you are about the cradling ceremony. But you just gave birth to a baby and have hardly had the chance to recover. Did you have to invite all fifty-six people on the guest list? Why couldn't we have invited fewer people?" he argues, drawing me into his arms.

I wince at his touch and retreat to the far end of our bed. Ever since Roshini's birth, the old feelings of dread and worry have wormed their way back into me. I wail like a trapped animal and thrash my head with both hands, trying to stop my thoughts from racing.

Ram stares at me, baffled. His eyes mirror the terror I feel inside. Every time he tries to hug me, I recoil from his touch. After a while, he gives up and goes to bed. Finally, I slip under the sheets, too, and muffle my sobs beneath the comforter. The house is quiet except for the rise and fall of Ram's breathing. I feel terrible for screaming at him, but I don't know how to apologize. My ego keeps me tongue-tied. I glance at Roshini lying next to me in bed. She smiles in her sleep. I am wracked with guilt. *What if I can't be good mother to her? Am I losing my mind?* The thoughts send shivers up my spine.

Ram stirs awake. "Gayu, you have to calm yourself," he says, rolling over. "Why don't you chant a prayer until you fall asleep."

"Sri Ram, Sri Ram," I chant, until I fade into a restless sleep.

I wake up at 6 the next morning, shower hurriedly, and get dressed in the new red silk sari Amma had sent—a gift from Chitra's wedding. I hear Roshini stirring awake.

"Good morning, Rani." I kiss her on her forehead, nurse her, change her diaper, and dress her in a lacy pink frock and panty set that I had picked up for the cradling ceremony. I slip a pair of matching pink booties on her feet and swaddle her in her favorite yellow waffle-knit blanket.

"Good morning," Ram mumbles, kissing us both.

"You'd better get ready before the guests arrive," I tell him, placing a black dot on Roshini's right cheek with my eyeliner pencil—a dhrishti *pottu* to ward off the evil eye.

By 8 a.m., the house is brimming with guests. We perform the puja and pray God to bless Roshini with a healthy and happy life. While Bismillah Khan's shehnai plays in the background, the women gather around the decorated bassinet and join my mother-in-law and me in performing the cradling ceremony. We anoint a smooth, round rock I had picked up on one of my trips to Cannon Beach with vermillion and offer it milk and honey and place it in a corner of the bassinet. We pray that the rock, symbolic of God, blesses the baby with the fortitude to face all of life's ups and downs with the equanimity and strength of a rock. We then place Roshini in the bassinet and sing lullabies as we take turns rocking her to sleep.

The commotion rattles Roshini. She begins to cry.

"Shhhh . . . You are almost done, Rani," I say, picking her up.

Our friend Anil is assigned to taking pictures, and Ram is busy capturing everything on videotape. "Please make sure you send us lots of pictures and the video of the entire event," Amma had requested in her letters. "We are not fortunate enough to be there in person."

I invite our guests to help themselves to the buffet. I excuse myself to nurse Roshini and lay her down for her afternoon nap. By the time I make it downstairs again, the guests are starting to leave. Heaps of gifts lie beside the bassinet, wrapped in colorful paper and tied with pink ribbon and bows. I thank each of our friends for the gifts and their blessings. Anil and Latha offer to stay behind and help clean up.

"Don't worry about it," Ram says, "I can do it."

As dusk turns to dark, so does my mood once again. I drag myself to my bedroom and close the door behind me. I pull the sheets over my head and lie in bed, motionless, tears soaking my face. That night, I don't go down for dinner.

"I am not hungry," I say, pushing the plate away when Ram brings me dinner in bed.

"What's wrong? Why are you crying again?" he asks.

"Nothing." I shake my head and roll over to the other side.

"I am sure someone has cast an evil eye on you," he says, and asks his mother to perform dhrishti to rid me of the evil eye.

I lie mute as my mother-in-law performs the ancient ritual, skeptical of its powers to rid me of my plight.

"Don't worry, it's not uncommon for a new mother to have emotional upsets," she says, trying to comfort Ram. "Just let her rest. The poor girl must be worn out from all the cooking and running around for days. Besides, she must be missing her mother at a time like this. Perhaps she should visit her mom with the baby soon," my mother-in-law suggests.

"Not now," Ram replies. "The baby is too young. But I have a sabbatical coming up next year. Gayathri, the baby, and I will come home to India for a couple of months then."

Two days later, Ram, his parents, Roshini, and I take a ten-day road trip across California. Ram wants to show his parents the sights and sounds of the Golden State before they fly back to India from Los Angeles. Except for the day we visit the Venkateshwara temple in Malibu, Roshini and I stay with friends or relatives while Ram and his parents take day trips to the Golden Gate Bridge, Disneyland, Universal Studios, and Sea World.

*I am suffering from postpartum depression, a major public health problem with negative emotional and physical effects on the mother, child, and family —but none of us know that yet. Many doctors believe that the hormonal changes that occur during pregnancy and childbirth are primarily responsible for the illness. Postpartum depression may also be caused or aggravated by exhaustion from childbirth, stress, or lack of sleep in the early weeks of a newborn's life. As a woman with a history of depression and anxiety disorder, undiagnosed as it was, I was particularly at risk to develop postpartum depression. Yet, like many of the nearly 10 to 16 percent of women suffering from postpartum depression, I am unaware of its symptoms and the fact that it is highly treatable. Afraid I might be labeled crazy and lose custody of my baby if I disclosed my struggles, I retreat deep within the chaos of my mind.*

On the drive back home to Portland after my in-laws board the plane in Los Angeles, each of us is crying for a different reason—Ram weeps quietly, but never once says how much he misses his parents. Ram and his family, I have learned by now, speak volumes in their silence. Roshini screams her lungs out, miserable from being trapped in the car seat for hours. I sit in the back seat along with Roshini and stare at the magnificent Siskiyou mountain pass, tears streaming down my face. I cry not as much from missing my in-laws, but more for the inconceivable sorrow I feel inside—the emptiness, the nothingness. Surrounded by the lush green mountains brimming with life, I struggle to find meaning in the graveyard of my mind. Despite it all, Roshini somehow keeps me tethered to sanity. She is my only ray of sunshine.

Back home, life takes on a different rhythm. Ram returns to work, and I immerse myself in raising Roshini. At first, I feel overwhelmed with all the chores. But gradually, I fall into a routine. I shower, cook, and clean while Roshini naps, and organize my life around nursing, naps, and bath times. Regardless of what my emotional barometer reads, the routine carries me through the days.

Months roll by and Roshini grows more radiant by the day. She learns to smile, sit up, scoot, and crawl. I capture each of the magical milestones on camera and print two copies of each picture, one for my album and the other to mail Amma and Appa.

"I can't wait to hold her in my arms, Gayu," Amma writes. "When will you visit us?"

"Perhaps next year," I reply. "Ram has a sabbatical coming up."

Roshini is a happy baby most of the time, except when she is hungry or sleepy, or when people visit us. She is wary of strangers and clings to me like a little chimp. Our house begins to look like Toys "R" Us. She loves all the popular toys we bought her, but her most favorite thing in the world is to be read to—her favorite books are *Mother Goose Rhymes, Winnie the Pooh,* and Dr. Seuss's *One Fish, Two Fish.* She crawls into my lap with a book in one hand and her favorite yellow waffle-knit blankie tucked in the other. She carefully wads a corner of the blankie in her palms and twirls a lock of my hair around her little fingers while I read. Every once in a while, she looks at the pictures in the book and then at me and breaks into a smile that lights up my world. In moments like this, I feel invincible, and convince myself that with my baby's love, I can overcome any darkness that may befall me.

Bath times are a breeze with Roshini, especially with the help of her favorite yellow rubber ducky. But mealtimes are yet another story. Our little princess expects to be entertained with songs and stories for every bite. Bedtimes are a battle for all of us. Roshini prefers to stay snuggled in my arms. Ram and I prefer her to sleep in the crib in her own bedroom. I don't know who weeps harder, Roshini or Ram and I. After multiple trips to her room to soothe her and several lullabies later, she eventually falls asleep. No matter how tiring my day was, watching my little angel sleep always revives me and fills me with love.

I finally get my driver's license and enroll her in a playgroup at the local church. We attend swimming classes at the local recreation center twice a week. Roshini takes to the water like a fish and breaks into giggles each time I dunk her in the water.

Ram can't wait to come home and play with his daughter. Our weekends are filled with trips to the park and potluck dinners. At one of the parties, I meet four other Indian women—Sahana, Anika, Neema, and Parimal—all first-time moms with daughters a few months younger than Roshini. All their husbands work at Intel as well. Soon, we start our own Moms' Group to support one another and socialize our babies. While our babies play, we share remedies for teething pain and tips for potty training. We gripe about how tired we are, eternally sleep deprived, and how much we miss our families in India. But, none of the moms ever mentions what I long to hear—that they, too, suffer from the dark moods and irrational fears that I do. I don't dare ask them, however, afraid that they may think I am crazy. Some days I can keep my worries at bay; other days I can't shut out the frightening thoughts.

*What if the knife drops out of my hands and stabs Roshini while I am chopping vegetables and she is playing with pots and pans by my feet? What if I don't pay attention to the traffic lights and jam into the car in front of me? What if I forget and leave Roshini unattended in the bathtub and she drowns herself?*

Irrational questions repeat themselves in my head over and over again—rewind, replay, repeat; rewind, replay, repeat; rewind, replay, repeat . . . I don't know how to shut them off. The only way I can cope with them is to let them run through me while I focus on the task at hand. There are times I can cope and times I can't; I somehow soldier on until Ram gets home. Once he changes and settles in to play with Roshini, I slip out of the family room and cower behind my clothes in the walk-in closet in my bedroom, banging my head against the wall over and over, beating it to numbness. The physical pain dulls the emotional turmoil, at least for a few moments.

The commotion brings Ram running upstairs, perturbed. "What's wrong with you, Gayu?" he asks. "Why are you bashing your head?"

"Go away!" I scream. "Leave me alone. I don't want Roshini to see me like this."

"People only see the glamour of America and don't understand how lonely and isolating this country can be, Gayu," he says. "I'm sure you are homesick. A visit with your parents will do you a world of good. Next fall, when I take my sabbatical, let's take a four-month trip to India," he suggests, trying to comfort me. "But in the meanwhile, why don't you visit your aunt in Ohio this summer? Perhaps your brother, Ravi, can meet you there."

In June, Roshini and I take our first flight together. Ravi and my aunt's family are enamored with Roshini. While they compete to take turns to play with her, I struggle to keep a serene front.

"You are going to have a nervous breakdown if you don't relax and take care of yourself," Ravi says, watching me get up four or five times through the night to nurse, sing, and rock Roshini back to sleep.

My heart leaps into my throat. For a moment, I panic. *Does he know?* Somewhere deep inside me, I long to bare my soul to my brother, to tell him about the emotional wildfire raging through me. But I don't, afraid that he might tell Ram and my parents, and they might take Roshini away from me.

"Raising a baby is hard work, Ravi. I am just tired," I say, turning over and biting my lip to keep myself from crying.

Roshini turns one on January 11, 1987. We rent the recreation room at a friend's apartment complex, invite nearly a hundred people, and have a gala party to celebrate the milestone. Roshini looks adorable in the long, red silk skirt and blouse that Amma had mailed and the gold earrings that my in-laws had shipped. That night I perform dhrishti for my little angel to protect her from the evil eye.

For the next several months, I shop, pack, and ship boxes full of diapers, baby wipes, baby cereal, pureed vegetables and fruits, milk powder, toys, and Roshini's favorite books to Amma, in preparation for our homecoming. I include a first-aid kit, just to be safe. I make sure Roshini and I get all the travel vaccines in time. Ram helps me cram our clothes, and armloads of gifts for our family, into four suitcases. He carefully weighs each one to make sure they are within weight limits. In early August, Roshini and I bid farewell to Ram and embark on the thirty-six-hour journey back home to India.

"I will miss you both very much," Ram says, hugging us tight at the Portland airport, tears trickling down his face. I am surprised to see him cry. Having a daughter has already begun to soften my otherwise silent and stoic husband.

"We will see you in October," I say, wiping my tears.

"Call me as soon as you reach India," he reminds me.

"I promise," I say, smiling, and board the plane.

# PART 4

# Descent into Darkness

CHAPTER 9

# Breakdown

IT IS THREE O'CLOCK IN THE MORNING, August 1987, in Chennai, India. Roshini and I inch forward through the immigration line along with hundreds of fellow passengers on board Singapore Airlines. It is unbearably muggy, even at this early hour. The air is stagnant with the smell of sweat and coffee. Most of us feel as crumpled as our clothes. The ceiling fans aren't working. A power shortage has forced the government to ration electricity and enforce mandatory power cuts throughout the day.

Roshini starts fussing and wants to be nursed. I drape her blanket over my shoulder and nestle her to my bosom, tossing modesty to the winds. People stare in discomfort. I don't give a darn. I am too tired to care.

"Next!" The immigration officer, a middle-aged man dressed in starched whites, summons me with the flick of his finger.

"Reason for your visit, madam?" he asks, flipping through my passport with one hand and twirling his handlebar moustache with the other.

"I am coming home to visit my family in Bangalore," I answer, cradling Roshini in one arm and balancing the diaper bag and stroller in the other.

"How long are you staying?" he inquires, "Did you bring any gold or electronics?"

"I'll be in India for four months. And, no, I am not bringing any gold or electronics," I reply.

The officer stamps my passport and slides it toward me. Relieved to have been spared any harassing questions, I hurry through the customs check and security gates.

"Welcome home, Princess," Appa says, grabbing Roshini and me in a hug. I sink into his arms, hoping I don't black out. The thirty-six-hour journey had been a test of endurance. Roshini hadn't slept a wink and neither had I. She had insisted on sitting on my lap throughout the flight and even accompanied me to the bathroom. My throat was parched from singing "Mary Had a Little Lamb" a million times.

"Welcome home, Gayu," Amma hugs me. "Hi, Roshini Rani!" she says stretching her arms out. To my surprise, Roshini glides into my mother's arms and stares at her, smiling.

"I am amazed she is letting you hold her, Amma," I say. "She hardly lets anyone except me and her dad hold her."

"Hi, Roshini, darling!" says Appa, tickling her toes. Roshini crinkles her nose and frowns.

"Not fair," Appa smiles. "You girls always gang up on me."

Except for the strands of gray hair and a few wrinkles of time etched around their eyes and forehead, my parents look much like they did when I had bid them good-bye three years ago.

Skinny porters clad in white dhotis mill through the crowds, grabbing people's luggage even before they are asked to help. Careful to keep the porters at bay, Appa ushers us into a taxi and directs the driver to my aunt's house. Appa slides into the front seat next to the driver. I sink into the back seat, and rest my head on Amma's shoulder. Roshini sits in Amma's lap playing with her bangles.

"I have waited to see this picture for so long, Gayu," Appa says, glancing at the three of us in the rearview mirror.

"Thank God for Sri Rama's blessings," Amma says, drawing Roshini closer. My heart fills with joy to see my parents happy. For all the pain I had caused them in the years past, this is my moment of sweet redemption.

"How many pieces of luggage did you bring, Gayu?" Appa asks, unloading the suitcases.

"Four suitcases and two carry-on bags," I say.

"There are only three suitcases and two carry-on bags here," my father panics.

"Don't worry, Appa, we can collect the missing suitcase tomorrow," I suggest and start walking toward my aunt's house. Aunt Sarasa and her family have gathered at the door to welcome us.

"What do you mean, we can collect it tomorrow?" my father shouts. "This is India, not America! If we don't get it right now, we may never find it tomorrow. Do you at least remember what is in the missing suitcase?" he asks.

"I think it had all my wedding saris," I reply, unperturbed. My calm angers my father.

"How can you just stand there calmly and tell me we can collect it tomorrow, Gayu?" Appa explodes. "We can't ever afford to replace those saris." He jumps back into the taxi and heads back to the airport.

"Don't worry, Gayu, I am sure your father will find your suitcase," Amma comforts me. "You must be tired. Why don't you sleep for a few hours before we take the train to Bangalore?" she suggests. "I will take care of Roshini."

"Thanks, Amma," I say, sinking into the mattress and pulling the sheets over my head. My body aches from sitting for hours, my ears buzz with the drone of the airplane, and my mind races back to the last time I was lying in this very bed, a few years before. My parents and I were in Chennai to get my green card at the American consulate. I was sicker than I had ever been in my life. My parents were frustrated with my mysterious illness, which no doctor could diagnose and no medicine could heal. I had felt completely estranged from my family. I toss and turn, trying to shut out the memories. But they repeat relentlessly in my mind's eye. Upset, I pray I don't get sick again.

"I can't fall asleep," I say, sitting up, tired of all the tossing and turning.

"It is okay if you can't sleep, Gayu," Amma says, stroking my head, "at least rest for a while."

I look to see where Roshini is. She has fallen asleep in my mother's arms. Eventually, I drift into sleep.

"Time to wake up, Gayu." Amma wakes me up a few hours later. "We need to catch the train in an hour."

I drag myself out of bed and stagger to the bathroom to brush my teeth.

"Don't use the tap water, Gayu" Amma says, handing me a stainless steel Thermos filled with boiled water. "I don't want you to get sick."

"I can't believe your mother," says my aunt Sarasa, shaking her head in disbelief. "She has carried that water all the way from Bangalore."

"It's just that the water in Chennai isn't as sweet as it is in Bangalore," my mother explains.

Soon, we bid my aunt and her family good-bye and take a taxi to the train station.

"I am glad I found the missing suitcase," Appa says, loading my luggage into an air-conditioned berth in the Brindavan Express and settling next to Amma and Roshini. I sit across from them, deeply grateful. The train ride rocks Roshini and my father to sleep within minutes.

"Is Appa okay?" I ask my mother, knowing that my father is fast asleep. Riding in the taxi from the airport, I had noticed a slight stoop in his shoulders, and a tinge of sadness in his eyes.

"He is fine, Gayu," she assures me. "He decided to quit his job a few months ago, and he has been very stressed about it."

"Oh, my God, why did he quit? Why didn't you tell me about it before?" I ask.

"We didn't want to worry you, Gayu," Amma says. "He had a disagreement with the management."

For as long as I have known my father, he worshipped his work. It was his identity and purpose in life. I can only imagine the pain he must be feeling. Despite the fact that money was tight, I realize that my parents had splurged by buying us tickets to travel in the air-conditioned coach. They did not want to compromise Roshini's comfort or mine. I feel guilty for imposing on my parents at a difficult time like this.

Later that afternoon, we arrive in Bangalore. Hours later, Roshini and I visit my in-laws. Sitting in the auto rickshaw, I wrap a shawl around Roshini to protect her from the deafening sounds of auto rickshaws, the honking, and the bellowing clouds of exhaust fumes trailing behind buses. I feel overwhelmed by the crowds and clatter of everyday life. As much as I try, I cannot understand why I need to trek across the city to visit my in-laws the very day of my arrival in Bangalore. The patriarchal dictate that rules this land and my life irritates me. *Why can't they visit me? After all, my baby and I had endured a thirty-six-hour intercontinental journey and hours on the Brindavan Express. Couldn't they have had the courtesy to visit us at my parents' house instead?* My in-laws are delighted to see us, especially Roshini, and their joy lessens my frustration.

The next few days are a jet-lagged blur. The twelve-and-a-half-hour time difference is playing tricks on me and Roshini. We can't fall asleep at night or stay awake during the day.

"You have to keep yourself awake during the day, Gayu. It is the only way to get over the jet lag," Appa insists. But all I want to do is sleep. Ever since Roshini's birth, I have rarely slept through the night. With my mother watching over my baby now, I feel at ease to let go and sleep at all times of the day.

"Why don't you take Roshini for a walk, Gayu?" Amma suggests one morning at seven thirty. "It will be good for you and the baby. I bet the neighbors would love to see you both."

A soft breeze wafts through the windows, and sunlight dances on the walls. A walk sounds like a great idea. Roshini had been fussy all night. I hope the fresh air will lull her to sleep. Besides, I can't wait to visit with my neighbors.

"Sure, Amma," I say. I strap Roshini into her navy blue umbrella stroller and step out. I feel woozy, like I am walking on clouds. Within minutes, we are swarmed by our neighbors.

"How are you, Gayuma?" Mrs. Nair asks, hugging me. "What a cute baby!" She pinches Roshini's cheeks. "She looks just like her father."

Mrs. Nair's daughter, Anu, jiggles Roshini's pink booties. "No, she looks just like her *ajji*," she says, referring to my mother, Roshini's grandmother.

"Do you still remember me?" asks Leela, picking Roshini up, the stroller dangling behind her. Roshini starts screaming.

"I am so sorry," I apologize. "She just needs a little time to get to know you all. She's rather shy of strangers."

I unhook Roshini from the stroller and pick her up. All at once, blood rushes to my head. I feel dizzy. My heart races, my chest tightens, and I feel out of breath. The distorted faces and voices of my neighbors swirl around me. Roshini feels unusually heavy in my arms. Afraid I will drop her, I squat on the sidewalk, clutching my chest, drenched in sweat. Waves of nausea wash over me. I feel completely detached from my body and my surroundings. I am terrified that I must be having a heart attack. My world goes dark.

"Gayathri, are you okay?" I feel someone shaking my shoulders. I squint, shielding my eyes against the blinding sunlight.

"Have a sip of water," Leela offers. "What happened?" she asks.

"I don't know," I shake my head.

Amma and Appa are concerned when I return home escorted by my neighbors, my face ashen. I hand Roshini over to my mother, rush to the bathroom, buckle over, and throw up. Scenes from the years past rush through my head. Determined not to give in to my worries, I clean myself up and join my parents sitting at the table, waiting to eat breakfast. I pick at my idlis while Amma feeds Roshini.

"Are you okay, Gayu?" Appa asks. I nod yes without looking up. I sense his concern, fear, and disappointment. In the blink of an eye, I revert back into the terrified teenager sitting at the table with my father glaring at me. "You are going to do it again, aren't you?" I can hear him shout, lips clenched, fists pounding on the table. I see myself running to the bathroom, hands clutched to my mouth.

Sitting at this table with my parents staring at me unleashes the trauma of the years past. The brief reprieve I had enjoyed from my symptoms in the first couple of years in America had led me to falsely believe that I had conquered my demons. But since Roshini's birth and subsequent troubles, I feel fragile, empty, and surrounded by darkness.

"She'll be just fine," Amma insists, handing me a glass of water.

Over the next few days, I develop severe stomach cramps and diarrhea. I can hardly eat, sleep, or think straight. The only thing I can do, and do so uncontrollably, is cry. I am eternally tired and literally feel like jumping out of my skin. I am attacked by recurrent bouts of dizziness, heart palpitations, breathlessness, sweating, nausea, and vomiting. At times, I feel like a freight train without a driver, zooming at breakneck speed, completely out of control. And at other times, I can barely move. I feel caged in a body and mind that has suddenly gone berserk. I begin to worry that I am going insane. Just as in the past, I don't tell my parents about my fears. Besides, they have no clue of my struggles in America following Roshini's birth. And I don't want to tell them. I see no point. For years they had insisted there was nothing wrong with me, and that my suffering was all in my head, and so had the many physicians that had treated me.

"Hello, Gayathri, how are you? Is America treating you well?" Dr. Mahesh asks, proceeding to check me. Amma and Appa had insisted I see him. "It must be the sudden change in climate and diet," he explains. "Hope you haven't been eating any fresh fruits and vegetables, or *panipuris* on the street side," he teases. "Be careful and drink boiled water at all times, and avoid eating out as much as you can. Things in India may not be as sanitary as they are in the United States. Perhaps you have lost your immunity over the last three years," he suggests.

"It could be a mild case of amebiasis," he speculates, and suggests having my stool tested. The results are inconclusive. But I grow sicker. So, he prescribes a course of antibiotics. My mother puts me on a bland diet. It doesn't help.

Friends and relatives pour in to visit Roshini and me, each curious to learn about America and see how much I have changed. "Remember me?" they ask. "Hope you haven't forgotten us," they say, implying that I might have developed selective amnesia while I was away.

They all want to know the same things: How big is your house? How many cars do you have? Do you have an American maid? Is it true that even the maids in America drive cars? Can you get all the vegetables and fruits you do in India in America? How old is Roshini? Does she like India or America? Is she daddy's little girl or mommy's? Does she understand only English, or does she understand Telugu and Kannada? (These are the languages Ram and I were raised to speak; Telugu is our mother tongue and Kannada is the regional language in the State of Karnataka, where we grew up.) When is Ram coming? How long are you staying? When will you come to our house for lunch or dinner? Do you still like Indian food, or do you prefer only American food now?

They come bearing gifts for Roshini, packs of Parle-G milk biscuits and Jems candies. Some even stuff a hundred-rupee note into her hands. All of them want to hold her and play with her. But, the only thing Roshini wants is for me and her to barricade ourselves in my parents' bedroom and emerge from our fortress once Amma assures us that our guests have left. And that is exactly what we do.

"How odd," our friends and relatives comment. "She is probably not used to seeing this many people in America."

"Perhaps it would help Roshini to meet other children," Amma wonders and sends word to my cousin Uma to visit us with her little girl, Seema, who is just four months older than Roshini. Although Roshini is wary of Uma, she tolerates Seema as long as she doesn't grab her blankie or toys.

"Why don't you and Uma go to the matinee?" Amma suggests, offering to take care of the children. "It will be a good break from your girls. I am sure you have lots to catch up on."

"Great idea!" Uma agrees excitedly.

Catching up with my cousin sounds wonderful, but I am not sure I have the energy to drag myself out of the house, drive through the maddening traffic, and squeeze through the crowds of people at the theater. But I don't have the heart to disappoint Uma. When Uma and I finally settle into our seats in the air-conditioned theater, I am relieved, at least until the movie starts to play. The sound system literally knocks me off my seat. I had forgotten how loud Indian theatres were. I plug my ears and stare at the screen.

"Don't you like Indian movies anymore?" Uma asks, accusingly.

"I love Indian movies," I say, "I am just shocked at how loud it is."

Partway through the movie, I am under siege. The actors on the screen merge into strange creatures and lunge at me; their screams boomerang in my ears. My heart leaps off my chest and the theater begins to spin like a Ferris wheel gone awry. My throat goes dry and chokes my breath.

*This is it,* I tell myself, *I am going to die.*

"I don't feel well," I mumble to Uma. "We need to leave."

"You are probably hungry," she suggests, her eyes glued to the screen, "Perhaps we can get hot *samosas* during the intermission."

People around us shush us and glare. I sink deeper into my seat and close my eyes. I sense the walls closing in on me. I panic, scramble to my feet, and stagger out of the theater and hail an auto rickshaw. Confused, Uma chases after me and hops in.

The next thing I remember is waking up in my mother's bed, staring at the ceiling fan whirring over my head, grateful that death had spared me, but terrified I was really going crazy this time.

Appa takes me to Dr. Mahesh again. The doctor starts me on another course of antibiotics, which only worsens my stomach cramps and diarrhea. Amma decides that it is best for me to wean Roshini. Even at eighteen months, Roshini loves to nurse a few times during the day and at least once at night. No matter my struggles, I had always cherished cuddling her in my arms, and losing myself in her sweet embrace. I had also reasoned that continuing to nurse her would protect her from waterborne diseases in India. However, I hardly have the energy to nurse her lately.

"Let me help you wean and potty train Roshini when you visit us," Amma had written in her letters. "It can be difficult." And, so, I have waited. Amma was right. Roshini hates the bottle at first and eventually accepts it only if her grandmother gives it to her while rocking her in her arms. When my father tries feeding her at night, wanting to give my mother a break, Roshini wakes up screaming, feeling his hairy arms with her little hands.

By early September—the time of *Gowri puja* and *Ganesh Chaturthi*, the festivals celebrating Goddess Gowri and her son, Ganesh—both Roshini and I are dehydrated. She is running a high fever and refuses the bottle, and my diarrhea and vomiting continue to spin out of control along with my mind, which is touched by the wings of madness. The new chocolate-brown silk sari that Amma had bought for me sits untouched in a box in the almirah, next to the gorgeous red silk *langa* with the blue border and the tiny blouse with puff sleeves Amma had tailored for Roshini. For four long years, my mother had waited to celebrate the festivals with me and especially with her first granddaughter. She had invited most of the neighborhood women for the *haldi-kumkum*—an ancient tradition where neighborhood women gather to sing songs in praise of the deity worshipped. The women are traditionally served homemade lemonade and *kosambari*—a lentil and diced cucumber salad dressed with lemon juice, seasoned with asafetida and black mustard seeds, and garnished with chopped cilantro. Before they leave, the women are offered turmeric, vermillion, strands of fresh jasmine, and a coconut nestled atop beetle leaves, with a rupee or two tucked underneath. Hundreds of coconuts Amma had stockpiled for months for the occasion remain untouched underneath the granite countertop in the kitchen.

My parents are exhausted rushing Roshini and me to doctors. For days, we lie limp in bed; Roshini survives on Pedialyte to keep her hydrated, and I can only tolerate tender coconut water. Once her chores for the day are done, my mother cradles Roshini in her arms and sings lullabies that she used to sing to my siblings and me when we were kids. Some afternoons, my father reclines on the sofa in the living room with Roshini lying across his chest and sings Mother Goose rhymes along with her and her little Playskool cassette player. They sing "Mary Had a Little Lamb," "Old McDonald Had a Farm," and "John Jacob Jingleheimerschmidt" over and over again.

Gradually, Roshini recovers, but I don't. I become completely withdrawn and lose all interest in caring for myself or Roshini. Days come and go as I sink deeper and deeper into the growing darkness of my mind. Here, in what has become the desolate landscape of my life, I feel completely alienated from both my inner and outer worlds. I lie in bed, mute with guilt and grief, paralyzed by a profound sadness. For most of my life, I had fought these emotions for fear that acknowledging them would make me weak, and perhaps cost me the love, acceptance, and respect of my family. And now they are back with a vengeance, holding me hostage in their vicious grip. Death becomes an alluring presence. I fantasize about killing myself. It is not that I want to die; but ending my life seems to be the only escape from the hopelessness and despair.

*Perhaps I can smother myself with a pillow when my family sleeps.* But I worry that the sounds of asphyxiation might wake my mother and Roshini, with whom I share a bed. For all the grief I have caused them in life, I want to spare them the pain of watching me die. *Maybe I can hang myself with a sari. But where? How?* I can't decide. *What if I throw myself in front of a bus?* Not a good option. I can't bear to disgrace my family in public.

My aunt Neena, Amma's younger sister, and her husband, Vinay, come to visit us one evening, and they are horrified to see me.

"We have got to get her out of bed," they insist. After hours of coaxing, they finally help me into their car and take me for a ride. Amma suggests we stop at the shopping complex in Jayanagar 4th Block and buy Roshini a potty seat. At first, I refuse to get out of the car. But I relent when Roshini fusses for me to join her. I hang on to my mother's arms as we make our way through the busy marketplace. Appa and my uncle decide to wait in the car.

"That one," Roshini points to a tiny red potty seat with Winnie the Pooh painted on the back rest. At a year and eight months, Roshini has grown into a chatterbox with enough vocabulary to convey her desires and distress. Her eyes light up with joy at the sight of Pooh Bear, perhaps conjuring up all the times Ram and I have cradled her in our arms and read her about Pooh Bear's adventures at bedtime. When she was six months old, Ram had bought Roshini a soft, cuddly Pooh Bear, and she and "Poo Be," as she later called him, had become inseparable. In fact, she had insisted on bringing him to India with her and took him everywhere she went. "Is it okay, Gayu?" Amma asks. I can't decide. I can barely think or stand up straight.

"Yes," I nod and beg Amma and my aunt to take me back to the car. I take a couple of steps and collapse on the street. I close my eyes shut and plug my ears with my hands, trying to shut out the dizzying images and jumbled voices swirling around me.

"I cannot live like this anymore, Amma!" I wail. "I want to die. I want to kill myself."

"What's wrong, Gayu?" my mother asks, kneeling beside me, cupping my face in her hands.

"I want to die, Amma, I want to die. I want to die," I repeat in a trance, tears flowing down my face. I spot the shock in my mother's eyes. But it pales in comparison to the horrors I have kept locked up in my heart for the past seven years of my life.

"Can you please help me die, Amma?" I beg, clutching her feet.

A crowd gathers around us, their breath mingling with mine. "Is she all right?" the voices ask. "Can we get her some water?"

Amma and my aunt hoist me up forcibly, and help me back into my aunt's car.

"Is everything all right?" Appa asks, peering over his shoulder, his voice tinged with pain and disappointment. I lower my head and pray that I die before I cause him any more grief and shame.

"Don't worry, Gayu," Amma says, holding me tight. "Sri Rama will set everything right."

"Neither you nor your God Rama can rescue me from this hell!" I want to scream. Instead, I say nothing. I simply stare out the window and into the dark night of my soul. My aunt sits next to me, trying to hold Roshini in her lap. Roshini winces and climbs into mine. I despise the madwoman that I have become, and I am convinced that my child would be better off without a mother like me.

That night, I writhe in bed like a fish out of water, gasping for air.

My nerves are on fire. My body jerks uncontrollably as if it were jolted with electricity every few minutes. My eyelids flutter constantly. I cannot close or open my eyes. My heart pounds and my thoughts race with one compelling thought—*kill yourself!*

"Do you love me, Amma?" I ask.

"Of course, Gayu," she says, clasping my hands. "Why would you even ask such a question?"

"If you love me," I plead, "please help me die."

Amma and Appa stare at me, tears running down their cheeks. Confused, Roshini begins to cry. Amma cradles Roshini in her arms and calms her down.

"How can you possibly want to die, Gayu?" my mother reasons. "Look around—you are the luckiest girl in the world. You have a loving husband and a beautiful baby girl. Don't you want to live at least for Roshini's sake?"

Roshini reaches out to me. I clasp her little fingers with mine. I desperately wish I could will myself to live, but I am tired of fighting the demons in my head. I just want to lie down and die.

"Please focus on the music, Princess, it will ease your mind," my father insists, playing yogic chants on the stereo. He sits beside me, stroking my head. I cling to his hands and beg him again, "Please, Appa, help me die."

"I know how hopeless you feel, Gayu. I promise we will take you to the doctor tomorrow. He will definitely help you get better," Appa comforts me. Deep within the dark wells of my father's eyes, just for a fleeting moment, I spot a sorrow that mirrors my own.

A mournful hush descends upon the house, except for the tick-tock of the grandfather clock. I can faintly hear the rise and fall of Roshini's breath beside me. She has fallen asleep in Amma's lap. I lie awake, staring at the ceiling, waiting, praying for death to come. Appa sits beside me, his head bobbing in exhaustion, the yogic chants blaring in the background. Amma massages my feet, chanting the *Lalitha Sahasranamavali.* Revered as the most favored form of prayer to Goddess Lalithambika, it is believed its regular chanting purifies the environment, invigorates each nerve in our body, and releases subtle energies to awaken the healing powers within to ensure a long and healthy life.

"Repeat after me," my mother coaxes me. "I promise it will revive you."

My faltering mind cannot concentrate long enough to chant even one of the one thousand *shlokas*—verses—in the prayer. I had grown up listening to Amma chanting the *Lalitha Sahasranamavali* and had witnessed her faith in its life-affirming powers. But today I find no salvation in its presence. The emotional wounds that had taken root in my youth have since festered into a raging infection, obliterating my body, mind, and spirit. As award-winning novelist William Styron describes the panic and depression that overcame him in his memoir *Darkness Visible,* I, too, am under siege of "a veritable howling tempest in the brain." And I believe no god, physician, or person can rescue me from the wrath of its ultimate destruction.

To my great disappointment, morning comes but death does not. My hands keep crawling up to my neck under the sheets, eager to snuff the life breath out. But I can't do it. Appa sits sentry watching my every move.

"Good morning, Princess," he wishes. I nod my head, roll out of bed, and walk toward the bathroom. On my way, I stop at the kitchen door and stare at my mother chanting prayers and lighting the nandadeepa.

She drapes the gods with garlands of fresh jasmine, rings the brass bell, lights incense, and offers fruits. These sights, sounds, and smells have awakened and comforted me ever since I was a child. But today, they enrage me. Over the last few years, I have secretly begun to hate God. I cannot understand how a loving, benevolent God can inflict such pain on his children. *For as long as I can remember, I have tried to be a good daughter, wife, and mother. What did I do wrong? Why do I deserve to suffer like this?*

"Good morning, Gayu," Amma says, sensing me standing behind her. "Come take the *managalarathi.*"

"I hate you!" I scream, "I hate you and your God! You are not my mother, are you?" I hiss. "You have always hated me, haven't you? You hate my eyebrows, my clothes, my makeup, and everything about me. I could never make you proud. No matter how much I tried, I was never good enough for you, was I?" The words spill out and seep into my mother like venom. I can see it in her eyes.

"What are you talking about, Gayu? I have always loved you," she says, walking toward me.

"Don't lie," I spit. "Don't lie to me standing in front of your almighty God."

"I don't understand you at all, Gayu," Amma says, coming closer. "I made sure you went to college, found you a good husband, and even sent you to America. I have prayed for your health and happiness each day, and thanked God knowing that you have been living the life of your dreams. What more could I have done for you, Gayu?"

"Don't touch me!" I scream, shoving her back with all my strength. Amma tumbles onto the floor. "You have no idea of the nightmares I have lived through. Not that you will ever understand my pain even if I told you!" I shout. "All I want you to do is help me die, and you can't even do that, can you?"

The pain that I have locked up in my heart for so long comes pouring out, unleashing a storm of conflicting emotions: relief that I have at last spoken my truth, and remorse for having hurt my mother.

"Popsi!" Amma screams out to my father. "There is something terribly wrong with Gayu." She looks at me, her eyes wide with terror. I sink by the wall, my head tucked between my knees, and mumble incoherently.

Appa calls Dr. Mahesh frantically and is advised to take me to Dr. Kiran, a psychiatrist, immediately.

"I pray no one we know sees us here, Gayu," Amma whispers, scooting closer to me in the waiting room. "You never know the vicious rumors people can spread."

Growing up, Amma always warned me, "Don't you ever believe in gossip, Gayu. The human tongue has no backbone. It can, therefore, roll any which way it wants to."

Most Indians, I knew, lived and died worrying about what other people thought of them. Saving face was of utmost importance. Although

I was born and raised in India, I had long imagined that I would dare to be different and live my truth. But today, the fear in my mother's eyes fuels mine and burns me with shame.

I sit beside my mother, head hanging low, trying to avoid the curious glare of the receptionist, who, I recognize, was my classmate in college. I don't want her or the world to know that I am crazy. *But perhaps she already knows. Why else would I be sitting in a psychiatrist's office?*

Our turn comes. "Hello! I am Dr. Kiran," says a middle-aged doctor, peering over the rim of his glasses and inviting us in with a quick smile. "How can I help you, Mrs. Kasinath?" he asks, as if he has known my mother forever.

"We have no idea what is wrong with Gayathri, doctor," Amma says. "Ever since she came for a visit from America a couple of weeks ago, she has been very ill. She can't eat, can't sleep, and she cries endlessly. She is nauseous and throws up all the time. She has lost fifteen pounds over the last two weeks and has absolutely no interest in life. All she wants is to die, and she keeps begging me and her father to help her kill herself." Amma dabs her tears with the tip of her pallu.

"Is it true, Gayathri?" the doctor asks, checking my vitals.

"Yes," I nod, my head glued to my chest. I am too ashamed to look at him.

"I think your daughter is suffering from clinical depression, Mrs. Kasinath," Dr. Kiran proclaims.

*Depression . . . mental illness . . .* the doctor might as well have handed me a death sentence. My suspicions are confirmed. I am *crazy!* Terrified, I wait for the doctor to call in the orderlies and have me institutionalized for life. *Isn't that what they do to crazy people?* To my relief, however, the doctor calmly says, "Don't worry. Depression is a very common mental illness—debilitating, but treatable."

"Depression?" Amma asks, incredulous. "How can a girl like her, who has everything one can dream of, have depression, doctor? She has a loving husband, a beautiful little girl, and a fabulous life in America."

"Depression doesn't discriminate, Mrs. Kasinath," Dr. Kiran explains.

"It can afflict anyone. It is caused by chemical imbalances in the brain. Medication can help."

Amma and I are in shock. His words merely pass through our ears. Just for a moment, I breathe a sigh of relief, knowing that my illness has a name. But almost immediately, the stigma associated with depression tightens its noose around my neck. I am paralyzed with fear of the consequences of my diagnosis on the future of our family.

*What if our family and friends find out? Will they ostracize us? Will Ram divorce me? Will he take custody of Roshini? Will Appa, my brother, and sister be able to get jobs? Who will want to marry my brother? What if the medications don't help? What if I get sicker? Will I be locked up in a mental hospital?*

Dr. Kiran scribbles a prescription for doxepin, a tricyclic antidepressant, and asks Amma to schedule a return appointment in two weeks.

It has taken me nearly seven years since the onset of my debilitating symptoms to arrive at a psychiatrist's office. And it has taken Dr. Kiran less than seven minutes to diagnose me as suffering from clinical depression. Having no documented record of my prolonged suffering, Dr. Kiran assumes that this is my first tryst with depression. And not understanding that my past trauma is related to my present breakdown, neither Amma nor I bring it to Dr. Kiran's attention.

Hours after receiving my diagnosis, Amma, Appa, Roshini, and I move in with my aunt Neena and her family. My aunt, uncle, and parents reason that Roshini and I will be more comfortable at my aunt's house, since it has Western toilets, showers, phones, and a car—all the amenities of my American home that my parents' home lacks.

With each dose, the medication makes me sicker and sicker. It worsens my anxiety and depression and exacerbates my suicidal thoughts. My mouth feels dry like an emery board and has an unpleasant metallic taste. I suffer from severe constipation, headaches, nausea, blurred vision, dizziness, and vomiting. I have no energy or appetite. My mind is fogged with confusion, and sleep completely escapes me. I spend most of my days crumpled in bed, tossing and turning restlessly, my heart pounding, my body soaked in sweat.

*According to the World Health Organization, about 350 million people suffer from depression, a leading cause of disability worldwide. Depression is a common mental disorder that presents with depressed mood, loss of interest or pleasure, feelings of guilt or low self-worth, disturbed sleep or appetite, low energy, and poor concentration. These problems can become chronic or recurrent and lead to substantial impairments in an individual's ability to take care of his or her everyday responsibilities. At its worst, depression can lead to suicide, a tragic fatality that can be prevented. Every forty seconds, someone loses his or her life to suicide. Each year, almost one million people die from suicide, and nearly 90 percent of those who commit suicide are struggling with mental illness.*

*Although depression can be reliably diagnosed in primary care and 60 to 80 percent of those affected can be effectively treated with antidepressant medications and brief, structured forms of psychotherapy, fewer than 25 percent of those affected (in some countries fewer than 10 percent) receive such treatments. Barriers to effective care include lack of resources, lack of trained providers, and the social stigma associated with mental disorders, including depression.*

*Looking back, I was fortunate to have received a diagnosis and access to mental health care at all. According to a recent study by the Indian government, there is only one psychiatrist for every 400,000 people. It is one of the lowest ratios anywhere in the world. There are a mere thirty-seven mental institutions to serve the country's population of 1.2 billion people—50 to 90 percent of people affected by mental illness, therefore, go untreated. Lack of awareness about mental health issues and resources, in addition to the pervasive stigma of mental illnesses, often compels people to seek help from faith healers and temple doctors, not mental health professionals. Fortunately, living in a major city like Bangalore and having a family able to afford mental health care ensured my access to a psychiatrist.*

Concerned, Appa calls Dr. Kiran and is told that the side effects will wane over the weeks and I should be patient for the medication to reach its therapeutic levels in my bloodstream. Amma and Appa take turns sitting by my bed singing *bhajans*—religious songs. Roshini doesn't budge from my side. A couple of times a day, Amma chants the

*Lalitha Sahasranama,* beseeching the goddess to invigorate my body and awaken the healing powers within.

"Please take me back into your womb, Amma," I plead, clinging to her feet one day. "I can't live like this anymore."

"I wish I could, Gayu," she says, brushing back her tears and mine. "I can't bear to see you suffer."

Day by day, the dreams that my parents and I had cherished for my homecoming turn into a deadly nightmare. We are experiencing how depression debilitates not only the affected individual, but also the family. Amma and Appa are heartbroken, but they do not give up hope.

I threaten to kill myself constantly. Abraham Lincoln, who fought clinical depression all his life, expressed my feelings best when he said, "to remain as I am is impossible. I must die or be better." Knowing that I won't get better, I decide to kill myself.

One morning while showering, I swallow my gold earrings, and calmly disclose it to Amma, who is standing guard by the bathroom door. She panics and calls Dr. Kiran. He is away on vacation, and suggests that I should get checked out by his colleague, Dr. Prashanth. Amma and Appa rush me to the doctor. After reviewing X-rays of my innards, Dr. Prashanth decides that the earrings present no threat to me and should be expelled from my system on their own in a day or two. He puts me on suicide watch and advises my parents to stay vigilant through the night and contact Dr. Kiran the next day.

Getting dressed the next morning, I try to strangle myself with my *dupatta*—a chiffon scarf. Amma pries it from my hands and rushes me to Dr. Kiran's office. Concerned, he insists on immediately administering ECT—electroconvulsive therapy, commonly known as shock treatment.

"The medications can take up to four to six weeks to help. We can't wait that long and risk her life," he explains. "The ECT will help her in the meanwhile."

Early next morning, I lie on a bed at Shanti Nursing Home, Dr. Kiran's clinic. The phenyl vapors wafting from the freshly mopped red oxide floors make my stomach churn. Except for Amma, me, Dr. Kiran, an anesthesiologist, and a nurse, there is hardly anyone else awake at the nursing home. Dr. Kiran places two electrodes on my scalp and slips a metal plate into my mouth. "To protect your jaws from clenching shut," he explains.

The anesthesiologist, Dr. Amir, a tall, fair-skinned man with a goatee, positions a mask over my mouth and nose and instructs me to breathe deeply. "You will drift into sleep within a couple of minutes. There is nothing to worry about," he reassures, standing beside my bed.

The nurse straps my feet and hands into leather harnesses on either side of the bed to keep them from flailing and getting hurt when the ECT is administered.

"You will feel a tiny prick now," alerts Dr. Kiran, injecting me with a muscle relaxant.

Terror spreads through my body like wildfire. I feel like a fugitive prepped for execution. I want to bolt out of bed and run. But my body feels like lead. In seconds, my world goes dark. When I wake up minutes later, my life is a blur. Scared that my brain might completely shut down at any minute, I beg Amma to call Ram and tell him to come to Bangalore immediately. I want to make sure that Roshini is safe in her father's arms before I become an invalid.

Not wanting to alarm Ram with the disturbing turn of events, Amma calls and tells him that I am suffering from a severe case of amebiasis and, while doctors are taking good care of me, it would be very helpful to have him home.

Even here in India, the land of Gandhi, where our national motto proudly proclaims *satyameva jayate—truth alone triumphs,* the truth about mental illness imprisons me and my family, exiling us into lives of shame and secrecy. To protect the honor and future of our family, my parents decide to lie about my ill health and tell Ram and others concerned that I am suffering from a severe stomach upset. And I don't dare to speak the truth.

Three days later, Ram arrives in Bangalore, a week earlier than he had planned. I have no recollection of Amma helping me shower at two in the morning, getting dressed in Ram's favorite sari, meeting him at the airport, or of the days that follow. The ECT has marred my memory.

Roshini and Ram are delighted to see one another. While I am deeply relieved to see them together at last, I am terrified at how Ram will react to the fact that I have been diagnosed with depression and have begun receiving ECT and antidepressants. He is shocked and saddened to say the least, but he remains steadfast in his faith that I will recover.

"Don't worry, Gayu," he says, wrapping his arms around my shoulders, "you will be fine."

Having never met anyone who has recovered from depression or any other mental illness, I don't share Ram's faith or my parents' hope. Neither do I believe Dr. Kiran's expert opinion that depression is treatable. The only people suffering from mental illness who I knew were locked up in the mental hospital at NIMHANS—the National Institute of Mental Health and Neurosciences—relegated to live like prisoners in their own homes, or abandoned by their families to wander the streets.

A few days after Ram's arrival, he insists that Roshini and I move in with his family. My mother tries to convince him that it would be best for us to stay with my parents, especially given the circumstances. But with Diwali arriving in a couple of weeks, Ram and his family want us to join them in the celebrations. A new wave of fear, guilt, and shame drowns me in its wake. *What will I tell my in-laws? When they find out I am suffering from a mental illness, will they send me back home to my parents? Will they make Ram divorce me and get him remarried? Will they take my baby away from me?*

Not knowing what to say, I say nothing, and they don't ask. I suspect that Ram and my parents have informed them of my diagnosis. My guilty heart, however, perceives the sorrow brimming in my mother-in-law's eyes, mourning the misfortune of her dearest son.

Just as Amma had suspected, Roshini is rattled by the move to my in-laws' house and the sea of strangers floating in and out. And I continue to struggle in choosing life over death. Every other day, Amma is called to come revive us. My husband and his family have no clue how to care for either of us. Not knowing what else to do, my mother-in-law, a deeply religious woman, requests Amma to seek the services of the local shaman, and my mother reluctantly follows the shaman's instructions. Years later, Amma weeps as she tells me of her desperate actions—she had placed halved lemons anointed with vermillion at the intersection of four streets before sunbreak and prayed that the person crossing the lemons be possessed with the evils spirits that possessed me.

"I knew how wrong it was to wish ill upon another innocent person, Gayu," Amma had pleaded. "But I was just a helpless mother who was driven to do anything to help her daughter heal."

In the weeks that follow, I receive several more ECT treatments, and grow deeply concerned about my memory loss and the confusion clogging my mind.

"Short-term memory loss is an expected side effect of ECT. Don't worry about it; it is short-lived," Dr. Kiran assures me. But I fear that the ECT is destroying my brain.

"Is it safe to take Gayathri to Tirupathi?" Ram asks the doctor. Concerned that my suffering could be a retribution for my past sins, Ram and his family hope to have special pujas—prayers performed to pacify the gods—and beg for a miracle cure at Tirupathi, the famed temple of his family deity, Lord Venkateshwara.

"Sure," Dr. Kiran says, and asks me to bring him some *prasad*—blessings from God.

"I am sorry, I can't," I tell the doctor calmly, determined to jump off the hill on which the temple stands and end my miserable life. Dr. Kiran shrugs his shoulders and wishes us a safe trip.

Much to my dismay, I am unable to fulfill my wish, and the trip is uneventful. I am worn out by the long drive and have no energy left to climb the mountain steps leading to the temple. Roshini, my sister-in-law, and I take the bus to the temple instead, while Ram and his brothers climb up the hill. Once at the temple, I never find the opportunity to break loose from my family, and my fear of heights spoils my plans to plunge to my death. So I return home dejected and retreat to bed.

Worried at my deteriorating health, my parents have special pujas performed at the Hanuman Temple. They bring home a talisman and tie it on my right arm to infuse me with courage. When that doesn't help, my mother-in-law, afraid that I might be possessed by evil spirits, summons a priest to exorcise me. She stands outside the room with reverence as the priest's turmeric- and vermillion-stained hands roam inside my sari blouse, purportedly to locate the pulse of the demons that possess me. I feel utterly violated. A primal scream emerges from the hollows of my stomach, part animal and part human. I stuff my fist into my mouth to muffle it. I want to curse the priest and the God he worships. I don't. Terrified that my actions would be witnessed as further evidence of my insanity, I toss aside the priest's hands and roll away from his body, which reeks of sweat and sandalwood paste. The priest leaves with a huff, and my mother-in-law follows suit.

For days I remain in a catatonic stupor. Concerned, my in-laws send word to my mother, who rushes to my bedside again. Heartbroken to see me lying mute and motionless, staring at the wall with vacant eyes, Amma asks to take me home with her. But Ram and his parents insist that Diwali is just a couple of days away, and they would like Roshini and me to celebrate the festival with them, especially since Ram's sisters and their families were coming home from across the country to join us. Not wanting to upset my in-laws, Amma relents. Even as Diwali bathes the world around me in joyous light, I continue to be engulfed by darkness.

Day by day, the medications turn me into a zombie. But Dr. Kiran insists on increasing the dosage to reach therapeutic levels. And when that doesn't help, he advises it is best that I wait to return to America to reevaluate my meds and dosing. "Any change with your meds will take four to six weeks to take effect," Dr. Kiran explains, "and you won't be here in India long enough for me to monitor you." In the meanwhile, he suggests that I meet Dr. Kincha, a renowned psychotherapist in town.

The following week, Ram takes me to Dr. Kincha's home office. A pleasant man in his sixties, he proposes that ongoing therapy would certainly help address any underlying conflicts and interpersonal problems, and teach me coping skills to enhance my well-being. He speculates that my move to America and the cross-cultural conflicts, in addition to the hormonal changes caused by pregnancy and childbirth, might have triggered my depression. Knowing that we will be leaving India in a couple of weeks, he recommends I work with a psychotherapist when I return home to America.

On December 14, Ram's brother Girish gets married. I have no memory of attending the wedding.

On December 21, Ram, Roshini, and I leave India to return to Portland, accompanied by my mother. She is deeply concerned about my well-being and Roshini's, and she wants to nurse me back to health. Besides, my sister, Chitra, is expecting her first baby in three months. Convinced that her absence during my pregnancy and childbirth had in fact triggered my breakdown, Amma is determined to save my sister from a similar fate.

Appa has finally found a job in Hyderabad and decides to stay in India. He looks broken as he bids us good-bye. As I hug my father, I want to tell him how sorry I am for the pain I have caused, and more importantly, that I now know about his secret. A day earlier, Ram and I had visited Dr. Kiran for the last time. To ensure continuity of care, Ram had asked Dr. Kiran to provide us with medical records specifying my diagnosis and treatment plan to carry with us to Portland.

"Did you know that Dr. Kiran had diagnosed your father with depression a year ago and treated him, Gayu?" Ram had asked me, reading the report on the way back to his parents' home. It was pouring rain, and each time the auto rickshaw hit a road bump or another vehicle passed by, we were splashed with slush.

"What?" I had asked, in shock. Ram had repeated the question.

"No, I didn't know." I had stared at him in disbelief. I could not understand why Appa would have kept it a secret from me. *Why didn't Amma or Dr. Kiran say anything? Perhaps they didn't want to burden me. But still, I wish they had disclosed the truth.* I finally understand why Amma and Dr. Kiran had greeted each other with such familiarity when we first met.

The Scottish writer Robert Louis Stevenson once said, "The cruelest of lies are often told in silence." Silence is always an option, I know, and sometimes a noble one. But holding back information that would ease another's pain, I believe, is cruel. I feel deeply betrayed by my father's silence.

When I confront my mother about Appa's struggles on the long flight back to Portland, she reluctantly tells me about his descent into darkness and his fight to stay alive. I am shattered to learn that my once-vibrant father, having lost all hope, had threatened to lay himself down on the railway tracks or throw himself underneath an oncoming bus. Finally, he had sought Dr. Kiran's guidance. Although antidepressants had not helped him, my father had crawled back into life, one painful step at a time, through the regular practice of yoga and sheer self-determination.

Heartbroken, I wish desperately that my father had trusted me to share his pain. Perhaps then I would have known that I was not alone. Knowing his struggles would have offered me strength, and in learning how he had freed himself from the death grip of depression, I might have discovered hope. Sharing his truth might have possibly prevented me from living a life entrapped in shame. I tell my mother that I want to talk to my father about his depression as soon as I get home. But she insists that I shouldn't discuss these matters with Appa for fear that it would further endanger my broken mind.

CHAPTER 10

# Prisoners in Paradise

AFTER A HELLISH FEW MONTHS in India, Ram, Roshini, and I return to Portland with my mother. It is her first trip to America. Throughout the journey, I am obsessed with thoughts of losing control and erupting into a maniacal frenzy. I feel compelled to jump off the plane, but I can barely move. Roshini's feverish body is lying limp on my legs, and I can't bear the thought of waking her up. She had just slept after hours of crying. When at last I make it to the toilet, I plan to strangle myself with my dupatta—my chiffon scarf. As I tighten the noose around my neck, I am wracked with guilt knowing the pain I will cause my family, and the public disgrace. The only thought that comforts me is the certainty that I will kill myself when I get home.

Our friends Anil and Latha are shocked to see me when they pick us up at the airport.

"Oh, my God! You have lost so much weight. Are you okay?" Latha asks.

Amma convinces her that I had a severe stomach upset and am fine now. Ever since Dr. Kiran had diagnosed me with depression, my family and I have an unspoken pact never to disclose my disease. The truth, we believe, will destroy us all.

"I am sure you are all exhausted," Latha says, dropping us off at home. "I have left some dinner on the countertop and some groceries in the refrigerator." Anil helps Ram unload the suitcases. Over the last few years, Latha, Anil, Ram, and I have grown into best friends, sharing the troubles and joys of our lives. But now the stigma of mental illness creates a wall of silence between us.

My brother, Ravi, arrives in Portland late at night on December 23. He hasn't seen Amma in more than a year since starting graduate school at Marquette University and plans to spend Christmas Eve with us before flying to College Station, Texas, to be with Chitra. Chitra is seven months pregnant and has been suffering from fainting spells. Her husband is in India, participating in the first death anniversary of his mother.

Ever since our return from India, despite my mother's relentless efforts to get me back into the flow of life, I have buried myself in bed, contemplating how best to end my life. But, although my mind compels me to kill myself, my body can barely move. I feel suspended between surreal states of mental agitation and physical paralysis. A million hammers pound on my head, my mouth is dry, and my vision is blurred. Somewhere amid all the chaos, however, I sense an inkling of calm as everyday objects transform themselves into tools for self-destruction. The bathtub becomes a potential drowning pool, the car in my garage a gas chamber, and my wedding sari a deadly noose. After carefully considering my options, I decide instead to slash my wrist with the kitchen knife when everyone is asleep. Convinced that my family would be better off without me, I tiptoe into the kitchen, careful not to wake anyone up. Hands trembling, tears rolling down my face, I grab a knife from the drawer by the stove and stand in front of the altar in the kitchen cabinet and beg God to watch over Roshini and forgive me for killing myself.

Suddenly, out of nowhere, Ravi pounces off the couch and grabs the knife in my hands. He must have slept on the couch the night before.

"Leave me alone!" I scream, wrestling with the knife. "Please let me die."

"Let go of the knife!" he shouts, tightening his grip.

"Please don't make me hurt you, Ravi," I tug at the knife with all my might. He doesn't let go.

"I hate you! I hate you all!" I howl.

Hearing the commotion, Ram and Amma run downstairs.

"What are you doing, Gayu?" Ram shouts. "Stop it! Stop the madness!"

Roshini starts screaming in her crib upstairs.

"Gayu, please give Ravi the knife. Everything will be all right," Amma coaxes. "If not for us, at least for Roshini's sake."

Ram runs upstairs and races back to the kitchen with Roshini screaming in his arms. The minute I see my baby, I let go of the knife, grab her in my arms, and collapse on the floor, terrified of the monster I have become. But I have nowhere to run or escape from the demons in my head.

"Don't worry, Gayathri. You will be fine," Ravi tries to comfort me.

"We need to get her to a hospital immediately," Ram insists, his eyes wide with terror.

Ravi is scheduled to fly out later in the day. Ram decides to drop him off at the airport and drive me to the emergency room at Kaiser.

"Promise me you won't kill yourself. Promise me!" my brother begs.

I bid him good-bye with vacant eyes.

It is Christmas Eve. The streets are deserted, but the emergency room is not. The waiting room is filled with the sick and dying. Incredibly agitated, I can barely sit straight. Terrified that any misbehavior might get me locked up for life, I brace myself and stay put in a chair. After an agonizing hour of waiting, I slump in a chair, sobbing, as Ram recounts the sordid details of our trip to India and my recent suicide attempt to the doctor. I don't say a word. The physician recommends hospitalization. I become hysterical. Growing up in India, my only image of a mental hospital was of a deathly hollow where people, once admitted, were locked up for life.

"Please don't hospitalize me," I beg. "I promise I will behave. I promise I won't kill myself." But the doctor insists that I need to be admitted for my own safety and the safety of others around me.

As people across America celebrate the birth of Christ, their homes decked with joyous lights, I am admitted to 5A, the psychiatric ward at the Oregon Health & Science University Hospital.

"Please take me home," I beg Amma, clinging to her. "I am scared to stay here. I am afraid of the other patients."

"Don't worry—there is nothing to be afraid of. We will take good care of you," a nurse comforts me and offers me a little pill and a tiny paper cup filled with water. "It's Ativan," she explains. "It will help calm you down." Hoping that my cooperation will earn me an early discharge, I pop the pill in my mouth and swallow it with the water.

"Don't worry, Gayu. We will stay with you for as long as you want," Ram says, sitting beside me on the bed. He covers me with the blankets and turns the lights off. I hold on to his hands and shake with fear. Amma squats on the floor beside me, whispering lullabies to Roshini, who is fast asleep in her lap. Gradually, I begin to doze off.

Hours later, I wake up with a start, shocked to see Naveen, our physician friend, sitting in a chair beside my bed.

"How are you doing, Gayathri?" he asks softly. I begin to cry. *Does he think I am crazy?*

"I am scared," I say. "I want to go home."

"Don't worry, Gayathri. They need to observe you for a while and adjust your medications. You should be home soon," he reassures, and urges me to let Amma, Ram, and Roshini go home for a few hours.

"Please, please don't tell any of our friends about my stay in the psych ward," I beg Naveen as he prepares to leave. "I am scared they won't understand."

"Don't worry. If anyone asks, we can tell them we had taken your mother to Seattle for a sightseeing trip," Ram suggests.

It is nearly midnight when my family and Naveen finally leave. They promise to come back in a few hours. The psychiatric ward is silent except for the footsteps of the staff checking in on patients. I pull the sheets over my head and lie awake, eyes darting in the dark, vigilant of any wayward patients who might break into my bedroom and harm me. No one does.

Amma, Ram, and Roshini return with a change of clothes and toiletries around midmorning. And, to my relief, they spend the rest of the day with me. Amma helps me shower and shampoo my hair. I am terrified to leave my room or go the bathroom by myself.

Naveen stops by with a home-cooked meal. After lunch, I cuddle up with Roshini and take a nap. Dr. Bell, a psychiatrist, visits me later that evening. Ram and Amma answer most of his questions. Paranoid that wrong answers might get me institutionalized, I decide not to speak at all. The doctor changes my antidepressant from dothiepin to nortriptyline, hoping that the new medication will have fewer side effects.

"Continue to take the Ativan as needed for anxiety," he suggests, handing me a brochure about depression. "It might take four to six weeks for the medications to work. Please be patient. It is important for you to take the medications regularly, Mrs. Ramprasad. Don't hesitate to page me if things get worse," he adds, leaving to check on his next patient.

Having been lax about visiting hours the day before, the nurse explains to me that my family can visit only during prescribed hours. Panicked, I beg and plead the nurse to let me go home. But she insists I should stay until the doctor thinks I am strong and stable enough to go home. Concerned any noncompliance with hospital protocols could get me confined, I decide to cooperate. And over the next couple of days, afraid and ashamed to venture out, I barricade myself in my hospital room, except for playing Ping-Pong with Ram for a few minutes and attending a group therapy session upon the nurse's behest. I take my medications on time and read the brochure about depression over and over again. But it offers me no comfort. Each time the nurse and doctor check on me, I beg them to let me go home. I promise them over and over again that I will take the medications and call them if I feel suicidal. Finally, on December 28, Dr. Bell consents to my release, after scheduling an appointment for me to see Dr. Richards, a psychiatrist at Kaiser Permanante, my health care provider, on January 6.

Although I am relieved to be home, I continue to struggle with persistent thoughts of suicide and the side effects of the medications—drowsiness, dizziness, dry mouth, blurred vision, constipation, racing heart, and nausea. I sleep through much of the day and night, only to wake up around three or four in the morning with heightened anxiety, and lie in bed dreading the demands of the day ahead.

Amma insists that having a routine will help normalize my life. Scared that any mention of my persistent suicidal thoughts might land me in the hospital again, I follow her cue like a robot and go through the drill: shower, pray, eat, help with Roshini's care, go for a walk, help with the meals and household chores.

One morning after breakfast, Amma suggests we go to the grocery store together. Hands shaking, sweat dripping off my forehead, I strap Roshini into the car seat, grab onto the steering wheel, and back the car out of the garage. I stop abruptly in the driveway and wonder which way to turn from my neighborhood to get on Highway 217 south. Confused, I begin to cry.

"Don't worry, Gayu, take your time," Amma rubs my back.

"I can't do it, Amma," I sob. "Ram can take us to the store when he gets home."

"Gayu, I understand how scared you are. But if you lose your confidence, you lose everything in life. Take a deep breath and try to remember the way. It's okay if we don't make it to the store. We can at least take Roshini for a ride."

After many deep breaths and Amma's continued encouragement, we finally arrive at the store. I strap Roshini into the shopping cart, and we make our way through the aisles. I feel wobbly and can't decide whether to buy Cheerios or corn flakes, one bunch of cilantro or two, a pound of beans or more. Betrayed by my wayward mind, I have lost all confidence in myself, second-guess every move, and find it difficult to make even the simplest of decisions. I suspect everyone in the grocery store is staring at me. And I don't dare lift my head to see if it is true.

*Perhaps they all know I was recently released from a psych ward.*

*Idiot! You can't even make simple decisions, can you?*

*You are nothing but a worthless piece of junk, a burden to your family.*

*Who do you think you are, pretending to be normal? You will never be normal.*

*Everyone knows you are crazy. Just do yourself and your family a favor and kill yourself.*

My heart starts pounding. I can't breathe. I run out of the grocery store, desperate to call Ram and beg him to come pick us up. I pick up the receiver on the pay phone just outside the automatic doors and panic. I can't remember Ram's office phone number. I close my eyes and try hard to remember it. My mind goes blank. I crouch underneath the pay phone, sobbing, praying I could just disappear.

Ever since my diagnosis of depression, I feel like my body is tattooed with indelible labels: *depressed, deranged, demented, dangerous, crazy, lazy, weak, possessed.* I fear that everyone around me perceives me as such, and worse yet, I define myself with these labels.

"Are you okay?" a couple of shoppers stop and ask.

"Yes," I nod and look away.

"What happened?" Amma asks, rushing out of the store. Roshini wiggles into my lap.

"Do you need any help, ma'am?" a store clerk asks, standing beside my mother.

"Can you please bring us a cup of water?" Amma requests.

The store clerk leaves and returns with a plastic cup filled with water.

"Thanks," Amma says and tells him we will be fine.

"I can't breathe, Amma. I can't even think straight," I cry once the store clerk leaves. "I can't live like this anymore."

"Shhhh . . ." Amma strokes my head. "You will get better, Gayu, I promise. Drink some water first. Don't worry about the groceries. Ram can get them in the evening when he gets home from work. Why don't we go home? You can have lunch and take some Ativan and rest. I am sure it will help you relax."

Roshini wraps her little hands around my neck and kisses me on my cheeks. Her love is the only thing that tethers me to life. Each time I want to give up and die, she gives me a reason to live. I struggle to my feet, wobble into the car, and slide behind the steering wheel. Half an hour later, with Amma's incessant prayers, we make it home safely. I force myself to eat a few bites, take an Ativan, and sink into bed.

"Never underestimate the power of prayer, Gayu," Amma insists, waking me up later that evening. She lights the silver diyas by the God's altar in the kitchen, asks me to squat on the floor, and teaches me to chant the *Lalitha Sahasranama.* Although I have lost all faith in God, I have no strength to fight my mother's conviction. To Amma's great joy, Ram insists on joining us. Over the next couple of weeks, each evening, when Ram returns home from work, he and I struggle to pronounce the *shlokas,* while Roshini sits in my mother's lap coloring her picture books. To my surprise, I memorize the one thousand hymns within a few weeks. Ram records my mother and me chanting the prayers on our cassette player so he can continue to practice with it.

Amma starts fasting on Mondays in honor of God Shiva, and Ram starts fasting on Thursdays in honor of God Raghavendra, hoping to secure their divine blessings to help me heal.

On New Year's Eve, a bunch of our friends gather at Anil and Latha's house to ring in the New Year. Not wanting to cause any suspicion, I agree to join them. As Dick Clark counts down and the gigantic crystal ball drops, I pray that I can safeguard my secret from my friends. While everyone is busy wishing each other a happy New Year, I discreetly thank Naveen for not disclosing about my diagnosis and recent hospitalization.

On January 6, Ram and I meet Dr. Richards. A soft-spoken, sandy-haired gentleman, he looks like he is about Ram's age. But he is a lot taller than Ram. He offers us a seat and patiently pores through the medical reports.

"Could you please tell me how to pronounce your name?" he asks, looking at me, "I am afraid I will butcher it."

Bolstered by his kind presence, I answer, "It is *Guy-a-three,*" knowing what a challenge my name is to most Americans.

"How are you doing?" he asks.

"Not great," I say, fighting to keep my tears at bay. "I feel depressed. I can't fall asleep at night, and I am nervous most of the day."

"Are you suicidal?" he asks.

"No," I shake my head, afraid that if I told him the truth, he would hospitalize me again.

"Tell me how it all began," he says.

Ram and I narrate the story of our trip to India, my breakdown, and the nightmare it has since unleashed in our lives.

"I am sorry for all your pain," Dr. Richards empathizes and suggests I continue to take nortriptyline and Ativan, and get back to him in a month. He explains the neurobiological, genetic, and environmental causes of depression and stresses the importance of medications and psychotherapy in treating it. He refers me to see Dr. Lin, a psychotherapist, and recommends that I exercise a few times a week.

"You need to be selfish, Gayathri," Dr. Richards asserts. "You have to take care of yourself before you can take care of others."

Having been raised to believe that selflessness is a virtue and selfishness is a sin, I am confused by Dr. Richards's recommendation. But the belief that doctors are gods and their words are gospel compels me to follow his advice.

Ram and I meet Dr. Lin a couple of weeks later. "Have a seat," she offers, and gets right down to business. She reminds me of Mrs. Shiela, my headmistress in school back in India.

"How can I help you?" she asks, flipping through the notes she has received from Dr. Richards.

"Dr. Richards suggested I come to see you," I say, having no clue how she can help me.

"Tell me about your depression," she says, settling into a tall wingback chair.

They say sharing our pain can be healing, but each time I tell my story, I feel like I am gouging my wounds until they are raw and bleeding. Choking back tears, I recount the details of my trip to India, the breakdown, the diagnosis, the ECT, the medications, the trip back to Portland, and the hospitalization. She listens intently, taking extensive notes.

"I understand how painful the past few months have been for you," Dr. Lin says, handing me a box of tissues. "But believe me, you will recover from these setbacks and move on with your life.

"I am afraid our time is up for now," she says, glancing at the clock on the side table, and she recommends I meet her in two weeks. "In the meantime, take your medications regularly, exercise, and do something to relax every day," she suggests, then bids us good-bye.

Ram, Amma, and I don't understand how recounting the horrors of my depression to a stranger will help me regain my sanity. But I decide to meet with Dr. Lin again.

I join Nautilus, the neighborhood health club, and attend aerobics classes three times a week. At first, I am terrified to leave home, afraid that my façade of normalcy might fall apart at any moment, and the whole world will find out about my mental illness and the crazy woman I am. But I force myself to go, and am pleasantly surprised to discover that I feel good, at least for a few hours after I exercise. Initially, I avoid talking to people in my class or making eye contact. But eventually, I start saying hello, and I am flattered when a young man in my aerobics class asks if I would like to go out on a date with him. I politely decline his offer and tell him that I am married. *Perhaps no one knows,* I comfort myself.

Late January, we celebrate Roshini's second birthday. I invite her playgroup and our circle of friends. Ram helps me decorate the dining room with streamers and balloons. We order pizzas and a banana cream bakery cake decorated with Big Bird, Bert, and Ernie—Roshini's favorite *Sesame Street* characters. Roshini looks darling in her ruffled pink dress. Her soft, wavy hair is swept into a side ponytail with a matching ribbon.

A few days later, Amma leaves for College Station, Texas, to pamper Chitra in the last few weeks of her pregnancy. Roshini and I miss her terribly. I am scared that I won't be able to take care of Roshini and the household on my own, and am relieved when Ram suggests that Roshini and I should visit Chitra in time to welcome the baby. I agree gladly. Mid-February, Roshini and I leave for College Station.

On March 3, 1988, Chitra gives birth to her first-born son. They name him Chandra, a befitting name for a beautiful, moon-faced boy. Roshini is mesmerized with her little cousin. She loves to hold him in her lap. Intellectually, I know I should celebrate my sister's joy, but emotionally, I feel nothing but sorrow. My moods remain as erratic as the new baby's sleep cycles. There are brief periods of time when I can conceal my anxiety and tears, and others when I lock myself in the bathroom and cry my heart out. I take my antidepressant regularly as prescribed and take Ativan frequently to keep the anxiety at bay. It has been more than six weeks since I started my new medications, but they don't seem to help. Weeks later, Roshini and I return to Portland.

When Ram gets ready to leave for work each morning, I panic. I am scared to be alone with Roshini. I worry that I might give in to my suicidal thoughts and kill myself or, worse yet, hurt Roshini accidentally. I want to beg Ram not to leave us.

"Have a good day," I wish him instead and kiss him good-bye at the garage door. I sit by the God's altar in the kitchen and cry for hours, begging for a way out. "What did I do wrong to be punished this way?" I ask God. "Why should I suffer like this?"

The minute I hear Roshini waking up, I dry my tears and rush to her room, hug her good morning, and resume the routine. Determined not to let my mangled mind ruin my child's development, I help her brush her teeth, change her clothes, and feed her breakfast. One morning a week, I drop her off with a playgroup mom and finish my grocery shopping and other errands before picking her up.

"Not fair," says Sahana, one of the moms. "I go to India and gain weight. And you go to India and lose weight. How did you do that?"

"I don't know," I shrug my shoulders and force a smile, trying hard to safeguard my secret.

Two mornings a week, I drop Roshini off at Mom's Morning Out, a program at the local community center. At first, Roshini screams her head off. But the teacher insists she will be fine, and asks me to leave. Feeling terrible for making my baby cry, I run back to the car and cry all the way to the neighborhood health club where I work out.

Concerned, I call Amma, and she recounts how much my brother, Ravi, hated going to school and that it had taken months before he stopped crying in class. Fortunately, Roshini settles down within days. She runs into my arms when I pick her up and proudly shows me her finger-painting portraits and the cat and dog figurines she has made out of play dough. "Head, shoulders, knees and toes, knees and toes," she sings, bouncing in her car seat, tapping her little body. Cruising along Cedar Hills Boulevard, singing along with my child, I am shocked by the sudden urge to drive into the oncoming traffic. I tighten my grip on the steering wheel and glance at Roshini in the rearview mirror. She giggles when our eyes meet. Her sweet, innocent laughter jostles me back to reality.

"Dear God, please don't let me kill my child or anyone on the street," I beg, keeping my eyes glued on the street and the cars ahead of me. Once home safely, I lay my head on the steering wheel and sob until my stomach hurts. On days like these, I wish I could rip off my "happy face" and let the world see the malignant tumors of my mind. But, I am afraid if I did, I might scare away my friends and family, and most of all, Roshini. Putting on a happy face is my only defense against the dark demons that lurk within.

"Mommy, Mommy," Roshini tries to wiggle out of her car seat. I pick her up, feed her lunch hurriedly, and lay beside her in my bed. I struggle to read Roshini her favorite book—Dr. Seuss's *The Cat in the Hat.* She has memorized many of the lines and pretends to read along with me. Midway through the book, Roshini dozes off to sleep, her little arms wrapped around my neck and her feet looping around my waist. Too restless to stay still, I carefully untangle myself from her embrace and tiptoe downstairs.

My mind searches for ways to end my misery. I pace up and down the house aimlessly, trying to shake off my crazy thoughts. But I can't. I frantically read the drug inserts for the millionth time, and can't for the life of me understand how these medications can potentially exacerbate the same symptoms they are trying to abate.

I call Dr. Richards's office, hoping he can change the medications or adjust the doses. Careful not to mention my suicidal obsessions, I leave a voice mail on his answering machine and tell him that the dizziness, dry mouth, constipation, and anxiety are worsening. I wait for the phone to ring. And when it finally does, Dr. Richard offers me the same old advice: "You'll have to ride the side effects out. It should subside over time. Meanwhile, why don't you take Metamucil to help with the constipation?"

I am eternally exhausted and develop chronic headaches, abdominal cramps, and a throbbing pain shooting from my shoulders down into my fingertips. I make multiple trips to my internist, who cannot find any clear answers. Finally, he suspects I have irritable bowel syndrome or chronic fatigue syndrome. But after many tests he rules them out. I am left to fend for myself against a body and mind that hold me hostage. I am perpetually angry at myself and everyone in my life. No one understands my pain. I feel like a freak, condemned to die a slow, excruciating death while everyone watches, and no one can help rescue me.

Growing up, I had heard my mother say *manorogakke maddilla—there is no medicine for the malady of the mind.* My father believed that the benefits of medications were marginal at best, and he feared they could be habit forming—perhaps they were right.

"It is your own inner strength that will revive you, Gayu," Appa had preached ever since my tryst with terror at eighteen. At twenty-six, I hadn't yet discovered the power within.

Trying to divert my nervous energy, I fold laundry, but I can hardly sit still enough to complete the task. Halfway through, I get up and start cooking dinner. My hands tremble as I cut the vegetables. I slowly raise the blade to the inside of my wrist and beg God to give me the courage to slash it. I can't do it. I think of Roshini sleeping peacefully on my bed, and the thought of her finding me bleeding to death on the kitchen floor horrifies me. I toss the knife down and collapse on the floor crying.

I hear Roshini's little footsteps coming down the stairs, and I spring back up, grab a yogurt out of the refrigerator, and flip to *Sesame Street* on the television. I cuddle with Roshini on the couch in the family room and feed her the yogurt as she sits transfixed by Elmo, Bert, Big Bird, and Snuffleupagus. While she watches TV, I hurry up and complete cooking dinner before Ram comes home at six. Caring for Roshini and cooking are my only saving graces lately. Although they seem to be insurmountable tasks, they give me a sense of purpose, and it is the only way I know how to show my love to my husband and daughter.

"Hi, Roshini Rani!" Ram scoops her into his arms first thing as he walks into the house and kisses her all over until she breaks into giggles. I love watching them together—their love, their joy. And yet, at the same time, I envy their simple pleasure, something I haven't felt for a long, long time.

"How was your day, Gayu?" Ram asks.

I shrug my shoulders and look away.

"I thought the medications would be helping you by now," he says.

"They are not," I say, gritting my teeth, "they are actually making my life miserable."

"I don't know what else to do," Ram slams his wallet on the kitchen counter, frustrated. "Perhaps you have to wait the side effects out like the doctor says? Why can't you just accept it as your karma?"

"Karma? Karma?" I mock Ram. "No. I will never accept this hell of a life as my karma. There must be something out there to help me heal." I divert my rage into setting the table for dinner. I bang the plates down and plop the meal with enough force to shake up the table and my husband. Roshini looks up at us, startled. I pick her up and feed her dinner. Except for Roshini's childish banter, the evening crawls along in painful silence. Around eight o'clock, I bathe Roshini and tuck her into bed. I dread going to sleep and dread waking up to face another day even more.

I see Dr. Richards once a month. He applauds me for complying with the treatment and continuing to exercise. Not wanting to displease him with my complaints, I remain quiet.

I meet Dr. Lin every other week. Contrary to my family's concern that I would grow dependent on her, she fosters independence in me.

"Tell me about your childhood," she asks. "How would you describe your relationship with your parents? How about your siblings? What was your life like in India? Tell me about your marriage? What do you think about life in America? How is it different from your life in India? How is depression perceived in your family and culture? What are your fears, your hopes and dreams?"

Dr. Lin is a great listener and a compassionate witness to my ongoing struggles. Like a seasoned detective, she uses my answers as clues to untangle the mystery of my life and unearth its fault lines—the genetic predisposition to mental illness, my utter dependence on my family, my desperate need to please others, and my perfectionist attitudes. She delves into the intricacies of my Indo-American life and identifies the diametric cultural forces that tug and tear at my very core.

"The interpersonal skills you needed to survive in India are almost opposite of the skills you need to thrive in America," she points out. "Your addictive need to please your family and gain their approval at all costs, coupled with the shame and stigma associated with mental illness, and your desperate need to safeguard your family's honor, is threatening your health and well-being.

"It is time to cut the umbilical cord with your family," she advises, and encourages me to distance myself from my family's misperceptions about mental illness and treatment. "It is time you take charge of your life and respect your own thoughts and beliefs," she insists, "Respecting yourself does not mean you disrespect others."

At first, I think Dr. Lin has lost her mind. *How could I possibly cut off my ties with my family? They are the roots that anchor my life and sustain me.* But slowly, one session at a time, Dr. Lin's wisdom begins to dawn upon me. In the months to follow, she teaches me to accept my individuality and discover my strengths. Embracing me with her unconditional acceptance and encouragement, she becomes the mother I desperately need now by providing the psychological perspective and emotional support my mother wasn't able to offer. "Sharing a burdened heart with another who has the wisdom, strength, and knowledge to carry it, frees us from its weight long enough to focus on solutions," says Liane Cordes, author of *The Reflecting Pond: Meditations for Self Discovery.* Dr. Lin embodies this wisdom and carries my burdens long enough for me to eventually discover solutions.

"You are not a hapless being shaped by the forces of gender, genetics, culture, or life experience, Gayathri," Dr. Lin insists. "It is time for you to learn about their impact and take charge of your life."

She gradually introduces me to the fundamental concept of cognitive-behavioral therapy (CBT): that our *thoughts* cause our feelings and behaviors. Our thoughts—not external things, like people, situations, and events. She illustrates how we can change the way we think to feel and behave better, even if the situation does not change. She teaches me that I have the power to *respond* to a given situation without *reacting* to it.

"Feelings aren't facts," Dr. Lin insists. "For example, the feeling that you will never get better does not make it a fact. You need to reprogram the negative tapes in your head with positive ones. You also need to learn how to express your emotions instead of bottling them up until you blow up or melt down."

Theoretically, it all makes sense—but I find it nearly impossible to retrain my thoughts. Still, Dr. Lin continues to encourage me to explore my thoughts and feelings without getting entangled by them and observe how they influence my behavior. She guides me on my inward journey and helps me identify and acknowledge emotions I have repressed over the years in my attempts to be the "perfect child." She creates a safe environment in which to express them without guilt or shame. She helps me experience my feelings without labeling them as good or bad. Slowly, I begin to feel in control of my thoughts and moods. Encouraged by my newfound skills and frustrated with the side effects of the medications, I decide to stop taking them and pursue exercise, progressive relaxation, and biofeedback to enhance my well-being. Over the next month, Dr. Richards reluctantly helps me taper off the medications. As I taper off the medications, however, the anxiety and depression slowly creep back.

Meanwhile, Appa, who had quit his job at Hyderabad, decides to join us in America. Excited beyond words to visit his dreamland at last, he flies into Chicago, visits Ravi in Milwaukee for a couple of days, and flies to College Station to join Amma at Chitra's house. In late May, my parents come to Portland to spend a couple of weeks with my family and me before returning to India.

Roshini is delighted to see her grandparents again. I put on a bold front and try to make their stay pleasant. But Amma and Appa can see through the cracks.

"Is everything all right, Gayu?" they inquire.

"Yes!" I nod, silently repressing my true feelings.

My parents reason that the demands of motherhood are wearing me down, and suggest that a job might give me a much-needed break. "Roshini can go to a day care, Gayu, and you can at least find a part-time job," they suggest.

I hesitantly agree and scout the day care centers in our neighborhood while Roshini clings to me in fear. I feel completely inadequate as a mother, forcing my child to let go of me before she is ready. But I realize that I simply don't have the energy to take care of her on my own. Besides, I worry that my deepening depression will jeopardize her normal development, and I believe that being away from me and in the midst of healthy adults and children her own age will safeguard her health. Ram and I finally decide to send Roshini to a local private day care.

My sister, Chitra, calls desperately one morning in June. Chandra, her three-month-old baby boy, is severely dehydrated and unresponsive. I advise her to rush the baby to the hospital and put my parents on a plane to College Station that afternoon.

"Please get a job, Gayu," my parents remind me at the airport. "It will be good for you."

Even before my parents arrive in College Station, Chitra calls to say Chandra's condition has deteriorated rapidly, and he has had to be air-lifted to the intensive care unit of a children's hospital in Temple, Texas. My parents join my sister and brother-in-law and keep vigil by Chandra's bedside for weeks on end as a team of pediatric experts try to save his life. While the physicians can't detect the exact source of Chandra's troubles, they suspect it is a rare viral infection attacking his intestines. Eight weeks later, Chandra is stable enough to be brought home, where he continues to recuperate. The doctors advise that he be quarantined at home for the next six months to rebuild his lost immunity.

Meanwhile, Ram agrees readily with my parents' suggestion for me to find a job, helps me write my résumé, and submits it at Intel, where he works. Within weeks, I get a call for an interview. It is a six-month opportunity to cover for Mindy, the software administrator, while she is away on maternity leave. The group I will be working with is located less than five miles away from home and is in the same office building as Ram's group.

As the day of the interview draws near, my anxieties steadily grow.

"Don't worry, Gayu," Ram reassures me, "the interviewers are all colleagues of mine. They are really nice people and will go out of their way to help you learn the ropes at work."

"Hi, I am John," "I am Julie," "I am Laila," "I am Mindy," my interviewers introduce themselves. They are dressed in jeans and T-shirts, and I stretch out my clammy hands to meet theirs. Fear races through my mind. *What if I can't do the job? Do they know I have a mental illness? Will they fire me when they find out?*

"Can you start in the first week of August?" Julie asks. I stare at her in disbelief.

Ram's delighted that I got the job. Fortunately, the day care is located just a couple of minutes away from work. Ram decides to drop Roshini off at day care on his way to work so I can have a few extra minutes in the morning. I decide to pick her up on my way home. It breaks my heart when Ram tells me how Roshini cries when he drops her off each morning, standing by the window in the day care, clutching her yellow waffle-knit blanket and Pooh Bear. When I pick her up in the afternoons, I see Roshini lying on her little mat, sobbing silently, while the rest of the children are taking their naps. The minute she sees me, she leaps into my arms, and cries, "No day care Mommy . . . no day care." I am filled with guilt for making her sad, but I have no other choice. Ram can't take time off from work. I have no other family in town, and I don't want to burden the playgroup moms by asking them to watch Roshini while I am at work. Having no other options, I decide to search for a better alternative.

I visit neighborhood schools along with Roshini after work. We fall in love with the Montessori School of Beaverton. Although the school does not have a building of its own and is tucked in the basement of the Cedar Hills Recreation Center, the classrooms are an oasis of calm. Maria, the petite preschool teacher and one of the founding members of the school, exudes a peaceful confidence that soothes Roshini's frayed nerves and mine. The three- to five-year-olds in the classroom are joyously absorbed in their work. Maria welcomes us warmly and walks us around the classroom, careful not to disturb the children engrossed in tracing sandpaper letters and working with metal insets.

"Would you like to join us for story time?" Maria asks, stretching her hand out to Roshini. To my surprise, Roshini lets go of my hand and takes Maria's and joins the circle of students. Soon, Roshini is drawn into the story. She turns back and glances at me every once in a while to make sure I haven't left the room. When at last Maria says, "The end," and closes the book, Roshini runs into my arms and hugs me tight.

"Do you like Maria?" I ask Roshini on the drive back home.

"Yes," she nods her head, bouncing in her car seat.

"Do you want to go back to see Maria and the other kids?" I ask.

"Yes" she says with a big smile.

Relieved to finally find a school that embraces Roshini's spirit, Ram and I enroll her in the Montessori preschool class. While Roshini delights in going to school, the very thought of going to work still stresses me out.

The first week at work, I shadow Mindy. I am amazed at her ability to run from meeting to meeting and help the team of engineers stay on track with their projects. I sit through the meetings in a daze, unable to understand much of what is being discussed. Everyone at Intel speaks a foreign tongue: Intelese, a language made up mostly of acronyms. Having never worked in a high-tech firm or with computers in my life, I'm certain that there is no way I can fit in or do Mindy's job.

"Don't worry," Mindy says, sensing my unease. "You'll be fine."

She assures me I can call her any time if I have questions, and she walks me through the files in the cabinet and on the desktop, explaining every minute detail of what my job entails. I nod my head in consent, although not much registers in my brain. Ever since my descent into depression, it has been nearly impossible for me to read or concentrate.

Desperate to belong in the world of "normals," I have learned to fake my competence. But when the pressure to perform exceeds my abilities, which happens almost every day, I crumble.

The morning of my first team meeting, I lock myself in a bathroom stall, stuff my fist into my mouth to muffle the sounds, and sob until I feel numb. Every time someone walks into the bathroom, I hold my breath in panic. Once I no longer hear any footsteps, I sneak out of the stall, wash my face, reapply my makeup, slip back into my office, and pretend to be immersed in work. I sit and stare at the computer, utterly overwhelmed. I hate myself and my masquerades. I want to quit my job. I want to tell my colleagues the truth: I have depression and I can't function. But I am scared it will eliminate my chances for future employment. I am also afraid it will ruin Ram's reputation and jeopardize his career forever. So, I decide to keep up the charade. But, it doesn't last for long.

"Are you okay, Gayathri?" asks Julie one day, as I literally crash into her in the bathroom. Having thought that the coast was clear, I had emerged from the bathroom, eyes swollen, and a wad of Kleenex stuffed in my hands.

"I am fine," I say, trying hard to hide my face from Julie, and I bend over the sink to wash my hands. My voice is hoarse from crying.

"What's wrong, Gayathri?" Julie asks, turning me around, "You can tell me anything. I promise to keep it confidential. Whatever it is, it is good to talk it out. It always helps."

Scared to face Julie, I dig my toes into the ground and cry.

"What is it?" she asks, "Is it Ram? Is it Roshini? Are they okay?"

"It's me," I sob, "I can't do this job."

"Yes, you can!" Julie says, hugging me tightly. "I am sure you feel overwhelmed right now. We all did when we started. Give yourself some time, and ask me and the team for help. We will definitely help you out. Everyone here knows how hard it was when we started. Besides," she adds, "you're a smart woman. You'll pick things up in no time."

*I have no idea who she is talking about. I haven't felt smart since the dreaded failing math grade in college when I was nineteen.*

"You don't understand," I cry. "Every day, I come to work, my thoughts race, my heart pounds; I am constantly fighting to keep myself from crying. I can't focus on anything. And, I feel like I am on the verge of a breakdown. I can't do it, Julie. I just can't do it anymore. The only thing I want to do is to kill myself. I am sure Ram and Roshini will be better off without me."

"Shhhhh . . ." Julie draws me closer into her arms. "How long have you been feeling like this, Gayathri?" she asks.

Her kindness breaks through the wall of shame behind which my secret lies. And, much to my shock, it comes spilling out without control—our trip to India, the breakdown, the medications, the ECT, the priest, the hospitalization, and my ongoing struggles with depression.

"Oh! You poor thing, I am so sorry you have been having such a rough time," Julie says. "Believe it or not, I know exactly what you are talking about—the sleepless nights, lack of appetite, restlessness, guilt, hopelessness, worthlessness, eternal sadness, emptiness, and the scariest of all symptoms—the horrible urge to kill yourself. I have been suffering from depression ever since I was fifteen." Tears roll down her cheeks. "It took me almost ten years to find the right doctor, the right therapist, and the right combination of medications that work for me. I still have tough times when I can't come to work some days," she confesses. "But I have learned how to manage my illness and move on with life. Don't worry, Gayathri, you will, too. If you want, I will give you the phone numbers of my psychiatrist and therapist. They have been incredibly helpful."

I am absolutely amazed at Julie's candor in talking about her struggles. I can't believe that a competent engineer like her could possibly be depressed. Somewhere in the bottom of my heart, I see a faint flicker of hope and wonder if, perhaps, in time, I too can recover and live a successful life like Julie.

"Thanks, Julie!" I say. "I am happy with my psychiatrist and therapist. But I will ask you for the phone numbers if I need to switch."

"How's Ram holding up?" she asks.

"It is hard. But he is doing his best. Please don't tell him or anyone else at work about our talk," I beg Julie.

"Don't worry, I promise I won't," she says. "How about getting ourselves cleaned up and going out for lunch? I will invite Laila and Elle to join us. You will love them," she smiles, sensing my fears. "Besides, a girl can never have too many friends."

Late that night, I lie in bed wide awake, worrying that I have made a grave mistake by confiding in Julie. *Will she breach my trust and tell Ram about our talk? Will he get mad and get me fired before I defame him any further? What if she tells the other colleagues? Will it ruin Ram's career? Will they fire Ram? Will they think I am crazy? Oh my God! What have I done?* I toss and turn restlessly.

"Are you okay, Gayu?" Ram asks, stirring in his sleep.

"Yes," I answer, and stay still.

The next morning, I sit nervously at my desk, bracing myself for the worst.

"Hi, Gayathri, how are you doing?" Julie, Laila, and Elle take turns stopping by my office to ask if I need help.

"I am fine," I say, breathing a sigh of relief, and I make plans to meet them at lunchtime. From that day on, Julie, Laila, and Elle take me under their wings. They check in on me every day and go out of their way to help me with my work. By accepting me as a competent co-worker and embracing me as a friend, they ease my anxieties and restore my sense of self-worth. Despite my doubts and ongoing struggles, they support my every step.

Ram and I are happy to see Roshini thrive at the Montessori school. Over Thanksgiving break, the three of us go to Milwaukee to attend Ravi's wedding. Chitra and her family join us as well. It is wonderful to watch Roshini and Chitra's son, Chandra, play together. We are all grateful for his amazing recovery from the mysterious infection that had nearly claimed his life. After spending months in the intensive care unit of a children's hospital and several more months quarantined at home, he has finally recuperated well enough to be back home and in the midst of people again.

My parents are delighted to have all three of their children and their families together for the first time in many years. We celebrate the wedding in a temple in Chicago. It is a far cry from the three-day weddings with hundreds of guests in India. There are hardly fifty people: Ravi's bride, Priti, and her family, a few of their friends, and a couple of Ravi's friends.

Amma and Appa return to India in the first week of December. Ram and I resume our jobs at Intel. After Christmas break, Roshini returns to school, and I begin the countdown to the last four weeks of my work at Intel. In late January, Mindy comes to visit with her new baby boy. He is gorgeous: rosy cheeks, big blue eyes, and blond curls spilling over his head.

"You did great, Gayathri," says Mindy, smiling as she looks through the files and the transition notes I have made for her.

"Thanks," I answer, deeply relieved. "Julie, Elle, and Laila helped me a lot." I am eternally indebted to all of them. If it weren't for them, I doubt that I could have lasted through the six months at Intel. On my last day at work, January 31, 1989, my co-workers take me out to a farewell lunch at my favorite Chinese restaurant.

Alone at home, after dropping Roshini off at school, I miss my colleagues, but not my work. I am convinced that the high-tech field is not for me. I find the world of computers alien, and nothing about it excites me or speaks to my soul. Bored and lonely, I decide to volunteer at Roshini's school a couple of days a week, until I find another job. Excited about the prospect of collaborating with other parents to raise money to build our own school, I sign up to work on the Auction Committee, and I am delighted to meet other mothers, especially Barb. Her energy and enthusiasm are infectious. Her daughter, Kristin, and Roshini are in the same class and are good friends. Barb and her family live by the park, a couple of blocks away from our house. Her husband, Mike, also works at Intel. They have a son, Patrick, who also attends the Montessori school. He is a couple of years older than Kristin and Roshini. Soon, Barb and I begin carpooling to school and meet at the neighborhood park after the girls have had their naps. We get to know each other while the children spend hours playing on the seesaw and merry-go-round. In time, Barb introduces Roshini and me to the world of after-school activities—ballet, gymnastics, and swimming—and takes us to the local library one day. Roshini and I fall in love with the hundreds of children's picture books and pop-up books, some of which are as wide as our coffee table. I am completely surprised to learn that we can borrow the books and videos for free. "Our tax dollars pay for the services," Barb explains. She takes us to the zoo and the Oregon Museum of Sciences and Industry. Over the months, Roshini and Kristin become bosom buddies, and so do Barb and I. I embrace the emerging normalcy of my life with gratitude and pray that my newfound skills of cognitive-behavioral therapy, exercise, and volunteering, and the support of family and friends, will shield and protect me from the maelstrom of my mind.

I miss my period in February. Ram and I worry that I might be pregnant. I go in for a pregnancy test and our fears are confirmed. Despite the joy of having a new baby, I worry that my depression will return. I share my concerns with Dr. Munroe, my OB/GYN. She acknowledges my fears and comforts me that I can always go back on medications to help me cope. Terrified that the medications might deform the baby, I pray I won't have to take them.

I call Amma in India to tell her about the pregnancy.

"Congratulations, Gayu," she says. "God bless you with a healthy baby."

"I am scared, Amma," I confess.

"Don't cry, Gayu, you are stronger than you think," she comforts me. "Women are like the pumpkin vine. We may look frail, but we are strong enough to bear the burdens of life. Just keep your mind focused on Roshini, Ram, and the growing baby. Leave the rest in God's hands. He will take care of you."

Unfortunately, within weeks, I spiral back into the dark pit of depression. I can't stop crying. My appetite wanes. I can't sleep. The old demons return with a vengeance. I worry constantly about Roshini, Ram, and our unborn child. I lie in bed, overwhelmed by the simplest of tasks—getting Roshini ready and carpooling for school, going to my exercise classes, or going to the supermarket.

I call Barb and tell her that I am pregnant. She is delighted. I tell her that I am struggling with morning sickness and ask if she can drop Roshini off at school and pick her up for the next few days. She agrees readily and asks if there is anything more she can do to help.

"No, thanks," I say, fighting back tears, scared I might need to be hospitalized again. *Who will take care of Roshini when I am hospitalized? Should I tell Barb the truth about my illness? Will she understand and help or will she shun me and my family?*

I decide not to risk sharing the truth and reconcile myself to the fact that I am crazy and will eventually be locked up in a mental hospital for life. My only consolation is in knowing that Ram will be a good father to my daughter and provide her a comfortable life. Day by day, I withdraw from Roshini, Ram, and the world around me. Ram grows increasingly concerned and wonders if it was a big mistake for me to stop taking my medications.

*Pregnancy is widely presumed to be one of the happiest times of a woman's life, but for many women it is a time of confusion, fear, sadness, stress, and even depression. According to the American Congress of Obstetricians and Gynecologists, between 14 and 23 percent of women will struggle with some symptoms of depression during pregnancy.*

"I can't deal with this anymore," he snaps, stepping out of the shower one morning. "I can't take care of you and Roshini, and deal with the pressures at work. I think it is best for me to resign my job and for us to move back to Bangalore," he says, tugging at his hair in frustration. "At least we will have our families to help us."

"Please don't do that," I beg Ram. "We will never have a future in India."

Ram has worked very hard in building a successful career at Intel, and has a great future ahead of him. I am wracked with guilt for ruining his career and our lives. My parents had toiled all their lives to ensure a bright future for my siblings and me in America. They had dreamed that their grandchildren would live in a country with limitless opportunities. I am about to destroy their dreams.

I remember the priest who molested me in my mother-in-law's house while he purportedly tried to exorcise my demons. I fear that the lack of understanding about mental health issues in India, and the resultant stigma and discrimination, will destroy our lives. Most of all, I worry that Roshini will never have the life of abundance and opportunities that America promised. "Please don't resign," I plead over and over again, grabbing Ram's shoulders. "I promise to pull myself together." He does not budge.

"We are running out of time, Gayu," he yells, pulling away from me, buttoning up his shirt. "I will resign today."

I feel the earth closing in on me, and have nothing to grab on to, no one to rescue me. I desperately want to stop Ram from making the biggest mistake of his life, but I don't know how. I feel absolutely powerless. A wild rage sears through me. Wanting to stop him from going to work, I lunge at Ram, grab on to his shirt collar and try to rip open his shirt. The force of my actions shocks us both.

"What are you doing?" he hollers, trying to shake free. His eyes are tinged with terror. "Get away from me," he screams, tossing my hands aside and buttoning his shirt back up.

Ashamed of my aggression, I let go. I stare at my trembling hands. I want to cut them off. Instead, I rip my white cotton nightgown into shreds.

Ram rushes past me and down the stairs. He grabs his wallet, hops into the car, and drives off to work. I stand at the garage door in my tattered clothes screaming hysterically, begging him to come back. He disappears around the bend.

*This is it! You have done it! You have crossed the line. You are not only crazy, you are a violent maniac! I am sure Ram will call the cops and hand you over. He will divorce you and take custody of Roshini. You will never see your child again.*

I hear Roshini waking up. I rush upstairs and change into my sweatpants and shirt. I steel myself, help Roshini get ready for school, and wait for Barb to pick her up. I kiss Roshini good-bye and silently beg her to forgive me. I stand by the door and watch Barb drive away with my child, and weep, wondering if this is the last time I will ever see her.

I lock the front door and rush to the kitchen to call Ram at work. He doesn't answer the phone. I continue to call him every few minutes. No answer. Determined to stop him from resigning his job, I call his manager, Roger. I take a deep breath and tell him that I am not well, and we need his help. I ask him to meet Ram and me at the Intel parking lot after work that evening.

"What's wrong, Gayathri?" Roger asks.

"I am sorry," I say, choking up. "I can't talk right now. But I will tell you when we meet this evening."

I continue to call Ram every few minutes.

"I can't do it. I can't do it anymore," I scream into the phone when he finally answers. "You need to come home and take care of Roshini right now."

"I will be home at lunchtime," he says and hangs up. He is deeply disturbed to come home and find me sitting at the nook table in a catatonic stupor—eyes glazed over, muscles rigid. Roshini leaps into his arms.

"What's going on, Gayu?" he asks. I don't answer. I can't. I stare blankly, frozen in fear.

He calls Dr. Munroe's office and tells them it is an emergency. Minutes later, he straps Roshini into the car seat, forces me into the car, and races up highway 217 to the doctor's office.

"How are you doing, Gayathri?" she asks, proceeding to check my vitals. I sit speechless, mute with grief.

"You need to tell me what's going on inside you, so I can help you," she says. "Please, Gayathri, you need to help me help you."

"I want to die," I scream. "I want to kill myself. What good am I alive, anyway? I am not fit to be a mother or a wife."

"I know how scared you are, Gayathri. But believe me, your family is better off with you alive than dead," she reasons. "We can manage your depression."

Dr. Munroe insists I get back on my medications and advises Ram to hospitalize me if things don't improve. On the way back home, I beg Ram not to hospitalize me. I promise I will take the medications and try harder to cope. He agrees.

Later that evening, I ask him to drive me to the Intel parking lot. He is furious when I tell him about my phone call to Roger. A fiercely private man, he is angry that I had dragged our dirty laundry into his workplace.

"Can you please ask Roger to come meet us in the car?" I beg. "I don't want to make a scene in your office."

Ram slams the car door and returns with Roger a few minutes later.

"Hi Gayathri, how are you doing?" Roger says, sliding into the backseat next to Roshini. "What a cutie," he says, tousling her hair. "She has grown a lot since I last saw her."

"Thanks for agreeing to meet us, Roger," I say, my voice trembling with shame. "I am severely depressed and might need to be hospitalized. I can't even take care of Roshini, and I am pregnant again. And now Ram wants to quit his job and move back to India. But I don't want him to do that. We have no future in India," I cry. "Not with my mental illness. Ram has worked hard to build a career here at Intel. I don't want him to throw it away. Roger, please promise me that you won't let him quit. Please Roger, I will do whatever it takes to get better," I plead.

"Don't worry, Gayathri," Roger says. "You will be fine. I promise I won't let Ram quit."

Roger turns to Ram. "Hey man, what's wrong with you?" Roger asks him. "Why didn't you tell me anything? For heaven's sake, she is depressed. It is not the end of the world. With the proper treatment, she will be fine. If you need some time off, just let me know."

"Thanks, Roger," I say, grabbing his hands. "Thank you for saving our family."

Ram and I don't say a word to each other on the way home. That night, I have recurrent nightmares. I see myself lunging at Ram. He is trying to run away from me. So is Roshini. I chase them. I hear them scream. A million deformed babies are floating all around me. "Murderer, murderer," I hear them shout, pointing their bony fingers at me. I wake up in a sweat, agonizing over whether I should have an abortion. But I worry that aborting a baby is the same as murdering it. I can't make myself do it. And yet I am terrified that my baby will be born deformed by the medications I am taking or, worse yet, dead. Careful not to wake Ram and Roshini up, I sneak into the garage and bash my head with both my hands, trying to get rid of the dreadful images in my head.

It is said that we are only as sick as the secrets we keep. Had I been suffering from diabetes, heart disease, or even cancer, I am sure Ram and I would not have kept it a secret. We would have reached out to our friends for support, and they would have helped. But the stigma associated with mental illness has filled us with shame and exiled us into lives of secrecy. Despite the escalating crisis in our life and our utter inability to cope with it, Ram and I decide to keep my illness a closely guarded secret. Our desperate need to save face within our community triumphs our dire need for support and understanding. Even our closest friends have no clue of our struggles. In their unsuspecting eyes, we are living the American dream—a house in the suburbs, a beautiful baby girl, and a promising future. Yet Ram and I live in quiet desperation: prisoners in paradise.

# PART 5

# Awakening

CHAPTER 11

# Finding the Light Within

AMMA'S LETTER ARRIVES one afternoon. *Sri Rama,* she has inscribed at the top of the letter, as she always does. The letter is full of inquiries about Roshini and Ram and advice about my pregnancy. Halfway through the letter, she writes, "Gayu, if only you prayed with a purer heart, you wouldn't be depressed the way you are." I read the sentence over and over again in disbelief. Her sermon completely unnerves me. I tear the letter into pieces and toss it in front of the God's altar in the kitchen.

"I hate you, God! I hate you, Amma!" I break down sobbing. *Why can't my mother understand that I have a disease that can't be cured by prayer alone?* After years of trying unsuccessfully to secure her love, understanding, and support, I suspect that she is not my mother at all. Perhaps, I reason, in an utter state of disassociation, that like Goddess Sita, I had no mother—at least not a biological one. Growing up, Amma often told us the stories from the revered epic *Ramayana.* She idolized Goddess Sita, the heroine of the fable, as the epitome of womanhood and extolled her virtues of stoic sacrifice. In an irrational attempt to earn my mother's respect, I decide that my only salvation is to follow in Goddess Sita's footsteps and retreat back into the womb of my real mother—Mother Earth—just as Sita had done at the end of her trials in life. I toss the shredded letter into the trash can and plan to bury myself in my backyard later that evening. Knowing that the end to my miserable life is near, I finish cooking dinner with a resolute calmness.

When Roshini wakes up from her nap, I brush back her tousled hair and kiss her rosy cheeks. I cuddle with her on the couch while she eats her string cheese and apple slices. I turn on the TV and switch to *Sesame Street*, Roshini's favorite show. As Cookie Monster chomps on cookies and sings about his undying love for them, Roshini giggles and bounces up and down in my lap. I stare at my daughter, trying to etch her image in my heart. In my twenty-seven years of life, hers is the only unconditional love I have known. I thank God for blessing me with her presence and apologize profusely for failing her as a mother.

"Mommy will be right back, bangara," I lie to my daughter, and kiss her good-bye. I close the sliding glass door behind me and head into the backyard. Roshini's eyes remain glued to the TV. I turn back to steal one last look at my little girl, and am relieved to see her smiling and singing along with Mr. Rogers. I know Ram will be home soon. He had said he would be back early.

"Please, dear God, watch over Roshini and Ram," I pray, crouching in a corner of my backyard tucked between our garage and my neighbor Mary Jo's house.

"Dear Mother Earth," I plead, "please take me back into your womb." I clear the ground around me and start digging furiously with my hands. I don't remember how long I sat there digging my grave. As the evening light fades, so does my memory. I vaguely recall Ram and my friend Latha carrying me forcibly into the house.

Surprised to see Roshini watching TV alone when he had returned home from work, Ram tells me he had looked for me everywhere, and when he couldn't find me, he had panicked and hurried to my best friend Latha's house a couple of homes away. Concerned about my disappearance, Latha had followed Ram home and insisted on checking the house and backyard again. They were horrified to find me utterly disoriented, muttering to myself, digging frantically.

"What's wrong with you, Gayathri?" Latha keeps asking. I sit next to her on the couch, mute. Ram stares at us helplessly. Sensing something is amiss, Roshini crawls into my arms.

"Drink some water, Gayu," Ram offers. I can barely grip the glass in my trembling hands. Now that my fantasy of following Goddess Sita's footsteps has been foiled, I realize I am no mythical goddess, just a madwoman. Unable to accept the painful reality, I let out a scream that explodes through the house. Scared, Roshini howls and runs to Ram. Flustered, he picks her up, rushes upstairs to our bedroom, and slams the door.

"Don't cry, Gayathri," Latha says, hugging me tightly. "Please tell me what is wrong with you." Each time I open my mouth to say something, my throat goes dry and the words escape me. Latha and I sit in silence for what seems like an eternity.

"Whatever it is, Gayathri," Latha insists, "I promise to stay with you as long as it takes to help you get well again."

I finally collapse in Latha's arms and spill the truth about my struggles with depression. Fully expecting her to discard me and run, I am shocked at first and then profoundly relieved when she promises her undying friendship and support.

"Why didn't you tell me anything all these days?" she asks.

"I thought you wouldn't understand," I cry. "I was scared you might think I am crazy."

"Come on, Gayathri," she says, "you are not crazy, you are sick."

Shackles of stigma, shame, and secrecy that had long held me hostage slowly begin to come undone as Latha continues to hold me in her arms and promises to support me on my road to recovery. Her understanding and compassion revive my faith in humanity, and strengthen me for the difficult journey ahead.

"Why isn't your family here to help you?" she asks. I say nothing.

"Doesn't your sister live in College Station?" she inquires. I nod yes.

"I am going to call her right now and ask her to come immediately," Latha says, asking me to give her Chitra's phone number.

"Let's not bother her, Latha," I suggest, not wanting to trouble my sister and her family. Having tucked Roshini to bed, Ram joins Latha and me and agrees that we shouldn't disturb my sister.

"But she is your sister," Latha argues. "She should be here helping you out." Ram relents and gives her the phone number.

"Hello," I hear Chitra's voice on the phone. It's about eleven o'clock in College Station.

"Hi, Chitra, this is Latha. I am a friend of Ram and Gayathri. I am sorry to call you this late," Latha apologizes.

"Hi, Latha," Chitra says, sounding irate.

"Do you know that your sister is very ill?" Latha asks. "I can't believe you are not here taking care of her and Roshini. You need to come to Portland immediately."

"Why isn't Gayathri on the phone?" Chitra demands, her voice rising, "and who are you to intrude in our family matters?" Just as I had feared, my sister is angry at an outsider interfering with our lives and telling her what to do.

"Did you know that Gayathri was trying to bury herself tonight?" Latha shouts. "I am her friend, and I am telling you she needs her family's help right now."

"The only help your friend needs is for you to call the cops and hand her over to them," my brother-in-law says, getting on the phone. "She is nothing but a rich, spoiled brat."

"I can't believe you both!" Latha screams and slams the phone down.

"I am sorry they were rude to you," I apologize to Latha, shocked at my sister's and brother-in-law's behavior.

"Don't worry, Gayathri," Latha says before leaving to go home. "I promise I will take care of you."

The next morning, Ram drops Roshini off at school and takes me to see Dr. Lin, my therapist. I squirm in my chair while Ram recounts the details of my recent nightmares and suicide attempt.

"Gayathri, you are very, very sick, and you need help," Dr. Lin says. "The unfortunate truth, Gayathri, is that I can't keep you alive, even if I tried. You have a disease that distorts your thoughts and behavior and compels you to kill yourself. And unless you accept the lethal impact of this disease and learn how to manage it, you will continue to endanger your life and that of your family," she continues. "I highly recommend you get hospitalized and learn how to cope with your illness."

Perhaps it is the painful realization that I have indeed lost my mind and have become a danger to myself and others, perhaps it is Dr. Lin's reassurances that the hospitalization will help me recover and rebuild my life, perhaps it is my love for Roshini and the unborn child, perhaps it is the power of Latha's promise to stand by and support me—finally, despite fears that I might be locked up for life, I relent and agree to get hospitalized.

"What are we going to tell our friends?" Ram asks.

*What are we going to tell our friends?* My blood boils with anger. I bet Ram would have never asked the question if I were being hospitalized to treat a heart attack or a hernia. Yet I have learned, over the years, that when it comes to mental illness, values of honesty, humanity, and compassion cease to exist. Instead, shame and fear loom large in the hearts and minds of all involved.

Dr. Lin looks perplexed at my husband's question.

I stare at Ram with absolute disgust.

Growing up in India, I was brainwashed into believing that, as a woman, I needed my husband and family to protect my honor and well-being. Now, I realize that in battling mental illness, I stand alone.

J. Krishnamurti, an Indian philosopher, once said, "It is not a sign of good health to be well adjusted to a sick society." Like millions of people across the world, my family and I have remained well adjusted to a society sickened by misperceptions and stigma about mental illness. I decide I no longer want to remain well adjusted to a sick society. I want to get well and live "well adjusted" in a world that honors my truth and humanity.

*What are we going to tell our friends?* Ram's question repeats in my ears over and over again.

"The truth." I spit the words out. "From now on, I will tell everyone the truth."

To continue to live the way I had, I realize, is to die a slow and suffocating death. The truth, however painful, I believe, will ultimately liberate me.

I ask Ram to drive me to Roshini's school. I walk into her classroom and ask her teacher, Maria, if I can speak to her in private for a few minutes. Between sobs, I disclose my struggles with depression and tell Maria that I will be hospitalized later that day, and I beg her to watch over my child. Although saddened to hear about my troubles, Maria promises to take care of Roshini. I pick Roshini up, and we drive to Latha's house. She has offered to take care of Roshini while I am away at the hospital.

"Mommy is not well, sweetie," I explain to my three-year-old daughter. "I need to go to the hospital for a few days. But, I promise, I will be back as soon as I can." Roshini stares at me, confused.

"Don't worry, darling," I comfort her, fighting back tears. "Latha aunty will take good care of you while I am away." Latha entices Roshini into playing with her one-year-old baby boy, Rohan.

Driving on Highway 26 on the way to the Oregon Health & Science University Hospital, I beg the stately cedars and pine trees to help my friend Latha watch over my little girl. *Please make sure she is given her afternoon snack and tucked to bed with her favorite story,* I plead the trees lining the very same path that had welcomed me to America when I had first arrived years before. Ever since then, these trees have stood witness to my life's joys and troubles, and there were times I had grown to trust them more than the people in my life.

Minutes later, I sit hunched over in a dimly lit room at the hospital, answering a barrage of questions from a psychiatrist. Ram hunches in a chair beside me, exhausted.

"What's your name? Do you know today's date? What day is it? What month? What year? Who is our president? Can you name the past five U.S. presidents? When did India win its independence from Great Britain? Can you count in sevens from zero to one hundred? Can you spell *world* forward and backward? What brings you to the hospital? What medications are you taking?" The physician continues to question and scribble in his notepad simultaneously until the very last question:

"Are you suicidal?" I answer yes and immediately panic that I might be locked up.

The physician stops writing and explains something to Ram and me in a soft monotone. I cannot comprehend his words. He stands up and motions for me to follow a nurse who seems to have appeared out of nowhere.

As if in a trance, I do as I am asked and follow the nurse through two sets of metal doors that automatically lock shut behind us. The loud bang sends shivers up my spine and explodes in my ears. The nurse hands me a gown to change into and gives me a bag to put all my belongings in. She leads me into a room and instructs me to leave the door unlocked. I don't dare ask her why. Once I have changed, she asks me to follow her. With each step I take, I fear that I am walking to my death. I want to bolt back into Ram's arms and beg him to take me home. But my feet are laden with lead. I can see the nurse speaking, but I can't hear her. She turns and leaves the room. The door shuts with a thud. I rush to the door and try to pry it open. It doesn't budge. And that is when it hits me.

I am locked up in a mental hospital!

I clutch my pregnant belly and crumble to the floor. Crouched, then curled in a fetal position, I rock catatonically to calm myself. A torrent of tears streams down my face—tears of shame, sorrow, guilt, grief, and rage. Nothing matters anymore. The moment I have dreaded for nearly a decade has come true. I had come to the hospital looking to find freedom from the death hold of depression, only to discover to my horror that there is no hope or help, just a deathly darkness that engulfs me. There is no light, not in this cell, not in my mind.

Confined in the seclusion room of a psychiatric ward in America, thousands of miles from where I was born, I feel like a caged bird that has broken her wings, and I wonder if I will ever find my way back home again. Even if I do, I worry that my family might disown me and my community might ostracize me. I desperately long to traverse back in time and dwell in a life that was once filled with love and light, only to realize it will never be mine again.

For years, I had feared getting locked up in a mental hospital. Still, somewhere in the bottom of my heart, I had hoped that at least here in America, the land of the free, no one would rob me of my human rights. But my faith is now shattered and replaced with paranoia.

*Did Dr. Lin know I was going to be confined in a seclusion room? Did Ram know? Was this a carefully thought-out conspiracy between them?* Out of a deep sense of betrayal, I begin to wail, shattering the silence in the seclusion room. I plug my ears with both my palms and bash my head to the wall to drown the sounds out. I feel faint. I lean my head on the wall. Suddenly, my eyes catch the sheen of a camera lens. Concealed in a corner of the ceiling is a surveillance camera recording my every move. Clothed in a hospital gown that barely covers my shivering body, I feel violated, dehumanized. I scurry to cover myself, and realize that there is nothing around to cover my naked soul or my body, which is turning ice cold. The room is bare except for a bed, and I am afraid to get into it. I creep into a corner of the room, as far from the eye of the camera as I can get, and raise my hands to cover my face. I stare at my trembling hands and beg them to strangle my neck in one last deathly embrace. They do not budge.

*Rama, Rama, Rama,* I chant, begging God Rama to take my life. Deep in my heart, I know, however, even God will forsake a sinner like me. The room begins to spin. I squeeze my eyes tightly and wrap my arms around me to keep my body from keeling over. I rock back and forth, whimpering like a caged animal. Streaming through the kaleidoscope of my mangled mind, I witness glimpses from my childhood as vividly as if I were living them in the present.

I am eight years old. Jaya, my best friend since kindergarten, and I are hopscotching our way home from school. Pigtails flying, arms swinging in joyful abandon, we are oblivious to the world around us. We listen intently to each other's chatter about Sarita, the mean math teacher, and Ms. DeSouza, the prim and proper English teacher, whom we both adore. Our childish reprieve, however, is shattered by the commotion of screaming voices and hurtling stones. We turn to see what is causing the ruckus, and see a scrawny, forlorn, half-naked woman running for her life. A pack of rowdy boys is chasing the poor woman. "*Huchi, huchi!*" they scream, pelting stones at her, calling her crazy. A couple of stray dogs join the chase. Tears stream down the woman's skeletal cheeks. She looks like she has not showered in years. Her tattered rags hang awkwardly on her famished body. I feel angry and sad. I want to stop the boys from hurting the woman. I want to chase them away, but I can't move. My feet have turned into clay. Jaya runs after the trouble-makers, trying to catch a glimpse of the "huchi," leaving me all alone on the deserted street.

"Huchi, huchi, huchi . . ." I hear the boys shouting in the distance, followed by the helpless shrieks of the poor woman. I cover my ears with both hands, trying to shut out the scary sounds, but I can't.

"Huchi, huchi, huchi . . ." I hear the commotion growing louder and louder, getting closer and closer. I see the woman running toward me. She is bleeding. She is screaming hysterically, struggling to outrun the boys. I force myself to look into her face. I am horrified at what I see—the woman being chased is me!

*No!* I scream. My flailing hand strikes something in the room. A sharp pain sears up my right arm, jolting me back into reality. My body is bathed in sweat. I feel utterly disoriented. I hear a knock on the door and freeze.

In the door stands a lanky young man in scrubs. "My name is Sam. I am one of the nurses," he says. "You have a phone call from your sister." He asks me to follow him to the phone booth and tells me I have five minutes to complete the call.

"How are you, ma?" Chitra asks. I burst out crying.

"Please come, Chitra," I beg. "Roshini needs someone to take care of her."

At first Chitra agrees to come the next day, and even before I can say thanks, she changes her mind. "I am sorry," she says, "I can't." Heart-broken, I hang up the phone and turn to leave.

"Hey, Princess of Pakistan, would you like to go out on a date with me?" I hear a voice booming from behind. The hairs on the nape of my neck prickle and stand up straight. Scared to turn back and look,

I search for nurse Sam and am relieved to see him standing right beside me.

"Hi, Peter, how are you doing today?" Sam asks the towering six-foot man with an impish grin.

"Good," he responds. "It'll be great if the gal goes out on a date with me tonight."

"Leave her alone, Peter," Sam says. "Don't worry, Gayu, he is harmless," he reassures me and asks if I would like to use the restroom before going back to the seclusion room.

"Yes," I nod. He escorts me to the bathroom and asks me to leave the door unlocked. At first, I am uncomfortable peeing with Sam standing guard by the unlocked door. But I decide not to question why I need to leave the door unlocked. Hoping that my compliance will at least merit a transfer to the unlocked ward and eventually earn me an early release, I decide to follow hospital protocols without question.

Hours later, back in my room, a middle-aged woman with cropped salt-and-pepper hair knocks on the door before entering and sets a meal tray beside my bed.

"Hi! I am nurse Sue," she introduces herself. "Can I please ask you a few questions while you eat?" she asks.

"Yes," I nod my head and answer her queries while I pick at my pasta and steamed broccoli.

"I am so sorry to hear about your struggles," she says, stroking my shoulders. Her brief touch invokes a sense of compassion and trust.

"I am terrified of being locked up alone," I say. "I promise not to kill myself. Can you please move me to the unlocked ward?" She agrees to share my request with her staff and get back to me in the morning. Then she leaves the room.

I lie awake in my bed, worrying. *Is Roshini sleeping soundly? Is she missing me? Will Ram come back to see me in the morning? Or will he never come back? Will he resign his job, get sole custody of Roshini, and move to India? Will Amma and Appa disown me when they find out about my hospitalization? Is there life beyond the psych ward?*

Questions whip through my tired mind. I close my eyes and try hard to imagine Roshini tucked in bed, sleeping peacefully beside her father. But I can't. *I wonder if she is scared without me. Will Ram sing her favorite songs until she falls asleep? Who will get her ready and take her to school tomorrow? Will the carpool moms ask her where I am?*

Fear and shame whip me without mercy, and memories of my cousin Bala's wife, Suma, who had strangled herself the year before, come hurtling back. I wonder if Suma, a once-vibrant woman and mother of a six-year-old girl, had succumbed to the same demons that haunt me.

My mind wanders back to Roshini. I ache to hold her in my arms and rock her to sleep. I close my eyes and hum her favorite songs, hoping she can hear them in her dreams. I recall the promise I have made her, and resolve to do whatever it takes to earn my freedom and get back to her. Staring at the tiny barred metal window welded into the door of the seclusion room, I suddenly realize that I am the only person who has the key to set myself free—an insight that frightens and frees me all at once.

By midafternoon the next day, nurse Sue moves me to the unlocked ward and gives me back my clothes and shoes. I am deeply grateful and relieved.

"Sanya, this is Gayathri. She will be your new roommate," nurse Sue introduces me to a petite girl who looks exactly like Liesl, the eldest of the Von Trapp girls in *The Sound of Music.*

"Hi there, roomie!" Sanya springs off her bed and hugs me. She looks more like a college student than a patient in a psych ward. Sanya is dressed in a pair of blue jeans, a red-and-white-striped T-shirt, and a pair of red Keds shoes. Her auburn hair, held back by a headband, tumbles to her shoulders.

"Can you tell me your name again?" she asks.

"Guy-a-three," I parse the name like I have done a million times before.

"Guy-a-three, Guy-a-three, Guy-a-three," Sanya repeats my name over and over again. "I got it!" she smiles, delighted.

"I am sure you girls will get along great," nurse Sue says, and leaves to check on the other patients. The room Sanya and I share is a luxury suite compared to the seclusion room. It has two twin beds lined up against the walls, flanked by nightstands and lamps. It also has a built-in toilet. Most important of all, it is not what is in the room that matters, but what is missing—the surveillance camera. Its absence alone makes me feel less like a dangerous criminal and more like a patient.

"Where are you from?" Sanya asks, plopping back on her bed with her shoes still on. Had my grandfather Tatayi been here, he would have scolded Sanya for dragging the filth on her shoes into the room and onto her bed. He would have insisted that she take off her shoes at the door and rinse her feet before entering the room.

"I am originally from India," I answer, taking off my shoes and tucking them underneath the bed and sitting cross-legged, facing Sanya.

"Wow! How did you end up here?" she asks. I share her puzzlement.

Over the next couple of hours, Sanya and I piece together the stories of our lives and our struggles with mental illness. Sanya finds my traditional upbringing in India and my arranged marriage fascinating. Although we are the same age, I learn that our lives are as different as night and day. She was born and raised in Seattle and has lived all over the United States since her college years. At twenty-seven, she has had numerous boyfriends, but has never been married. At present, she works as a waitress in a restaurant, lives alone in an apartment in Tacoma, and has absolutely no contact with her family. She loves to drink, party, and travel, but is tired of her nomadic lifestyle. She hopes to recover someday soon, find a loving man to marry, have a couple of children, and settle down in life.

"Is this your first hospitalization, Sanya?" I ask.

"Heck no! This is probably my fifth or sixth time," she says, counting on her fingers. "I remember how shit-scared I was my first time in the psych ward. But that was ten years ago. Now, I am a pro. I check myself in and out of 'Club Med' whenever I get in trouble." She laughs, nonchalantly. "In fact, I have a suitcase packed and ready to go in my coat closet. I have bipolar disorder and am addicted to alcohol—deadly combination, you know? When things get bad, I check myself into the hospital and stay until I can get back on my feet again."

Sanya hops off her bed and runs to the light switch across the room. She flicks it on and off, on and off. I just stare at her, confused. "At first, I didn't know what the heck bipolar disorder was, you know," says Sanya. She leaves the light on. "When I am manic, my life is filled with sunshine. I feel on top of the world—unstoppable. I don't need to sleep, my mind races with a million thoughts a minute, and I am filled with grandiose ideas about how I can save the world."

"And then comes the darkness," Sanya says, turning off the light. "All I want to do is curl up in the dark hole and die. I bet that's how you feel when you are depressed," she says, turning the light back on. "Don't worry, you will get the hang of climbing out of the dark hole in time. You will learn how to switch on the light in the darkness of your mind."

I stare at Sanya in awe. Her simple explanation and reassurances comfort me. Her acceptance of bipolar disorder as an illness like any other transforms my own perceptions about depression. I am amazed at Sanya's candor and courage. Even her ongoing struggles and multiple hospitalizations have not dampened the twinkle in her eyes and sweet smile. Perhaps someday, I pray, I can be as strong as Sanya.

"Just stick to the hospital rules and stay on the good side of the nurses and docs," Sanya advises me later that afternoon, while we make stained-glass ornaments in the occupational therapy class. "You should be able to get out of here in no time." In the days to come, I heed her wisdom. I take copious notes in the medication management, stress management, time management, and progressive relaxation classes and force myself to participate despite my inhibitions. Each class offers me kernels of insights and tools to help me cope with my illness.

In one of the group therapy sessions, they discuss the healing powers of religion and spirituality, and encourage us to share our thoughts.

"If there is a f---ing God, why the f--- are we suffering the way we are?" asks Alex, one of the patients.

Another patient, Tracy, chimes in with a quotation. "Religion is for people afraid of going to hell, spirituality is for those who have already been there."

I completely agree with the wisdom of my colleagues. While the other patients take turns sharing their thoughts, I retreat within and wonder if my religious upbringing has hurt or healed me. When I was growing up, my mother's faith was my bedrock. I had blindly embraced her faith as mine. But my struggles with depression, unfortunately, have splintered my relationship with both God and my mother.

"Pray with a pure heart, Gayu," Amma often said. "God will relieve you of all your burdens." But no matter how sincerely I prayed, my suffering had only grown worse. So I began to question the very existence of a kind and loving God.

"Why don't you accept your suffering as your karma?" well-intentioned family and friends often suggested, implying that my suffering was a retribution for my past sins. Instead of comforting me, this connotation of karma confined me in an inescapable web of guilt, hopelessness, and helplessness. For if I was a child of God, as I was told, I could not understand what kind of God would condemn his own child for mistakes she had made in her previous births, mistakes that she had no recollection of. I struggled to understand: IS God forgiving or vengeful? Cruel or compassionate?

Over the years, my relationship with God had become entrenched in fear, rather than faith. To me, God was a stern taskmaster seated on a bejeweled throne high above in heaven with a karmic ledger in one hand and a pen poised in the other. His primary job was to watch every move we mortals make, note down all our right and wrong doings, and tally them up at the end of our lives to determine whether or not we would achieve *moksha*—liberation from the cycle of rebirth and death.

Considering that, despite my prayers, my life had become a living hell, I decided not to fear God and his karmic accounting. And I certainly didn't care about achieving moksha. All I longed for was an escape from the demons of depression, and if that was not possible, I welcomed death. But since meeting Sanya, I had discovered a ray of hope. Her acceptance, love, and compassion had revived my spirit and infused me with the courage to dream of a life beyond the limitations of my illness. Growing up, I had heard the adage *Jana seveye, Janardhana seve*—

serving people is serving God. When it is my turn, I say, "I was born and raised a Hindu. But I want to live the rest of my life as a humanitarian."

Ram and Roshini visit me every day and dispel the fear that they might desert me. The minute the locked metal doors into the psych ward open, Roshini runs into my arms and wraps her little hands around me, suffusing me with her love. Each day at the occupational therapy class, I make a little gift for Roshini—a souvenir of my undying love for her—a teddy bear made with brown yarn, stained-glass Christmas ornaments, and colorful beaded bracelets and necklaces with letters that spell *Roshini* and *I love you.* Roshini revels in receiving these gifts, and her joy lessens the pain of our separation when it comes time to say good-bye. It teaches me that even in my state of brokenness I can create gifts that bring joy to another soul.

Our friends Latha, Anil, Naveen, Kiran, and Das take turns visiting me. They bring home-cooked meals and books. It is said that "friends are angels that lift us to our feet when our own wings forget how to fly." The mere presence of my friends mends my mind, revives my spirits, and reassures me that I am worthy of being included in the circle of life.

Like my friends, I find the staff at the hospital kind and compassionate. They go out of their way to connect with me and my peers as people, not merely patients. Other than nurse Sue, I am particularly fond of Dr. Scott, a resident. The fact that he looks exactly like my favorite actor, Michael J. Fox, had drawn me to him at first, but it is his simple acts of kindness that touch my heart.

"Is that curry I smell?" Dr. Scott says, then pulls up a chair, sits beside me, and asks if he can taste a bite of my dinner. The ordinary gesture of him sitting next to me and partaking in my meal erases long-established boundaries between a physician and patient, and reminds me of our common humanity.

"I wish I could go to India someday," nurse Sue says dreamily, offering my medication one night. "It sounds like a fascinating country."

Having known my homeland's beauty and its burdens, I smile and say nothing.

"You are a lucky girl, Gayu," nurse Sue says. "Your husband loves you very much."

"Perhaps," I say, shrugging my shoulders, doubting that Ram could possibly love me since my illness had torn us apart.

"Honey, I know. I see him visiting you every day with your little girl and staying as long as he can. I see the look in his eyes. He adores you. I have seen so many marriages break up at the slightest troubles, let alone mental illness," nurse Sue continues. "It is as if there is a hidden clause in the wedding vows: *In sickness and in health . . . Till mental illness do us part.*"

She hands me a little paper cup filled with water. "What is the secret of your marriage? What keeps you together, Gayu?" she asks.

"Commitment," I say after several minutes. "It is commitment. We take our wedding vows seriously. Besides, divorce is not really an option in our culture. Perhaps it carries just as much stigma and shame as mental illness."

In the days to come, Sanya shepherds me through the daily drill: exercise class, group therapy, occupational therapy, self-esteem and stress management classes, time management classes, progressive relaxation classes, meals, medications, quiet time, and recreational time. Strangely enough, I begin to feel comfortable, even secure amid the rigid rules and confines of the psychiatric ward. For the first time in my life, I find true kinship among the other patients. For nearly a decade, I had wandered through the dark alleys of depression alone, ashamed, and afraid. And, now, for the first time, I meet people that truly understand my pain, *my tribe,* and know that I am not alone. Living amid the so-called lunatics of the world, I discover a deep strength and solidarity forged by our shared struggles. Their compassion gives me the gift of self-acceptance. And, in our collective quest for recovery, I see a flicker of hope.

Soon, a stranger named Aida visits me and fans the flicker of hope into a flame. I call her Aida the angel. Aida was my husband's colleague's mother-in-law's friend, visiting Portland from Los Angeles. She had heard about my battle with depression, multiple suicide attempts, and the recent hospitalization, and had insisted on visiting me.

"Look at me," Aida prods me upon her arrival, propping my face up with her fingers. I am too ashamed to look into her eyes. "Look at me," she keeps insisting, and when I finally do, I nearly buckle into her arms. Aida is an Armenian woman in her fifties with the grace of Jackie Kennedy and the compassion of Mother Teresa. The love in her eyes and her mere presence are healing.

"I bet the whole world looks at you and wonders what in the world you have to be depressed about," Aida says. "Look at you. You are young and beautiful. You have a loving husband, a gorgeous little girl, and a financially secure future in America. You have everything a woman could ever dream of. But I bet you look into the mirror some days and ask yourself the same question, only to be convinced that you are crazy. I know how horrific it feels to wake up each day, wishing you were dead. I know how scary it is to live at the brink of suicide. I know the deep sense of worthlessness and hopelessness that strangles you each day. I know the sorrow, and the flood of tears that you can't hold back. I know how guilty you feel for lashing out at your loved ones. I know that you believe that your family would be better off without a despicable woman like you."

I stare at Aida, wondering how this stranger knows the darkest secrets of my soul.

"But you are wrong, my darling," Aida says, pulling me closer into her arms. "You are suffering from depression, a disorder of the brain. You are not weak, lazy, or possessed. You have a disease that disrupts the way you think and behave. I know you think there is no hope, no treatment that will ever make you better," she continues, "but I promise you, you have the strength within you to overcome this disease. One day, one painful step at a time, you will get better, and you will rebuild a beautiful life for yourself and your family. I know it won't be easy, but you can do it. I know, because I have struggled with depression ever since I was eighteen years old."

I stare at Aida in disbelief. For the next thirty minutes or so, Aida holds me in her arms, recounting the details of her struggles with depression and her relentless pursuit of recovery. For years, although my family and doctors had insisted I would get better, I had no faith in their words. But I believe Aida because, unlike my family or doctors, she had walked through the dark abyss of depression and emerged into the light.

Growing up, my only image of a woman with mental illness was that of an unkempt, forlorn woman in tattered clothes muttering incoherently to herself. Meeting Aida completely transforms that perception, and, for the first time in my life, with Sanya's example and Aida's testimony and faith, I believe that recovery is possible. I learn that people with mental illness can look and function as "normal" people do. Although Aida's visit is brief, she gives me a gift that will sustain me for a lifetime—the gift of hope—*hope that sees the invisible, feels the intangible, and achieves the impossible.* Empowered with hope, I begin to imagine a life beyond the psych ward. Over the next week, I stick to my daily routine, comply with the hospital protocols, and earn the coveted day pass to go home for a few hours on the weekend.

Friday night, I can barely sleep. The anticipation of getting out of the hospital and tasting freedom, if only for a few hours, fills me with delight. When Saturday dawns, I rise with a smile, shower, get dressed, and wait for Ram and Roshini in the waiting room. It is a beautiful spring day in Portland, and my spirit soars with the warm breeze wafting through our car as we sail through the sleepy streets of Portland and make our way home. I dream of preparing my family a delicious lunch and taking Roshini to the neighborhood park.

But my dreams are shattered. Soon after getting home, I am wracked with pelvic cramps and low back pain. Ram suggests I rest while he makes us lunch. Unfortunately, the cramps intensify and I begin to bleed. Ram calls Dr. Munroe, my OB/GYN, who suspects I am suffering a miscarriage. She suggests I go to the emergency room or return to the hospital and inform the doctor and nurses of my predicament. Heartbroken, I return to the hospital from my hard-earned day pass and spend the next few days in bed trying to prevent a miscarriage. When the bleeding and cramping don't stop, I am wheeled to the radiology department for an ultrasound. Sprawled on the examination table in a semi-darkened room, waiting for the technician to arrive, I hear Amma's words echoing in my head. "Gayu, a mother's state of mind is of utmost importance in the development of the unborn child. Always think good thoughts and pray with a pure heart. Everything will work out just fine."

"I am so sorry my hands are cold," Nicole, the technician, says, proceeding to spread a gooey gel over my abdomen. Her eyes dart between the display screen and my stomach as she moves the ultrasound wand around my belly.

"Is everything okay with my baby?" I ask, hoping for a miracle.

"Well, um . . . I am not sure," Nicole says, concern clouding her eyes. "The doctor will get back to you later this evening with the results. You can change back into your clothes now and the nurse will take you back to your room."

Something in my gut tells me that my baby is dead. But I have no one to confirm or calm my fears. I wipe the goop off my stomach and stagger to the bathroom to change. I stare at my image in the mirror and despise the woman I see. *How could I have done it? How could I have killed my unborn child? Amma is right. Perhaps this is God's curse for my inability to think good thoughts and pray with a pure heart. How can I ever forgive myself? How can I face Ram and Roshini?*

"I hate you!" I scream voicelessly and raise my fists to shatter the mirror on the wall. I freeze just before my fists strike the mirror, certain that I will be confined to the seclusion room again if I cause any commotion.

"Is everything all right?" the nurse asks, tapping on the door. I splash my face with cold water, steady myself, step out of the bathroom, and get wheeled back into my room.

"I am so sorry," Sanya says, running her hands up and down my back. I creep away from Sanya, turn toward the wall, and cry.

Ram arrives later that evening without Roshini. Overcome with shame from believing that I have done something to cause the miscarriage, I again descend into the dark world of my depression and suspect that Roshini will be taken from me and I will never see her again. Throughout the last few years, Roshini has been the only anchor amid the stormy seas of my life. She is the only reason I have chosen to live.

And the thought that I may never see her again pushes me over the brink. I see no reason to fight. No hope to live.

"It's okay, Gayu, it is not your fault." Ram adjusts the blanket around me and sits next to me in bed.

"Don't touch me!" I scream and pull away from him and cower closer to the wall. I am filled with guilt, knowing how much Ram loves babies and how happy he was when we found out I was pregnant. I can't bear to look into his eyes. I don't know how to soothe his pain.

"Please, Gayu. Don't cry," Ram says and tries to turn me toward him.

"Go away and leave me alone," I sob, shrinking away from him.

Ram gets off the bed and stands helplessly in silence. After a while, he says he will come back the next day and begins to leave the room. I leap out of bed, grab his hands, and beg him to stay. He is just as confused as I am. When he is around, I feel guilty about the pain I have caused and can't bear to be with him, and when he leaves, I get scared that he may never come back and I beg him to stay. A bit shaken, Ram reassures me he will return the next day. Then he leaves.

A nurse stops by with brochures about spontaneous abortion. She expresses her sympathies and instructs me to examine the sanitary pads for clots. A little while later, a male nurse hands me a plastic utensil and instructs me to use it when I pee, and asks me to check for clots and fetal tissue and report it to the nurse on call. Running my fingers through the blood clots and fetal tissue, I am convinced I have murdered my baby and ripped its body into a million little pieces. Crazed, I begin to howl, "My baby is dead! My baby is dead!"

I become paranoid that Ram will divorce me, take custody of Roshini, and return to India, leaving me stranded in the psych ward. "They'll take Roshini away. I will never see her again!" I cry. Nurse Sue rushes to my bedside and tries to calm me. I am beyond reason.

I sit in bed, screaming, "I want to die! I want to die!"

Concerned, nurse Sue asks me to sign some papers. Petrified they may be commitment papers, I refuse to sign them. Nurse Sue pages the resident on call and is advised to move me back to the locked ward.

"What is it that you are wearing around your neck?" she asks, leading me into the seclusion room.

"It's my mangalsutra," I mumble.

"What?" she asks.

"It is my wedding necklace," I say.

"I am sorry. But you need to hand it over to me," she says stretching her hands out.

"You don't understand. I can't take it off," I cry, grabbing the mangalsutra with both hands and clutching it to my heart.

*Is she mad? Does she know what she is asking me to do? Does she realize that the managalasutra isn't just a wedding necklace, and that it is the most sacred symbol of a Hindu marriage? Does she understand how utterly inauspicious it is for a married woman to remove the managalasutra?*

"Please hand it to me," nurse Sue requests, inching closer.

"I can't!" I scream. "The only time I am forced to take it off is when I become a widow. And becoming a widow is a curse worse than death in my culture."

"I am sorry," nurse Sue says, "I am afraid you could hurt yourself with it."

"Please don't make me remove it," I sob hysterically. "I promise I won't hurt myself with it. Removing it means I won't be married anymore. Why didn't you take it away the first time you locked me up?" I cry.

"I didn't notice it on you then. If I had seen it, I would have asked you to remove it," nurse Sue insists. "I am sorry, Gayathri, but it is hospital policy. And it is for your own safety."

Shivers running up my spine, I hand over my mangalsutra to nurse Sue. As an Indian woman, I had grown up believing there were only two measures of success: marriage and motherhood. Convinced that I have lost them both, I completely lose control.

"I am no longer married!" I scream, over and over again at the top of my lungs. Nurse Sue tries to calm me. Agitated, I throw pillows at her. She insists I take Ativan to help calm me down.

"I need to call my husband," I beg nurse Sue between sobs.

She tells me I have five minutes to complete the phone call.

"They took my mangalsutra," I cry into the receiver. Distraught, Ram requests me to hand the phone to nurse Sue, and confirms to her that the removal of my mangalsutra does indeed symbolize the dissolution of our marriage. He is furious at the staff's lack of cultural sensitivity and insists he wants to take me home immediately. Nurse Sue apologizes and suggests that I stay a few more days in the hospital until my moods stabilize. She explains to Ram that I was suicidal and wouldn't sign a no-harm contract, and it was for my safety that she had insisted on having me hand over my necklace. She offers to connect Ram to the Patient Advocate Office to resolve the issue.

"It's your choice, Gayu," Ram says after nurse Sue hands the phone back to me. "You can choose to stay at the hospital for a few more days, or I can come right now and bring you back home." I sit silently for a couple of minutes, pondering my options. Finally, I feel that interrupting my treatment is in some way flunking out of psych ward. Indian that I am, I don't want to flunk out of anything, even a psych ward. So I decide to stay back at the hospital and complete my treatment.

But my resolve turns into terror as I follow nurse Sue back to the seclusion room for the second time in ten days. With each step I take, I feel like a convict on death row being led to the execution chamber. Having no escape, I collapse on the bed and surrender to the panic flooding through me. As nurse Sue turns to leave the room, questions that I had long buried in my heart scream through my mind: *Am I crazy or is the world around me crazy? Is psychiatric treatment traumatic or therapeutic? What is the purpose of my life?*

Just before she shuts the door, tears misting her eyes, nurse Sue turns back and says, "I am so sorry to confine you again. I wish the hospital policies were different. And I sincerely pray that you will perceive the psych ward as a place of learning, not a prison. Gayathri, you came to the hospital to learn how to cope with your illness, and you are doing a great job. I realize how painful the last two weeks have been for you. But I know you have the strength within to recover and rebuild your life."

"When the student is ready, the teacher will appear," says a Buddhist proverb. I am ready. Nurse Sue's compassion and belief in me transforms my perspective about my illness, the psych ward, and myself. I am able to see myself as a human being with potential, not merely a weak, immature, crazy woman. I realize that while mental illness can break my mind, and the mental health system can confine my body, there are no walls in this world that can contain my spirit.

Later that night, as the darkness in my womb and the world around threaten to engulf me, I have an awakening. In a startling moment of clarity, I see my choice: I can either die cursing the darkness, or I can light a candle. I choose to light a candle and emerge from this crucible a messenger of hope and healing. For every indignity I had suffered in shame and silence, I promise to fight to restore my dignity and the dignity of others like me around the world. For every moment that my family and I had lived in despair, I promise to bring hope to the lives of others like us.

On April 30, 1989, entombed amid the dark abyss of depression, I discover my calling to be *a candle in the dark*—a candle to dispel misperceptions about mental illness, a candle to incinerate the insidious chains of stigma and discrimination, and a candle to bring hope to the lives of others on their road to recovery.

For nearly a decade of my life, as the dark winds of depression blew out the lamp of my mind, body, and soul, I had looked outward, hoping that someone or something could light my darkness away. Yet, in my darkest hour, I discover my *antarjyoti*—the light within. It leads me to a still center that had long eluded me. Amid an ocean of chaos, I discover an island of calm. Beneath mounting waves of fear, I discover faith. In the midst of madness, I discover a new meaning to my life. I learn that the strength I had long sought in others had always resided in me. Despite despair, I discover the power within to transform my life.

Ever since I was tormented by mental illness as a teenager, I had looked outward, hoping to find love and acceptance from my family. *If only Appa knew that I was strong, as nurse Sue believed, if only Amma could acknowledge my illness and not perceive it as a curse brought on by my ingratitude to God, if only Ram understood that my broken life wasn't my karma.*

But today, alone and with no one to turn to, for the first time in my life, I turn inward and ask myself this question: Do I accept myself and my illness, and, more important, will I take responsibility for my wellness? Yes! Yes! Yes! I answer. Buddha says, "In order to be free one must accept, even embrace suffering." I decide to embrace my suffering and take the first step to finding peace and solace.

CHAPTER 12

# On the Road to Recovery

AFTER SEVENTEEN DAYS in the hospital, Ram brings me home on May 3, 1989. I stand at the threshold of our doorway as Roshini tugs at my hands and jumps into my arms. "Go in, Gayu," Ram urges me softly. And I do. I step back into our life. That night, as I tuck Roshini into bed and fall asleep in Ram's arms, my fears begin to fade: fear of him divorcing me, taking sole custody of Roshini, and moving back to India.

"Happy anniversary!" I wish Ram as he stirs awake the next morning. It is our sixth wedding anniversary. Having lost and earned my freedom, I cherish every moment of our life together. All the things I had taken for granted before, I embrace with a deep sense of gratitude now. Whether it is waking up in my husband's arms, or taking a shower with the bathroom door closed, or taking Roshini to school without having to ask anyone's permission, I marvel at the many gifts that freedom affords. Yet at times I find freedom both exhilarating and frightening.

At first, even simple tasks like taking care of Roshini or going to the grocery store seem insurmountable. I feel judged by everyone around me, for there are no more secrets to hide behind. My friends and neighbors know about my illness. I feel as if they, like me, are waiting to see whether I will heal or crack open again. There are days when I crave crawling back into the secluded safety of the hospital. But I realize that it is time to face my fears and overcome them. So, one painful, purposeful step at a time, I persist in creating a life outside of the hospital and in the community. I discover the Serenity Prayer at a friend's house and embrace it as my mantra: "God, grant me the serenity to accept the things I cannot change, courage to change the things I can, and wisdom to know the difference." With time, I pick up the threads of my life and, with tenderness and understanding, weave them back into a life of love and healing.

Recovery is a journey, not a destination, I learn. Driving to the day treatment at the hospital, days after my release, I am terrified that I might lose control of the car and kill myself or others on the road. Having never driven much on high-speed roads before, I feel my heart leap into my mouth and my eyes fog with fear as I turn onto Highway 26 and make my way through the three-lane traffic and up the winding roads leading to the hospital at the top of the hill. Not wanting to give up, I clutch the steering wheel and mutter a million prayers begging God to help me drive safely. The triumph I feel when I finally park the car and join my peers at the day treatment program far supersedes the terror I had felt on the road. Most important, it teaches me the meaning of facing my fears and the joy of overcoming them, a skill that comes in handy as I transition back into life outside the hospital.

Since my return from the hospital, I had feared that my friends might not trust me with their children anymore. But I am deeply relieved when they welcome me home and invite me to take my turn in the carpools, playdates, and potluck dinners. In so doing, they give me three precious gifts—social inclusion, trust, and support—gifts that all of us crave, but few people with mental illness receive. While most of my friends treat me with compassion, there are a few who simply cannot comprehend how a woman like me, who is blessed with all the trappings of material success, could have possibly been depressed enough to attempt suicide. One friend, a woman I had known for years, tells me that the only way we could remain friends is if I never mentioned my mental illness again, as if its mere mention would infect her with madness. Her request stings me, but I find comfort in the quote "Three men are my friends: he that loves me, he that hates me, and he that is indifferent to me. Who loves me teaches me tenderness. Who hates me teaches me caution. Who is indifferent to me teaches me self-reliance" (anonymous). Elie Wiesel, a Holocaust survivor and winner of the 1986 Nobel Peace Prize, once said, "The opposite of love is not hate, it is indifference." My friend's indifference inspires me to become self-reliant.

My mother arrives by the end of May and stays through the end of September. She is deeply saddened by my recent hospitalization and miscarriage, and is determined to help me heal. Roshini is delighted to have her grandmother back, and Ram is relieved. Wanting to overcome her misperceptions about mental illness and get a better understanding of depression, Amma studies the brochures given to me at the hospital with as much devotion as she does the chanting of her mantras. While I sincerely appreciate my mother's interest in learning about my illness, and I am deeply grateful for her love and caring, I struggle with the resentment I still feel for all the years she had failed to understand and support me. I realize, however, that she, like me and the rest of our family, was imprisoned in ignorance about mental health issues. Longing to rebuild our relationship and move on with life, I decide to cherish every moment I have with my mother. I forgive my mother for her lack of understanding and forgive myself for the resentment I had harbored. Forgiveness sets me free to focus on the hard work of recovering and rebuilding my life.

Wanting to further support me on my road to recovery, Amma accompanies me to day treatment one day. Meeting my peers and learning of their struggles through mental illness, their fears, hopes, and dreams, offers my mother a greater understanding of my struggles and deepens her empathy for me. It also lets her see for the first time that my family and I were hardly alone in our struggles. She is amazed to discover that people of all ages, genders, races, and socioeconomic status are affected by mental illness. For the first time in my life, my mother expresses how sorry she is for my suffering and applauds my strength and resilience. The little girl in me leaps with joy for having gained my mother's approval and respect. For the first time since I was a teenager, I feel truly loved and understood by my mother.

Amma takes over the daily cooking and insists I exercise regularly, attend my therapy sessions, and practice my relaxation techniques. She calls my father, brother, and sister, and tells them to learn about depression and how best to support me on my journey to wellness.

Everything seems to be going well in my life except for the cocktail of medications I am taking. I continue to struggle with their side effects: heightened anxiety and panic, restlessness, recurring bouts of debilitating depression, dizziness, mental confusion, muscle spasms, exhaustion, dry mouth, stomach cramps, constipation, headaches, joint pain, nausea, blurred vision, rapid heartbeat, and, worst of all, continuing thoughts of suicide. Suspecting that my depression is resistant to treatment, and might perhaps respond better to an additional drug, my psychiatrist decides to prescribe lithium. However, within days of taking lithium, it proves disastrous. My body and brain go haywire like a chemical experiment gone awry. I feel like the drugs are racing through my body, setting my nerves on fire. My eyelids flutter without control, and I feel like jumping out of my skin. Unable to cope with my racing thoughts or stand still in the shower one morning, I bolt through the house, jabbering. Shocked to find me running around the house buck naked and mumbling incoherently, my mother chases me up and down the stairs, finally forcing me back into the shower. The blast of cold water takes my breath away but calms me enough for my mother to coax me into some clothes. She makes me swallow an Ativan to calm me down and tucks me into bed. As I lie in bed lashing around like a fish out of water, she places a warm towel over my eyes to keep them from fluttering and literally holds me down until I slip into a drug-induced stupor.

Even after weeks of dose adjustment and periodic blood tests to make sure that the lithium doesn't exceed therapeutic levels, I fail to experience any benefits. Finally, my psychiatrist asks me to stop taking it. Wanting to pursue other options, however, he prescribes Prozac, which doesn't help me, either. It worsens my restlessness, depression, and suicidal ideation. It also induces tremors in my hands, which makes it hard to brush my teeth, feed myself, do housework, drive the car, or take care of Roshini. Hoping that the side effects would recede with time, my psychiatrist asks me to stay on Prozac for a couple of months. But when the side effects worsen and I can no longer cope, he recommends I stop it.

Amma returns to India with a heavy heart. With her absence and lack of support, I spiral back into severe depression. On October 20, 1989, I end up in the emergency room at St. Vincent Medical Center and spend the next six days at the hospital. Concerned that my doctor might have missed an underlying disorder that is causing my misery, I suspect I could probably be suffering from hyperthyroidism. I had recently read in a health magazine that symptoms of hyperthyroidism mimic and often exacerbate underlying depression. I insist the doctor does the necessary diagnostic tests, and the results confirm my hunch. The doctor prescribes Inderal, a beta blocker to control the hyperthyroidism. When it doesn't help, the attending physician recommends radioactive iodine and antithyroid medication. Ram and I decide to seek a second opinion. Given the traumatic events of the past year, the endocrinologist suggests giving my body and mind a chance to recover. He recommends we wait things out for a few months and resort to more aggressive treatment if things get worse.

Hopeful that the Inderal will eventually offer some relief, I return home on October 27 and struggle though the following weeks. Unfortunately, I end up at the St. Vincent Hospital again on December 3 following yet another suicide attempt. Ram had found me sobbing in my closet, with a handkerchief tightened around my neck.

Staring out of the fifth-floor hospital window one day, I witness the world go by. I see cars cruising up and down the street, people milling around briskly to avoid the winter chill, and a mother taking her baby for a walk. I long to take Roshini to the park and watch the crisp, cool air kiss her rosy cheeks. I ache to hear her giggles. I desperately want to be part of that normal world. I am sick and tired of being a chronically mentally ill patient—the medications, side effects, suicide attempts, and hospitalizations. I just want to be well.

Like millions of people suffering from depression around the world, I had hoped to discover a miracle pill that would cure my ills and promise me *nirvana*. But, somewhere deep in my soul, I am convinced now that the medications are making me sicker instead of helping me heal. Despite being raised in a culture where I was taught to implicitly follow the directions of doctors, I decide to listen to my inner wisdom and wean myself off all medications under the supervision of my psychiatrist and explore holistic avenues to healing. Fortunately, my psychiatrist supports me in my decision, and so does Ram.

After nearly a decade of struggling through recurrent depression and suicide attempts, my physicians and I had failed to find the right treatment to alleviate my suffering. The antidepressants and antianxiety medications had made me more agitated, depressed, and suicidal. Although the electroconvulsive therapy might have prevented me from committing suicide, and the cognitive-behavioral therapy had been helpful in retraining my thoughts and behavior to some extent, I find that Western medicine has its limitations. Unlike Eastern modalities of healing that take a holistic approach to treating the mind, body, and spirit, Western medicine is focused on controlling symptoms instead of fostering systems change. I learn at last that wellness does not come encapsulated in a pill that can be patented by pharmaceutical companies and traded for profits. Rather, it encompasses the way I live.

Recalling that an intern at the hospital had recommended I decide to learn to practice *pranayama*, a meditation discipline involving breath control that originated in ancient India, and transcendental meditation to heal my mind and foster overall well-being, I contact a local teacher. I find it ironic that although these healing practices originated in my home country, India, I had to travel clear across the world and nearly lose my sanity and life before finding an American teacher to teach me these phenomenal life-affirming practices. Growing up in India, I had often heard the adage *Hitthala gida madalla*—an age-old wisdom alluding to the fact that we often ignore the healing potions that can be found growing in our own backyard.

Sitting cross-legged on a Persian carpet across from my meditation teacher, Pat, in the dining room turned shrine in her home in Beaverton, I marvel at her healing presence.

"Close your right nostril with the thumb of your right hand and inhale

**Healing from Depression**

*Like millions of people struggling with depression around the world, I longed to discover a magic pill to cure my ills and promise me nirvana. Now, finally, I was learning to look inward. Over time, I discovered eight keys that have helped me recover and thrive no matter what obstacles I've faced. Today I share them with others who struggle. Together, they spell "recovery":*

**R**esponsibility
**E**mpowerment
**C**ourage
**O**ptimism
**V**ision
**E**mpathy
**R**esilience, and
**Y**ou!

*Over time, I have created a Personalized Wellness Action Plan that has helped me live a fulfilling life despite recurrent bouts of depression. I learned that there are eight dimensions of holistic wellness that I must attend to in creating an integrated plan: emotional, social, spiritual, intellectual, physical, financial, occupational, and environmental. These wellness practices have helped me put my plan into action:*

- *Pranayama – Breath work*
- *Transcendental Meditation*
- *Journaling*
- *Exercise*
- *Hydration*
- *Nutrition*
- *Meaningful work*
- *Social connectedness*
- *Spirituality*
- *Service*
- *Joyful hobbies*
- *Sleep*

*Most importantly, I learned that wellness begins with me.*

deeply using your left nostril," Pat says, teaching me the ancient practice of *nadi sodhana pranayama*—one of many forms of pranayama. I follow her instructions and take a deep breath. "Now, close the left nostril with the ring finger and baby finger and exhale using the right nostril." I follow suit. "Repeat on the other side," she says. "With the left nostril still closed, inhale using the right nostril and exhale with the left nostril. Let's repeat the complete breath cycle fifteen times."

At first, I fumble with my breath and fingers. But with Pat's persistence and encouragement, I learn to focus on the ebb and flow of my breath. And, for the first time in my life, I begin to notice the connection between my *prana*—the life force of my breath—and my mind, body, and spirit. With each breath, my mind becomes calm and centered, my body relaxes, and my spirit feels renewed.

"Good job, Gayathri." Pat smiles and proceeds to instruct me in the art of performing transcendental meditation. She reminds me to sit comfortably with my eyes closed. She offers me a mantra—a phrase—and invites me to repeat the mantra silently.

"Just focus on your mantra and allow your mind to effortlessly transcend your thoughts," she says, breathing in and out deeply.

While Pat sits still, Buddha-like, eyes closed, breath steady, body relaxed, face serene with peace, my breath is erratic, my eyes flutter like the wings of a hummingbird in flight, and my "monkey mind" runs amok. *Oh, my God! Does Pat think I am crazy? What if I can't sit still? Will my eyes ever stop fluttering?* As hard as I try, my mantra keeps floating in and out of my consciousness, and a million thoughts muddle my mind. Within minutes, I grow restless.

"Don't worry, Gayathri," Pat says, sensing me squirm. "With practice you will experience a deep state of restful, alert consciousness."

Although I don't believe Pat at first, eventually, with daily practice, I learn to tap into the hitherto unexplored tranquility of my mind. Despite my mind's tendency to wander, much like a mother lovingly guides her wayward child back to its task, I learn to gently guide my mind back to its still center. Therein I discover a reservoir of energy, clarity, creativity, and restful calm. Meditation also offers me a sacred space to reflect and look back on my life, which in turn teaches me to become an observer of my thoughts and emotions instead of getting entangled in them. Eventually, the daily practice of pranayama and meditation regulate my emotions and help me live each moment with gratitude and mindfulness.

The *Hatha Yoga Pradipika*, a classic Sanskrit manual on hatha yoga written by Swami Svatamarama in the fifteenth century, states, "When the Breath wanders, the mind is unsteady, but when the Breath is still, so is the mind still." Much to my surprise, with months of practice, I begin to experience fleeting moments of bliss. Here in the stillness of my mind, I hear the song of my soul—a song that fills me with love and hope.

"If you can control your breath, you can control your life," say the yogis. One breath, one day at a time, I begin to take control of my life.

The dark clouds of depression gradually recede and often return a week or ten days before my menstrual cycle begins. My OB/GYN suspects it is premenstrual dysphoric disorder. Cognizant of my adverse reaction to psychotropic drugs, she suggests I try St. John's wort—an herbal remedy to treat depression. Although it doesn't eliminate my distress, it alleviates the symptoms enough for me to continue with my life. Much like a person with diabetes learning how to manage his or her illness, I eventually learn to manage my moods and create a life of meaning and purpose.

Day by day I begin to enjoy life as I haven't done in years. I dream of having another baby and share my wish with Ram. At first, afraid that another pregnancy and childbirth could revert me back into a deep depression, he is adamantly against it. Eventually, I convince him to reconsider his choice and promise him that I will get pregnant only if I can stay healthy and stable for at least six months. Encouraged, I create and adhere to a wellness regimen with the intensity and focus of an athlete training to win a triathlon.

I wake up each morning around six thirty and practice pranayama for ten minutes and follow it up with twenty minutes of transcendental meditation.

"Your mind can elicit a healing response when even conventional medicine has proven ineffective" says Dr. Andrew Weil, an expert in integrative medicine and author of many best-selling books on health and wellness. Pranayama and transcendental meditation begin to heal me in ways that no medicine ever had.

Each morning after I meditate, I take a few minutes to write in my journal. Journaling provides me a safe avenue to express my thoughts, emotions, fears, hopes, and dreams. It helps me clarify my feelings, work through conflicts, and set goals. It also provides me the opportunity to express my gratitude for the many gifts of my life—a family to love, a cozy home to live in, a garden to tend to, friends to share my life with, a life filled with possibilities, and the random acts of kindness by strangers. Journaling also helps me celebrate the little miracles of life and the major milestones—the tender green shoots of the bleeding hearts poking their little heads through the winter-hardened earth to welcome spring, the dainty hummingbirds suspended in midair drinking nectar out of the crimson-red blooms of crocosmia in the summer, Ram's promotion at work, Roshini turning five and learning how to swim and ride a bicycle, my sister, Chitra, giving birth to her second son, Shekar, and my brother, Ravi, and his wife being blessed with their firstborn son, Surya—and my continued health. I am especially grateful that I have the luxury of devoting time to my healing regimen, knowing that so many people struggling with mental health issues do not have the time or resources to learn and practice wellness skills because of job, family, and financial responsibilities.

Most mornings, I drop Roshini off at school by eight fifteen, and I go the health club and work out three to five times a week. I attend aerobics and yoga classes and train with free weights. I love my yoga classes the best. They never fail to relax and rejuvenate my body, mind, and spirit. Exercise also energizes me and elevates my mood.

I return home from my workouts by ten o'clock, shower, get dressed, and pray. Although my relationship with God has been severely tested by my journey through depression, chanting prayers my mother had taught me as a child and lighting the diyas by the God's altar remind me to honor the divine light of life inherent in all of us. It connects me to a deeper spirituality that transcends all religions and unites us in a seamless web of universal consciousness. Knowing that there is a greater power—a cosmic consciousness that sustains us all—strengthens me and allows me to marvel at the interconnectedness of our lives. It also comforts me in knowing that my pain is not without purpose.

I eat a healthy breakfast around ten thirty and make sure to drink six to eight glasses of water a day. I do chores around the house, cook the meals for the day, or run errands before picking Roshini up at school at twelve thirty. Following lunch, I tuck her in for her nap and sink into the couch with a book. One of my favorites is *Feeling Good* by David Burns, M.D. It reinforces the cognitive-behavioral skills Dr. Lin, my therapist, had taught me years before. With practice, identifying negative, self-defeating thoughts and replacing them with positive, life-affirming thoughts and behaviors becomes as automatic as breathing. Albert Einstein once said, "The world we have created is a product of our thinking; it cannot be changed without changing our thinking." The tools of cognitive-behavioral therapy, in essence, help me change my thinking, and, therefore, my world. Reading *Man's Search for Meaning* by Viktor Frankl, *Seven Habits of Highly Effective People* by Stephen Covey, and *When Bad Things Happen to Good People* by Rabbi Harold Kushner further enrich my life.

Once Roshini wakes up from her nap, I give her a snack, and we watch her favorite TV shows, play together, go to the library, or meet her friends at the neighborhood park. Ram comes home around six thirty. We eat dinner, help Roshini with her bath, read to her, and tuck her into bed by nine. Ram and I watch the news or a comedy show on TV and go to bed by ten. I make sure I get at least eight hours of sleep a night. Inability to fall asleep and stay asleep had been one of the most debilitating symptoms of my depression. Fortunately, the consistent practice of pranayama, transcendental meditation, and exercise help me reestablish a healthy sleep cycle.

Well rested, I wake up the next day and do it all over again. Gradually, one day, one resolute step at a time, I inch away from illness and create a life of wellness. Eight months roll by. Having fulfilled my promise to remain healthy and stable for six months, Ram and I are excited at the prospect of having another baby. Much to our joy, I get pregnant within months, and cherish every moment of my pregnancy.

Having decided to immigrate to America, my parents arrive in Portland in mid-May, in time to pamper me through the last few weeks of pregnancy and get their green cards. Appa's dream of living in America comes true at last. Knowing how much my father longed to live in America, I had become a U.S. citizen and sponsored my parents.

On June 29, 1991, while Appa stays home with Roshini, Amma and Ram help welcome our baby girl into the world. We name her Diya. True to her name, she fills our life with light. Holding her in my arms, I thank God for my children. They are the reason and reward for living.

In the weeks following Diya's birth, just as suspected, I experience symptoms of postpartum depression. Although we are concerned it might escalate into a crisis, as it had after Roshini's birth, it doesn't. Greater awareness about the issue, my commitment to self-care, my mother's love and nurturing, and social supports help me manage the symptoms effectively.

When Diya is three months old, my parents move to Austin, Texas, to live with my brother and his family. I immerse myself in raising my daughters as Ram and I delight in watching our girls blossom. When Diya turns one, wanting a break from my career as a mother and homemaker, I enroll in a psychology course offered in the evenings at the Portland Community College. Ram is happy to watch the girls when I am in class. I fall in love with the subject and continue taking the full series of courses in psychology and enjoy learning about the human psyche and its mysterious workings. Collaborating with my classmates and earning A grades gratifies me deeply, boosts my self-confidence, and inspires me to dream of a world beyond motherhood. I recall the promise I had made in the seclusion room several years before and long to pursue my dream of serving my global community as a messenger of hope and healing. But I realize that my daughters, who are four and nine, need my time and attention more than the world.

Growing up, my mother often said, "Gayu, a mother's job is the most important job in the world. Our children are the building blocks of society. And, as mothers, it is our utmost responsibility to raise competent, compassionate children who will become good stewards of our world. If you fail them, you have failed yourself and the world."

As a young girl, I often dismissed my mother's advice as archaic and old-fashioned. "Shouldn't fathers be equally responsible in raising children?" I used to challenge her. But with Ram busy at work, I embrace my mother's wisdom and decide to revive my dream to serve the world when the girls are older and more independent.

As the years roll by, the girls flourish at school and Ram continues to climb the corporate ladder. We build a dream house, and I enjoy decorating it and making it a cozy home. In time, I create a beautiful garden, and it becomes my sanctuary. The changing seasons in my garden comfort me and teach me that there is a time to lie dormant and a time to come alive, a time to prune and a time to bloom. When at times I find myself weighed down by the dark winter of my mind, my garden reminds me that within me is an "invincible summer," as Albert Camus put it. The vibrant red and yellow parrot tulips that come so soon after the snow, the gorgeous blooms of pink peonies, golden showers of coreopsis, and the beautiful blue hydrangeas reassure me that all is well. When I tuck my garden into bed each winter, I know that with love and nourishment, it will burst alive in spring and smile through summer and fall. The cyclical nature of my garden helps me understand the cyclical nature of life and strengthens me to embrace my sojourns through darkness.

Now, in 1999, Roshini turns thirteen and Diya turns eight. They are in school for much of the day, and busy with after-school activities and homework in the evenings. I decide to go back to school and gather skills to pursue my dream to be "a candle in the dark." Convinced that I need to harness the power of the Internet to realize my dream, despite my aversion to technology, I enroll in the Management and Business Information Systems program at George Fox University in the fall of 1999. Over the next eighteen months, along with a cohort of twenty-five students, I attend classes on Monday evenings and a few Saturday seminars. I do my homework assignments when the girls are in school or while I wait in the car during their piano, swimming, and tennis classes. The program helps me overcome my fear of technology and literally puts the world in the palm of my hands, or, should I say, at my fingertips. On December 15, 2001, I earn my second undergraduate degree in Management and Business Information Systems.

Thrilled, I begin thinking of going to graduate school. For months, I research my options. Should I get a master's in psychology or social work and work as a mental health provider to help people transform their lives? Or should I become a social entrepreneur and transform the mental health system at large? I realize that although there are dedicated mental health professionals, lack of awareness, stigma, and discrimination have resulted in a fragmented, severely underfunded, understaffed mental health system. In the end, I decide to become a social entrepreneur and pioneer innovative programs to transform the mental health system and create social change. I apply to the Masters in Business Administration program at George Fox University, and am ecstatic when I am accepted.

Although Ram and my parents are delighted, they worry about how I will cope with the demands of graduate school in addition to those of a mother and homemaker. They have reason to be concerned—as do I. Throughout the years of accomplishment and joy, the dark winds of depression return from time to time. Periods of high stress, and especially my hormonal cycles, continue to trigger my descent into darkness. It is as if I had made a pact with God—for every three weeks of sanity, I have to endure a week of insanity. A week to ten days before the onset of my menstrual cycle, my world begins to crumble. Regardless of my blessings, at those times, my life seems worthless and without meaning. As hard as I try, I cannot discover a ray of hope. Sometimes death seems like an alluring escape. Usually a calm person, I erupt into an emotional tempest and lash out at my daughters and husband for the most innocuous reasons—perhaps a cluttered room or unwashed dishes. The rage fuels a deep sense of shame and guilt and an inexplicable grief, which further robs me of my will to live. Overwhelmed with the everyday demands of life and unable to concentrate or think clearly, I struggle to wade through the cobwebs in my mind. There are months when I can cope with the symptoms and others when they completely disrupt my life. At times, my daughters are the victims of my volatile moods, and it breaks my heart.

"I am so sorry," I tell my daughters. "It's not your fault. My body and brain go through changes that make me irritable and sad. I love you very much, and you have nothing to be afraid of.

"Please forgive me," I beg my children and Ram repeatedly, repenting for the pain I inflict upon them. Their love and understanding gives me the strength to forgive myself and forge ahead. Just like riding a bike, when I fall off, I get back on the seat and start pedaling again.

Fortunately, my troubles dissipate within days after my period starts. I return to the stable, sane, loving wife and mother that I am. A software engineer who believes in the power of data, Ram begins to chart my menstrual cycles. Together, we make peace with my cyclical depression and do our best to manage it. Ram goes out of his way to be helpful at home and encourages me to take care of myself while he tends to the children. I often wonder what grounds my husband. I believe that it is his faith in God and a deep sense of duty that anchors and sustains him.

Despite the ups and downs of life, I adhere to my wellness regimen. Pranayama, transcendental meditation, journaling, exercise, cognitive-behavioral therapy, proper nutrition and hydration, spirituality, St. John's wort, adequate sleep, nurturing relationships, meaningful work, and pleasurable hobbies such as decorating, gardening, volunteering, and traveling become my recipe for recovery. Regardless of the periodic setbacks I experience, these wellness practices help me develop the resilience to thrive in life.

CHAPTER 13

# From Adversity to Advocacy

AS I CELEBRATE my progress through graduate school, I learn, sadly, that in my beloved family, we share a genetic predisposition to mental illness. My brother, Ravi, is debilitated by depression, and my sister, Chitra, succumbs to the ravages of schizoaffective disorder. When the phone rings, we never know if my siblings are alive or whether they have successfully committed suicide. Yet again our family is torn apart and tested by mental illness. My journey through depression, however, has educated my parents and me to better cope with the crises and support my siblings.

While Ravi embarks slowly but surely on his road to recovery, Chitra begins to deteriorate. Unable to drive away the distorted visions of decapitated people and quell their relentless voices in her head demanding she kill herself, she overdoses many times and struggles through multiple hospitalizations and electroconvulsive therapy treatments. Having exhausted all other avenues to help her heal, her psychiatrist decides that involuntarily committing her to the state hospital is the only option to ensure her safety and that of her family. Heartbroken, we pray for a miracle to rescue my sister. I offer to visit her and stay with her for a few weeks until she stabilizes, but she refuses vehemently. Although we were extremely close growing up, our journey through mental illness has tattered our relationship.

In the summer of 2002, Ram, the girls, and I go to visit our families in Bangalore with a heavy heart, not knowing if and when Chitra will be admitted to the state hospital. I rise early one morning to join my parents on their morning walk. Glancing at my sleeping daughters huddled together on a mattress on the floor, I am reminded of my childhood when Chitra and I used to do the same. For a moment, I long for my sister to be a little girl again. I remember the kindhearted, carefree tomboy she was, and hard as I try, I cannot reconcile that with the current trauma of her life. I kneel by my daughters and pray to God to bless them with health and spare them from the misery of mental illness. Raising them, I was often wracked with guilt that I had passed on my defective genes to them and feared that my ongoing struggles with depression had scarred them for life. Fortunately, they had defied my fears and were growing up to be spirited young girls with a love for life.

The girls stir in their sleep. I adjust the blankets to cover them, shut the door gently, and join my parents, who are waiting for me by the front gate. Every few yards, Amma and Appa stop and bend their heads, hands folded by their heart in prayer to the many deities at the temples that dot our path. Tears streaming down their faces, they tell me about their daily conversations with God, asking him to watch over their children and bless them with health and happiness. Touched by their undying love and our shared trials, I lower my head in prayer and promise them that I will one day find a way to honor our struggles. For all the years we had walked in silence with our heads bent low in fear and shame, for all the tears that we had shed alone, I promise I will transform our cries into a call for action. I tell them that I will spearhead a walk one day, a walk to symbolize our hope and solidarity, a walk that would literally bring us out of the dark and into the light of a bright new day. I envision a day when we would walk hand in hand, our heads held high in pride of our persistence—mothers, fathers, sons, and daughters, spouses, family, friends, and colleagues. Together we would stride with hope in our hearts and faith in our souls, celebrating our courage in overcoming the devastating impact of the dehumanizing disorders of the brain. My parents hug me and bless that my vision will come true.

Upon my return to Portland, I enlist the support of my teammates in the entrepreneurship course of my MBA program to write a business plan for the walk. We call it March for the Mind. Professor Rose questions its feasibility. But I point to the phenomenal success of the Race for the Cure presented by Susan G. Komen for the Cure, the global leader of the breast cancer movement; the AIDS Walk; the March of Dimes walk; and other similar events, and I convince Professor Rose and my teammates that March for the Mind is a viable venture that could greatly benefit humanity. Considering that an estimated 57.7 million Americans ages eighteen and older suffer from a diagnosable mental disorder in a given year, according to the National Institute of Mental Health, in addition to millions of children struggling with mental health issues, I impress upon my colleagues that people struggling with mental illness and their families are hungry for hope and solidarity, and the proposed walk would provide just that. I discover the inspiring story of how Nancy Brinker's promise made to her dying sister Susan ignited the Race for the Cure movement, and I pray that March for the Mind will someday become a symbol of my love for my sister, Chitra.

In the winter of 2002, my colleagues and I complete our business plan and conduct a mock march on campus. Inspired, I begin searching for a strategic partner to help launch the walk nationwide, and discover the National Alliance on Mental Illness (NAMI), the largest advocacy organization in America dedicated to improving the lives of individuals and families affected by mental illness. I contact Stephen Loaiza, at that time the executive director of NAMI Oregon, share my business plan for March for the Mind, and inquire if NAMI would be interested in collaborating with me to launch a nationwide walk. Speechless at first, he marvels at the timing of my phone call and the proposed plan, and tells me that he had just spoken to a consultant that NAMI National had hired to pilot a nationwide walkathon in May 2003.

"Portland is one of twelve pilot sites," he says, and asks if I would be interested in joining the Steering Committee to launch NAMI Walks for the Mind of America.

Thrilled beyond words, I jump on board and begin campaigning the length and breadth of my state to engage fellow Oregonians in the inaugural walk.

A couple of months before the walk, my colleagues and I in the MBA program are required to present a five-minute speech based on a quote in our Effective Communications course. After years of agonizing about the consequences of disclosing my illness in public, I heed to the wisdom of Martin Luther King Jr. that "our lives begin to end the day we become silent about things that matter." I decide to break my silence and speak about courage. Centered on the quote "Courage is fear that has said its prayers," I share my journey through mental illness with my class. I am overwhelmed by the positive response. I learn that by sharing my truth, I can set others free to do the same. Some of my classmates tell me about their own struggles through mental illness or the struggles of their family and friends. They applaud me for my courage and encourage me to follow my dream to become a mental health advocate.

Weeks before the walk, I stand trembling with excitement alongside Senator Avel Gordly and Governor John Kitzhaber on the footsteps of the capitol building in Salem and address a crowd of three hundred people. Together, we rally in support of passing the Mental Health Parity Act and invite Oregonians to join us at the NAMI Walk. Standing amid my fellow citizens fighting for our human rights and social justice, I experience the power of our voices in initiating change.

Days later, as a keynote speaker at the kickoff luncheon for the walk, I realize the power of stories to touch and transform lives.

"May I please speak to you in private?" a young woman in her twenties taps me on my shoulder as I step off the podium. Between the excitement of receiving a standing ovation and the sheer relief that I had delivered my speech without faltering, I hardly hear her soft voice.

"My name is Sarah. Thank you for sharing your story," she says, tears misting her hazel-brown eyes. "Tonight was going to be the night." She squeezes my hands tightly. "After years of struggling with depression, I had decided I was going to end it all tonight. But listening to your story has given me hope and helped me change my mind. Perhaps like you, one day, I will recover and be well again."

"Thank you for sharing your story!" she says over and over again, hugging me tight. Chills running up my spine, I hug the young woman and applaud her for her courage in choosing to live. I offer her my phone number and e-mail address and invite her to call me anytime. She thanks me again and disappears into the crowd. In the short time we had shared, Sarah teaches me that stories, when shared, heal both the speaker and the listener.

Excited about the walk, I call my parents and siblings to share the news. They are delighted to learn about it and pledge to offer a donation. I reach out to my sister and share my dream of us walking together, hand in hand at the inaugural walk. Much to my surprise, she promises to join me at the walk and raises hundreds of dollars on her own in pledges. Her psychiatrist's decision to admit her to the state hospital had been a wake-up call. Since then she had worked hard to accept her illness and focus her energies on learning how to cope with it. Delighted that my dream would come true, I build a team of 115 walkers and raise more than twenty-five thousand dollars in cash, and in-kind donations.

On May 18, 2003, Chitra, Ram, the girls, and I are joined by many friends and thousands of Oregonians to raise money and awareness about our country's need for a world-class treatment and recovery system for people with mental illness. As morning drizzle gives way to sunshine, mothers and fathers, brothers and sisters, sons and daughters, friends and co-workers, health care professionals and community leaders walk together just as I had envisioned, in celebration of our journeys. Together we emerge out of the dark and into the light of a new era where people with mental illness and their families will no longer hide in shame. Instead we stride with hope and solidarity, our heads held high in pride of our resilience. Together, we raise nearly $187,000 to support NAMI Oregon's programs of education, advocacy, and support.

The resounding success of NAMI Walks and my continued collaboration with NAMI draws me into the world of mental health advocacy. Mr. Loaiza invites me to serve on the board of directors at NAMI Oregon, and, to my delight, the board votes me in. Over the next couple of years, I gain a deeper understanding of the broken mental health system in my neighborhood and the nation at large, and its heartbreaking impact on the lives of men, women, and children across the country.

I learn about the lack of parity in mental health care—this was before the Mental Health Parity and Addiction Equity Act was signed into law in October 2008, which was a big step in giving people with mental illness access to insurance coverage. I learn of loving parents who were reduced to relinquishing custody of their children struggling with mental illness to the state in a last-ditch effort to secure health care. I discover that the prisons in America have become the new asylums: while fewer than 55,000 Americans receive treatment in psychiatric hospitals, almost ten times that number—nearly 500,000 mentally ill men and women—are serving time in U.S. jails and prisons. I also learn that a significant percentage of the homeless people on our streets, many of whom are veterans who had dedicated their lives to safeguarding our freedom, are struggling with mental illness.

I read in *The Oregonian* about the tragic suicide of twenty-one-year-old Garrett Lee Smith, son of Oregon Senator Gordon and Sharon Smith, who had shot himself in his apartment in Utah. And of a loving husband, father, and highly regarded employee of the City of Portland who jumped off the Ross Island Bridge to his death—both victims of untreated depression. *Who said mental illness isn't lethal?* These families blame stigma as one of the greatest barriers in their loved one's life, and plead for people living with mental illness to stand up and speak out to destigmatize mental illness, encourage people to seek help, and promote hope and recovery. Deeply saddened by these events and determined to make a difference, I decide to heed the pleas of these families.

On December 20, 2003, I graduate from George Fox University. Walking up to the podium to receive my MBA, I am filled with gratitude knowing that I am the first woman on my mother's side of the family to go to college, and I have earned not one but three diplomas, including a graduate degree. For all the unrealized dreams that my mother had cherished about going to college herself, I am deeply grateful for the opportunities I have had in my life. Clutching my diploma to my heart, I realize that I am the luckiest woman in the world: *India has given me roots and America has given me wings to fly.* As a child, India had given me a place to belong, a loving family, and a rich heritage. But, as a young woman struggling with depression, it had held me hostage. Eventually, it was America that had blessed me with the freedom and opportunities to discover the power within me to soar in life. To the world, an MBA implies Master of Business Administration. To me, it symbolized a Master in the art of Believing and Achieving.

Immediately after graduation, I get trained to present NAMI's unique public-education program, "In Our Own Voice," in which speakers are trained to share personal stories about their journey through mental illness and recovery. At the three-day intensive training, I meet the most courageous people. Listening to their stories, I am deeply touched by their struggles and inspired by their resilience.

Wanting to gain further mastery over the art and business of speaking, I enroll in the Candidate Program at the Oregon chapter of the National Speakers Association. Over the next nine months, I attend monthly classes along with twelve other aspiring speakers and learn a variety of skills to enhance my impact as a speaker. I also attend speaker labs, where I work on my material and presentation skills. During one such lab, the facilitator, a professional speaker whom I greatly admired, pounds me with questions—"Why do you want to speak?" No matter how hard I try to educate her about the devastating impact of mental illness and the need for speakers to promote mental health awareness, hope, and holistic wellness, she fails to see the value of my work. Deeply saddened yet determined to make a difference, I sit in my car sobbing and write a poem about why I want to speak.

**WHY DO I WANT TO SPEAK?**

*I want to speak, I want to speak,*
*to break the silence about mental illness.*

*I want to speak, I want to speak,*
*to give voice to the voiceless millions whose screams*
*for help are often unheard.*

*I want to speak, I want to speak,*
*to stop a thirteen-year-old from slashing her wrist.*

*I want to speak, I want to speak,*
*to stop a young man from shooting himself to death.*

*I want to speak, I want to speak,*
*to prevent a deranged mother from drowning her kids.*

*I want to speak, I want to speak,*
*to prevent parents from needing to relinquish their kids.*

*I want to speak, I want to speak,*
*to engage the global community to stop the human carnage*
*of a million innocent lives lost to suicide each year.*

*I want to speak, I want to speak,*
*to empower my brethren the beautiful minds of the world.*

*I want to speak, I want to speak,*
*to tear down the insidious chains of stigma and discrimination.*

*I want to speak, I want to speak,*
*to promote mental health awareness, hope, and holistic*
*wellness.*

*I want to speak, I want to speak,*
*to inform, inspire, and transform lives.*

The poem becomes my anthem.

To be certified as professional speakers, my classmates and I must also present twenty paid presentations within twelve months. Determined to be the first student in my class to earn my credentials, I present the In Our Own Voice program at more than twenty-five venues. Regardless of the diversity of the audience, whether they are members of the American Psychiatric Association or prison inmates at the Coffee Creek Correctional Facility for Women, they find hope and healing in my story. Their valuable testimonials gratify and energize me to continue my outreach. Inspired and fascinated by my cross-cultural odyssey through depression, many listeners ask if I have written a book. I promise them I will someday.

It is said in the Upanishads, the ancient Hindu scriptures, "You are what your deepest desire is. As you desire, so is your intention. As your intention is, so is your will. As your will is, so is your deed. As your deed is, so is your destiny." I am so grateful in finding such widespread support and acknowledgment of my intention to serve as a messenger of hope and healing, and I feel that a Greater Power is surrounding me with the people who can help me realize my deepest desire.

"Hi, my name is Chris Summerville," says a well-dressed, distinguished gentleman, stretching his hand out to me shortly after my panel presentation at a NAMI convention. "Do you have a couple of minutes?" he asks, pointing to the couch in a quiet corner of the lobby. "I would like to talk to you."

We sit down. "You were incredible this morning," Chris goes on. "I have been a mental health advocate for quite a while and have heard a lot of speakers. But I have never heard anyone as passionate and candid as you are. I really admire your courage and eloquence."

Even before I can thank Chris for his kind compliments, he adds, "I would like to connect you with Dr. Jagannath Wani in Calgary. He is a great guy and an incredible mental health advocate. I bet the two of you will find ways to collaborate." Chris hands me his card and promises to connect me to Dr. Wani. Besides struggling with mental health issues himself, Chris is the CEO of the Manitoba Schizophrenia Society, a certified Psychosocial Rehabilitation Practitioner, and an ordained pastor. I am filled with admiration for Chris's resilience and accomplishments, and soon discover that we share a passion for holistic healing.

Soon after the NAMI convention, my family, my sister, Chitra, and her family travel to Bangalore to visit our parents and extended family. The city is bursting at its seams. The IT boom and subsequent arrival of multinational companies over the last several years have propelled the city and its citizens into a pattern of unsustainable growth. Unfortunately, the unprecedented increase in job opportunities and salaries are coupled with a spike in suicide rates—up almost 40 percent since 2000. In addition to being dubbed the IT Capital of India, Bangalore has emerged as the suicide capital of India. The stress of a fast-paced lifestyle and the pressure to perform, coupled with the fragmentation of the extended family support systems, are literally destroying people's lives. And people's reluctance to seek mental health services due to stigma is proving to be lethal.

Wanting to promote mental health awareness within my community, I meet Dr. Kiran, the psychiatrist who had first diagnosed me with depression in 1987. Delighted to learn of my interest, he introduces me to his work at the Richmond Fellowship Society, which provides care and rehabilitation for people struggling with chronic mental illness. Next I meet Dr. Nirmala Srinivasan, the founder of the Association for the Mentally Disabled, Bangalore's first autonomous self-help group for families and patients of mental illness, and the founder and trustee of Action for Mental Illness. The mother of a bright young man suffering from bipolar disorder, she tells me about her lifelong efforts to raise awareness about mental health issues in India and to advocate for the human rights of those living with mental illness. Last, I meet Father Hank Nunn, the director and cofounder of Athma Shakti Vidyalaya, a unique therapeutic community promoting mental health.

Deeply inspired by their work, I ask if I may meet some of their clients. Touched by the stories of their struggles, I resolve to create a wellness campaign to promote global mental health awareness, hope, and holistic wellness.

At one of the meetings, a gentleman in his sixties approaches me with a warm smile. His slightly stooped body is etched with the love and labor of years of caregiving. "My son was a brilliant young man on his way to becoming a successful engineer when depression robbed him of his dreams," he says, tears misting his bespectacled eyes. "For years, I had looked in hope to find a person who had overcome depression, so that I could convince my son that he too could get better and reclaim his dreams. Meeting you today, Gayathri, has revived my faith that perhaps my son will one day recover and rebuild his life just as you have."

"I don't have much to offer you," he says, holding out a hundred-rupee bill. "Consider it my small contribution to help you bring hope and healing to people around the world."

I press the currency to my heart and promise I will pay his gift forward.

Upon my return to Portland, I start researching the state of mental health around the world. I am shocked to discover that according to the World Health Organization, an estimated 450 million people worldwide suffer from mental disorders. One in four patients using health care services has at least one mental, neurological, or behavioral disorder, but most of these disorders are neither diagnosed nor treated. For every person using health care services, I suspect there are many more people affected by mental health issues but with no access to health care.

Exploring further, I realize that although the scientific community has made significant strides in understanding the causes of mental illness and discovering treatments to promote recovery, society has lagged far behind in its understanding of mental illness. Despite growing knowledge of how to diagnose and treat mental illnesses, myths and misperceptions about these disorders persist, leading to stigma and discrimination toward those who suffer from them. And in India, we were slow to accept that these illnesses are real and lethal. We were slow in taking action to change public policies and provide the community supports to ensure that every man, woman, and child suffering from mental illness could receive the help they need to heal and become contributing members of our global community.

Attending mental health conferences and the Brain Awareness Lecture Series, I am delighted to learn about breakthrough technologies such as PET scans and deep brain stimulation in witnessing the inner workings of our brain and its many disorders. And I am deeply grateful for living long enough for science to substantiate what my soul had always known—that depression and other brain disorders are not caused by demonic spirits or a weakness in character. Neither are they a retribution for our past sins. These debilitating disorders are caused, instead, by a complex web of neurobiological factors.

Browsing through the Web one day, I weep reading a *Frontline* article about the tragedy at the Moideen Badusha Mental Home at Erwadi in Tamil Nadu's Ramanathapuram district. In chains, twenty-eight patients died on August 6, 2001, unable to escape the fire that engulfed the thatched shed that housed them. Although they had screamed for help, no one had come to their rescue.

Days later, I come across a 2003 photo essay by *Time Asia* photographer John Stanmeyer called "Lost Lives." The pictures, taken in mental health centers across Asia, deeply disturb me. My heart breaks at the horrific image of a young woman screaming behind metal bars at the Cipayung center in Indonesia, and a naked, emaciated man curled up on the floor beside a live chicken and some rotten wood. What haunts me most are the desperate faces of children as young as seven languishing behind locked bars, their little faces pressing against metal grates, their hands reaching out through the openings in the walls of a mental health facility at Edhi village in Pakistan where a thousand mentally ill patients live jammed together.

In the coming months, I learn that the deplorable conditions of these facilities are just an example of the dire state of the mental health system not just in Asia but worldwide. Sitting in the comfort of my home office, protected from the dehumanizing conditions under which my brethren live, I can still sense their crushing despair. I want to make a difference. I want to reach out to these lost souls and let them know they are not alone, that there is hope, there is help. Yet I feel overwhelmed by the enormity of the task. I don't know what to do or where to start.

After days of agonizing, I find comfort in Mother Teresa's wisdom: "We can do no great things, only small things with great love." And I discover my call to action in her quote: "We want to create hope for the person and acceptance in the hearts of the people. We must give them hope—always hope—and remove the bitterness that is harming them when they are avoided by everyone . . . compassion, love, understanding . . . that is what is important." Deep in my heart I believe that we, the people suffering from mental illness around the world, need hope, compassion, love, understanding, and inclusion more than mere medications and institutional care. Convinced that my life would be worthwhile if I can give hope to even one person suffering from mental illness, I decide to start local and eventually extend my outreach to the global community.

In December 2005, I start Mind Beautiful, a mental health consultancy dedicated to "Empowering Beautiful Minds around the World." I create and present customized keynotes and workshops to destigmatize mental illness, promote mental health awareness and holistic healing among the general public, and enhance cultural sensitivity among health care professionals. I am deeply gratified by the positive response from my audiences at schools of medicine, nursing, psychology, social work, and pharmacology, and at hospitals, community mental health facilities, civic organizations, college campuses, corporations, and conferences.

Meanwhile, true to his word, Chris Summerville, who had approached me after a panel presentation some time earlier, connects me to Dr. Jagannath Wani. I quickly learn Dr. Wani is not only a Professor Emeritus of Statistics and Actuarial Sciences at University of Calgary; he is also a renowned philanthropist and founder of more than eighteen nonprofit organizations, including the Schizophrenia Awareness Association (SAA) in Pune, India. His passion for promoting mental health, I learn, was inspired by his struggles as a care provider for his wife, Kamalini, who suffered from schizophrenia. The more I get to know Dr. Wani, the more in awe I am. He personifies the *power of one*—I marvel at his relentless passion to help those in need. Mustering up my courage one day, I ask if he will help me launch a global campaign to promote mental health awareness, hope, and holistic wellness. To my delight, Dr. Wani asks three pioneering organizations in India—the SAA, the Institute for Psychological Health in Thane, and Shanti Nursing Home in Aurangabad—to sponsor my programs, and they agree.

Amid all the excitement, I realize that I need to establish a nonprofit organization and raise funds for my global outreach. Although Ram suggests we invest our private funds to start one, I challenge myself to raise the money based entirely on the merit of my work as a mental health advocate. Miraculously, in February 2006, I win the Welcome Back Award for Lifetime Achievement, a program established by Eli Lilly and Company to recognize outstanding achievements in the fight against depression and the stigma often associated with the illness. In addition to the award, I receive $15,000 to donate to a nonprofit of my choice.

Dr. Samuel Kessler, who had grown into my mentor since I had first met him at the American Psychiatric Association's conference in February 2005, had nominated me for the award. A rare physician with the ability to reach beyond people's pathology and into their personhood, Dr. Kessler empowers me to realize my dream of starting a nonprofit organization.

In April 2006, along with Dr. Kessler and a distinguished group of mental health advocates, I finally transform my life's work into global action and start ASHA International (www.myasha.org), a nonprofit organization. After weeks of meditating on a name for it, I had decided on ASHA, which literally means "hope" in Hindi and also in Sanskrit—one of the world's most ancient languages, which originated in India. Our mission is to promote mental health awareness, hope, and holistic wellness. Our vision is to create a world in which people living with mental disorders are provided the resources and support they need to thrive in their communities. Seventeen years after the promise I made while hospitalized in the seclusion room, I finally realize my dream to serve as a messenger of hope and healing.

Filled with gratitude, I decide to visit the seclusion room before I embark on my multicity tour across India. Dr. Kessler graciously arranges for my visit. Much like a devotee visiting a temple to pray before a pilgrimage, I walk through the familiar halls of the psychiatric ward and into a seclusion room very much like the one I'd found myself lost in seventeen years before. During that time, I had realized that all the wealth, prosperity, and good fortune in the world hadn't protected me, and without health and peace, very little else matters. In the cell that first night, as day ebbed into darkness and the sliver of light through my tiny window had disappeared, I was terrified of the dark. There was no light, not in the cell or in the darkened recesses of my mind. Yet, in the days to come, as the darkness grew and threatened to engulf me, I had reached and discovered the light within. And so my life, the fullness of life, with its depths and shadows and its incomparable drunken sun, began.

Glancing at the doors of the seclusion room that had once confined and threatened to annihilate me, I realize that *getting locked up had set me free.* Getting locked up set me free to imagine a life beyond the confines of the isolation cell and the limitations of my illness. Getting locked up set me free to realize that while mental illness could break my mind, and the mental health system could confine my body, there were no walls in this world that could contain my spirit. Getting locked up set me free to create a life of meaning and purpose.

I sit on the floor, legs crossed, eyes closed, and meditate in gratitude for the journey I have endured and the journey I am ready to embark on.

# EPILOGUE

My mission as a mental health advocate has taken me around the world and given me the opportunity to meet and collaborate with a wide array of amazing people. Together, we continue our collective quest to create a world of equity, dignity, hope, and humanity where every man, woman, and child struggling with mental health issues is provided the love and support needed to thrive in life.

According to the World Health Organization, more than 450 million people suffer from mental disorders. Globally, 350 million people struggle with depression, and it is the leading cause of disability worldwide. It costs employers billions of dollars in lost productivity. Treatment works. People can recover and live healthy, meaningful lives. But nearly two-thirds of those affected do not seek care. Stigma, discrimination, lack of awareness, and lack of access to affordable care deter people from seeking lifesaving treatment and social supports. Unfortunately, one million lives worldwide are lost to suicide each year, a life lost every forty seconds. Nearly 90 percent of those who commit suicide are struggling with mental illness. People are hungry for hope and healing.

While my mission is far from complete, I am deeply grateful to my colleagues at ASHA International. In the eight years since the 2006 launch of our wellness campaign, Healthy Minds, Healthy Lives, we have touched the lives of more than 26,000 people, nationally and internationally, with a resounding message of hope and healing. Over the years, we have learned that mental illness has no barriers of age, gender, geography, culture, or socioeconomic status. And hope and healing have no boundaries. One day, one person at a time, we strive to empower people struggling with mental health issues to overcome barriers to recovery and achieve wellness. Ultimately, helping others has helped me heal and become whole.

I am eternally grateful to my family for their love and support. They have given me both refuge and a reason to cherish life. I am also thankful to the many health care providers, friends, and strangers who have lifted me up each time I have fallen, held me in their hearts and prayers, and helped me heal.

Recently, my now-grown daughter, on the occasion of our twenty-seventh wedding anniversary, gave us a beautiful, handmade book of questions for Ram and me to explore during a vacation we are about to take, to get to know each other better, she says. Under the canopy of a glowing Mexican sunset, quesadillas, and virgin margaritas on a table between us, I ask Ram, "What do you fear most?"

"Losing you to depression," he replies softly.

Ram's answer pierces through the cool evening breeze and cracks open the locked box within our hearts in which we have both stored away our fears. I realize that as long as we live, so will our fears. But we also know today that the possibility of Ram's losing me to depression is unlikely, and we know how far we have come, together. I am so glad this marriage worked out and that we have learned to see the beauty in each other, and in our lives. Left alone, I don't believe Ram and I would have chosen each other. Left to myself, that girl of twenty-one would have been exploring the world, her foot ever on life's accelerator, while that shy boy with the big future in America would be stuck, his foot on the brake. We are driven by different chemistries. And yet, without the other one, we understand that we would have been going nowhere. Together, we explore the world and live our lives, safely and with joy.

My question comes when he asks me what, if anything, would I wish to change about my life. I know Ram is holding his breath, expecting me to say, "My illness." But that's not quite right.

In a life filled with love and light, from time to time, my moods continue to cast shadows in the sun. But I no longer curse the shadows, for they have become my greatest teachers. Depression is no longer a demon I dread, but a teacher whose wisdom I seek. Although depression has caused a great deal of pain and suffering in my life, it has also blessed me with many gifts. It has taught me about the power of love to heal all wounds, the fragility of life, and the invincible resilience of the human spirit. Most of all, it has taught me not to fear the darkness in our lives. For it is in our darkest hour that we discover the *light within*—the light of love, wisdom, courage, and compassion.

"No," I say, thinking of my precious daughter and the gift she has given us for starting this conversation. She is now the same age I was when I married her father. Thank God, both my daughters and my husband have been blessed with good health. Some questions have no answers, I would like to tell her, but this one does. I extend my arms across the table, smile, and take my husband's hands in mine and say, "Not a thing."

# GLOSSARY OF INDIAN WORDS

**aarti** (also spelled *arathi*): a Hindu religious ritual of worship, a part of puja, in which light from wicks soaked in ghee (purified butter) or camphor is offered to one or more deities

**abhisheka:** devotional prayers offered to gods and goddesses

**abhyanga:** Ayurvedic oil massage—an integral part of the daily routine recommended by this healing system for overall health and well-being

**Agni Deva:** fire god

**ajji:** grandmother

**akshate:** rice confetti

**Amma:** a term to address or refer to one's mother

**antarjyoti:** the light within

**antarpata:** a cloth curtain

**Appa:** a term to address or refer to one's father

**asafetida:** a brownish, bitter, resinous material obtained from the roots of several plants of the genus *Ferula* in the parsley family and formerly used in medicine

**bangara:** a term of endearment meaning "my golden angel"

**bhajan:** a religious song of praise

**bindi:** the red dot worn on the forehead of Indian women that is an auspicious sign of marriage and guarantees the social status and sanctity of the institution of marriage

**chai:** tea

**chapatti:** whole-wheat flat bread

**charpoy:** a bed, used especially in India, consisting of a frame strung with tapes or light rope

**chole-batura:** a combination of chole (spicy chickpeas) and batura, a fried bread made with white flour

**churidar** (pajamas): tightly fitting trousers worn by both men and women in South Asia

**chutney:** a sauce or relish of East Indian origin

**dhal:** lentils

**dhare:** the main part of a South Indian Hindu wedding ceremony

**dhoti:** a traditional Indian male garment, a length of cloth wrapped around the lower body

**dhrishti:** an Indian ritual of ridding the evil eye

**Diwali:** the Hindu festival of lights, an important four-day celebration in October or November

**diya:** a clay lamp

**dosa:** South Indian crepe

**dupatta:** a chiffon scarf

**Gayathri mantra** (also called Gayatri mantra): a highly revered mantra based on a Vedic Sanskrit verse from a hymn of the Rigveda

**ghazal:** a poetic form consisting of rhyming couplets and a refrain, with each line sharing the same meter; may be understood as a poetic expression of both the pain of loss or separation and the beauty of love in spite of that pain

**ghee:** purified butter

**grihapravesha:** a housewarming ceremony

**haldi-kumkum:** an ancient tradition in which neighborhood women gather to sing songs in praise of the deity worshipped

**huccha:** a madman

**huchi:** crazy

**idli:** a South Indian steamed rice and lentil dumpling

**jamoons:** a popular dessert made with fried cheese dumplings marinated in sugar syrup

**kameez:** a long shirt or tunic

**kanyadaan:** the gift of one's daughter in marriage

**kesaribhat:** a sweet treat made of Cream of Wheat, diced mangoes, milk, and sugar, seasoned with crushed cardamom and saffron

**kurta:** a long-sleeved hip-length shirt worn by men in India

**laddu:** a popular Indian sweet often made to celebrate festivals or weddings

**lagna:** the anointed time for holy union

**ma:** a term of endearment used between girls and women in India

**mangalashtaka:** a composition of eight couplets chanted during a Hindu wedding ceremony to bless the couple

**mangalsutra:** a necklace that serves as a sacred symbol of Indian marriage

**masala:** a blend of ground spices

**mithai:** Indian sweets

**moksha:** liberation from the cycle of rebirth and death

**nagaswaram:** traditional wedding music

**namaste:** a conventional Hindu expression on meeting or parting, usually spoken while holding the palms together vertically in front of the bosom

**nandadeepa:** a traditional ornate lamp kept aglow all day and night in the homes of Hindus in India

**paan:** a betel leaf filled with betel nuts and other scented ingredients

**paanwali:** a person skilled at making paan

**pallu:** the fanciest, most patterned end of the sari, which is usually left hanging from the shoulder

**pani-puri:** a popular street snack in India, Pakistan, Bangladesh, and Nepal

**papad:** a deep-fried lentil wafer

**parijata:** a tropical flower grown in India

**payasam:** a rich milk pudding made of ground poppy seeds and almonds, simmered to perfection with generous mounds of brown sugar and a touch of finely crushed cardamom

**peni:** a traditional South Indian dessert served especially at weddings

**prana:** the life force of breath and mind, body, and spirit

**pranayama:** a meditation discipline involving breath control, originating in ancient India

**prasad:** blessings from God

**puja:** special prayers offered to gods and goddesses

**puri:** fried, puffed whole-wheat Indian flat bread

**rangoli:** intricate ritualistic designs drawn in front of Indian homes, on walls, and so on

**rani:** princess

**rasam:** a South Indian soup, traditionally prepared using tamarind juice as a base, with the addition of tomato, chili pepper, pepper, cumin, and other spices; steamed lentils; and often other vegetables

**sagu:** vegetable medley

**sambar:** a savory lentil stew cooked with eggplant

**samosa:** a savory pastry filled with spiced vegetables or meats, then fried or baked

**saptapadi:** literally means "seven steps"—an integral part of the Hindu wedding ceremony

**sari:** a garment worn by Hindu women consisting of a long piece of cotton or silk wrapped around the body with one end draped over the head or over one shoulder

**seemantha:** a bangle ceremony performed in the seventh month of pregnancy to pray for the health and well-being of the mother and unborn child

**shehnai:** an aerophonic instrument that is thought to bring good luck, and as a result, is widely used in North India for marriages and processions

**shikakai:** a paste made with soap nut powder and water, used as shampoo

**shlokas:** a category of verse line developed from the Vedic Anustubh that is the basis for Indian epic verse, and may be considered the Indian verse form *par excellence,* occurring, as it does, far more frequently than any other meter in classical Sanskrit poetry

**spatika:** a tropical flower grown in India

**stylewali:** all style and no substance

**supari:** a special blend of candied sugar, spices, and betel nuts

**tiffin:** lunch; Tiffin is also a brand of containers for lunch foods

**tithi:** death anniversary

**Ugadi:** Hindu New Year

**uppama** (upma): a common South Indian and Sri Lankan Tamil breakfast dish, cooked as a thick porridge from dry roasted semolina; various seasonings and/or vegetables are often added during the cooking

**vadais** (vada): a savory fritter-type snack from South India

**Vedic:** referring to a period in history during which the Vedas, the oldest scriptures of Hinduism, were composed

**vermillion:** a vivid red to reddish orange mixture of turmeric, alum, iodine, camphor, and other substances

# RESOURCES

I hope you find the following resources useful. For a more complete list, please visit **www.myasha.org/resources** and let me know if I can be of help. You can reach me at gayathri@myasha.org. Thanks!

—Gayathri Ramprasad

**Mental Health Information**

- Brain & Behavior Research Foundation: www.bbrfoundation.org
- National Institute of Mental Health: www.nimh.nih.gov/index.shtml
- Substance Abuse and Mental Health Services Administration: www.samhsa.gov
- World Health Organization: www.who.int/topics/mental_health/en
- World Health Organization: *10 Facts on Mental Health:* www.who.int/features/factfiles/mental_health/mental_health_facts/en
- World Health Organization: *Depression, A Hidden Burden:* www.who.int/mental_health/management/depression/flyer_depression_2012.pdf

**Advocacy Organizations**

- Active Minds: www.activeminds.org
- ASHA International: www.myasha.org
- Bring Change 2 Mind: www.bringchange2mind.org
- Depression and Bipolar Support Alliance: www.dbsalliance.org
- Mental Health America: www.mentalhealthamerica.net
- Movement for Global Mental Health: www.globalmentalhealth.org
- National Alliance on Mental Illness: www.nami.org
- National Coalition for Mental Health Recovery: http://ncmhr.org
- National Empowerment Center, Inc.: www.power2u.org

- SAMHSA's Resource Center to Promote Acceptance, Dignity and Social Inclusion Associated with Mental Health (ADS Center): http://promoteacceptance.samhsa.gov

**Wellness Resources**

- Benson-Henry Institute for Mind Body Medicine: www.massgeneral.org/bhi
- Life Force Yoga to Manage Your Moods: http://yogafordepression.com
- Mary Ellen Copeland—Wellness Recovery Action Plan: www.mentalhealthrecovery.com
- Transcendental Meditation Program: www.tm.org

# DISORDERS ON THE DEPRESSION CONTINUUM

The following are disorders related to depression that appear in the most recent editions of the *Diagnostic and Statistical Manual of Mental Disorders* (*DSM-IV-TR* and *DSM-5*), published by the American Psychiatric Association in 2004 and 2013, respectively. We are not including the bipolar spectrum (or manic depression) disorders here, except for the disorder of cyclothymia.

*Major Depressive Disorder*: A history of one or more major depressive episodes. A major depressive episode is a period of more than two weeks of either depressed mood or anhedonia (loss of pleasure) that causes severe distress or inability to function. In addition to this symptom, at least four of the following must also be present: significant weight change (gaining or losing more than 5 percent of body weight without intending to do so), significant changes in sleeping patterns (insomnia or its opposite: sleeping much more than is usual for the person), psychomotor changes (a noticeable slowing down or speeding up in movements and speech), constant fatigue, feelings of worthlessness or inappropriate guilt, trouble concentrating, and thoughts of death or dying or suicidal thinking.

There are several identified subtypes of major depression. Two of these include *postpartum depression,* in which an episode of depression occurs within four weeks of childbirth, and *seasonal pattern* (often called *seasonal affective disorder*), in which episodes of depression tend to occur at the same time each year and remit as the seasons change. *Bereavement,* or grieving, is also listed under depression in the *DSM-5.* Bereavement is extreme sadness following the death of a loved one. Although criteria for depression may be met during the period of bereavement, this period of sadness is recognized as a normal and even healthy response to loss that will begin to lift on its own after time.

*Dysthymia*: A period of depressed mood or anhedonia (loss of pleasure) that is less intense than that experienced in major depression and doesn't include suicidal thinking. However, it lasts much longer—at least two years without remission for longer than a one-month period. It also includes two or more of the following: changes in appetite, changes in sleep patterns, low energy or fatigue, low self-esteem, poor concentration or difficulty making decisions, and feelings of hopelessness.

*Depressive Condition Not Elsewhere Classified (CNEC)*: This diagnosis includes *minor depression,* which is a period of more than two weeks of either depressed mood or anhedonia that causes severe distress or inability to function. It also includes between two and three of the following: significant weight change, significant changes in sleeping patterns, psychomotor changes (a noticeable change in movements and speech), constant fatigue, feelings of worthlessness or inappropriate guilt, trouble concentrating, and suicidal thinking.

*Adjustment Disorder with Depressed Mood*: Significant distress or inability to function accompanied by depressed mood within three months of experiencing a major life stressor.

*Cyclothymia*: A period of two years or longer in which the person has recurrent periods of depressive symptoms that cycle with recurrent periods of hypomania. Some features of hypomania include: persistent elevated or irritable mood (at least four days at a time), inflated self-esteem, decreased need for sleep, being more talkative than usual, and excessive involvement in pleasurable activities that may have painful consequences (such as shopping sprees, sexual indiscretions, foolish business investments, or reckless speeding). This disorder is classified under Bipolar and Related Disorders in the *DSM-5.*

*Depressive Personality Disorder*: (This is not currently an official diagnosis, but a disorder that is slated for further study by the American Psychiatric Association.) This is a trait-like pattern of depressive thoughts and behaviors that begins in adolescence and includes five or more of the following: dejected, gloomy, or cheerless mood; low self-esteem; excessive brooding or worry; a blaming or self-critical nature; negative and critical attitude toward others; pessimism; and proneness to feel guilt and remorse.

*Premenstrual Dysphoric Disorder*: Marked feelings of depression, irritability, anxiety, and/or mood swings that cause significant distress or inability to function and are centered around the week before the onset of menses each month. It also includes some or all of the following: anhedonia, difficulty concentrating, overeating or food cravings, fatigue, changes in sleep patterns, a sense of being overwhelmed or out of control, and physical complaints such as tenderness or joint pain.

The *DSM-5* also includes categories for *substance-induced depressive disorder* and *depressive disorder associated with another medical condition.*

**Source:** Jefferson Prince, MD, and Shelley Carson, PhD, *Almost Depressed: Is My (or My Loved One's) Unhappiness a Problem?* Center City, MN: Hazelden, 2013.

# ABOUT THE AUTHOR

Gayathri Ramprasad is the founder and president of ASHA International, a nonprofit organization promoting personal, organizational, and community wellness. She received her first undergraduate degree in science from Bangalore University in India, a second undergraduate degree in management and business information systems, and a master's in business administration from George Fox University in Newberg, Oregon. She is a member of the Global Speakers Federation and the winner of the prestigious Eli Lilly Welcome Back Award for Lifetime Achievement and the Voice Award for Consumer Leadership sponsored by the Substance Abuse and Mental Health Services Administration.

For more information about Gayathri Ramprasad and her mission to promote mental health awareness, and bring hope and healing to people's lives, please visit www.gayathriramprasad.com and www.myasha.org, or email her at gayathri@myasha.org.